About the Author

LORRAINE EVANS studied Ancient History and Egyptology at the University of London and is an expert on the Egyptian priesthood. She is a regular Lecturer on the Egyptology circuit and is a tutor in ancient Egyptian history in Adult Education throughout London and the Middlesex area. Lorraine has worked on the internationally acclaimed TV documentary series *Secrets of the Dead* and is currently preparing for her doctoral research.

KINGDOM OF THE ARK

*The startling story of how the ancient British race
is descended from the Pharaohs*

LORRAINE EVANS

POCKET
BOOKS

LONDON · SYDNEY · NEW YORK · TOKYO · SINGAPORE · TORONTO

First published in Great Britain by Simon & Schuster UK Ltd, 2000
This edition first published by Pocket Books, 2001
An imprint of Simon & Schuster UK Ltd
A Viacom Company

1 3 5 7 9 10 8 6 4 2

Simon & Schuster UK Ltd
Africa House
64-78 Kingsway
London WC2B 6AH

Simon & Schuster Australia
Sydney

A CIP catalogue record for this book is available from the British
Library

ISBN 0-671-02956-8

Printed and bound in Great Britain by Omnia Books Ltd, Glasgow

This book is dedicated to my loving partner and best friend Gary Parsons, together with little 'J' and Hugo who, sadly, both never survived its completion

ACKNOWLEDGEMENTS

My sincere thanks go out to the following people who have helped in the conception of this book. They include Gary Parsons, without whose understanding and assistance this book would never have been completed; Graham Phillips, for his unquestioning friendship, help, support and infamous daily telephone conversations over the past two years – here's to Akhenaten and the knights of Ny! A big thanks to Andrew Collins, for his encouragement and advice; Andrew Salmon, for not only putting up with my Egyptological ranting and raving but who also became chauffeur and removal man in one go. To my agent Simon Trewin, at Peters Fraser & Dunlop, for his support and faith in me over the years and for fending off the bad guys when it was required. My gratitude to Ingrid Connell, for her initial foresight, and my Editor, Katharine Young, Editorial Director, Helen Gummer, and the rest of the team at Simon and Schuster, for taking a chance.

My thanks also go out to Dr Bill Manley for his friendship and advice whenever I would call out of the blue. In addition I would also like to express my gratitude to Bill and Dr Robert Morkot, who gave me the confidence to challenge the 'Establishment' all those years ago, even though they did not realise it at the time. My thanks go to the staff at the British Museum, especially to Gillian Varndell, Curator of Prehistoric and Romano-British Antiquities, for her assistance; Dr A J Spencer, and to all the members of the Department of Egyptian Antiquities, who kindly allowed me access to artefacts whenever it was required; to the staff at the British Library for their help in finding obscure books and to the staff at the Institute of Archaeology, University College London; Dr Helen Whitehouse, at the Ashmolean Museum, Oxford; to John Allan, Exeter Museum, for his hospitality; Roger Penhallurick, Truro Museum, for his kind assistance; Dr George Simkis, at UCLA, for sharing his research into maritime powers; Steve Ottery and Sarnia Butcher, on the Isles of Scilly, for their information and help; Gillian Hutchinson, National Maritime Museum; Historic Scotland; the National Library of Wales; Andy Halpin, at the National Museum of Antiquities, Dublin; Bob Partridge, at the Manchester Ancient Egypt Society, plus the various Egyptology and Archaeological Societies around the country for their support; Glynis Reeves, for her information on the Mouselow Stones; Anglo-Israel Archaeological Society; Dr Woolgar, at the University of Southampton; Dr Denford, at Winchester Museums Service; Somerset County Museums Service; Cornish Studies Library; Andrew Deathe at Salisbury and South Wiltshire Museum.

I would also like to say thank you to Tony Wakeford and Andrew King for the musical ideas. Keep them for the next book, lads! Also Chris Stewart and the numerous Egyptologists around the world who have provided me with information when I asked. And not forgetting my Nan and brother for supporting me over the past decade.

Lastly, I would like to say a big thank you to the 'most electrifying man in Sports Entertainment', the Rock, and the rest of the WWF team, for bringing fun and laughter into the house when the chips were down.

Lorraine Evans
London, April 2000

CONTENTS

ILLUSTRATIONS

AUTHOR'S NOTE

Following the practices of early Egyptologists, it has become the custom for some scholars to refer to ancient Egyptian names and places by their Graeco-Roman equivalent. The spelling of ancient Egyptian personal names continues to cause problems. Thus the kings cited here as 'Amenhotep' can be found elsewhere as 'Amenhotpe' or in its Greek form 'Amenophis'. I would like to stress that in the text of this book, the ancient Egyptian name has been used, except for particularly well-known places which have become more familiar over the years by their Greek or Arabic name, for example Amarna, the city of the pharaoh Akhenaten.

In addition, over the past few years there has been much variation in the chronology of ancient Egypt. For the purpose of this book, all dates are taken from J. Baines and J. Malek, *Atlas of Ancient Egypt*, Phaidon, 1984.

TIMELINE

Early Dynastic Period

3150-2686 BC – Dynasties 1-2

Narmer, the first king of Egypt, unites Upper and Lower Egypt.
This period laid down many of the concepts, such as religion, that were to govern later thought in ancient Egypt.
Memphis becomes the capital city.

The Old Kingdom

2686-2181 BC – Dynasties 3-6

Known as the Pyramid Age, whereby the power of Egypt expanded considerably.
Djoser builds the Step Pyramid at the necropolis of Saqqara.
Khufu builds the Great Pyramid at Giza.

The First Intermediate Period

2181-2040 BC – Dynasties 7-10

Decline in royal power.
A period of anarchy and chaos whereby a united Egypt divides, once again, into the separate kingdoms of Upper and Lower Egypt.
War breaks out between Thebes and the Delta.

The Middle Kingdom

2040-1786 BC – Dynasties 11-13

Monthuhotep II re-unifies Egypt.
Thebes becomes the new capital city.
Amenemhat I founds the 12th Dynasty.
They move to a new capital at Lisht.
The god Amun now becomes the state god of ancient Egypt with the emergence of a new Amun Priesthood based at Thebes.

The Second Intermediate Period

1786-1550 BC – Dynasties 14-17

The country disunites once more. Hyksos occupation of Egypt. They establish their kingdom at Avaris in the Delta.

The New Kingdom

1550-1050 BC – Dynasties 18-20

The Golden Age of Egypt (Amarna Pharaohs in bold type)

1550-1525 Ahmose: Expulsion of the Hyksos. Reunification of Egypt.

1525-1504 Amenhotep I: Capital city at Thebes.

1504-1492 Tutmosis I

1492-1479 Tutmosis II

1479-1425 Tutmosis III: Amun at the height of his power.

1479-1457 Queen Hatshepsut: Egypt becomes the most powerful and richest state in the world.

Amenhotep II

1393-1383 **Tutmosis IV** The kings of Egypt begin to fight back against the power of Amun.

1383-1345 **Amenhotep III** Birth of Scota. Continuation of the persecution of the Amun priesthood.

1353-1337 **Akhenaten** Amarna Period. The gods of Egypt have now been abolished. The rise of the Aten.

1338-1336 **Smenkhare** Scota flees Egypt and the restoration of Amun.

1336-1327 **Tutankhamun**

1327-1323 **Ay**

1323-1293 **Horemheb**

Dynasty 19

1295-1186 BC The age of Ramses the Great. Amun rises to power once more.

Dynasty 20

1186-1069 BC Invasions of the Sea Peoples and a decline in Egyptian power. At the end of the dynasty, Herihor, the

High Priest of Amun, theoretically claims the throne of Upper and Lower Egypt.

The Third Intermediate Period

1069-525 BC – Dynasties 21-26: The power of the pharaoh weakens as the strength of the Amun priesthood rises. The High Priests of Amun rule Upper Egypt from Thebes. Egypt divides once more.

The Late Period

525-332 BC – Dynasties 27-31: Egypt under Persian rule. Alexander the Great conquers Egypt.

CHAPTER ONE

⤙⤙⤙⤖⤖⤖

THE FORBIDDEN FINDS

In the early spring of 1955, archaeologist Dr Sean O'Riordain of Trinity College, Dublin, was excavating a prehistoric settlement at the Hill of Tara, just to the south of Trim in County Meath, Ireland. It was meant to have been a fairly routine excavation, but on 12 March Dr O'Riordain unearthed one of the most enigmatic archaeological finds ever to have been made in the emerald isle.

In Irish tradition the Hill of Tara was the seat of the high kings of Ireland, seemingly from the first arrival of the Celts at the start of the Iron Age around 700 BC.[1] However, its true history is something of an historical puzzle, on which the 1955 excavation had hoped to shed light. All that now remains of what had evidently been an important pre-Christian hill-fort are the earthen ramparts that encircle the flat-topped hill some 30 metres above the surrounding countryside. It was just to the north-west of the Hill of Tara, however, that Dr O'Riordain made his discovery. Here was a much older, pre-Celtic burial cairn called the Mound of Hostages: a circular man-made hillock, some 21 metres

wide and 3.5 metres high. Dr O'Riordain's team removed
the earth to the east of the mound to reveal a huge boulder
which sealed a narrow stonework passageway, some 4
metres long, which led into three separate chambers.[2] From
the many human remains and simple stone artefacts found
inside, the site was clearly a Neolithic, late Stone Age burial
mound, of the sort relatively common throughout Britain
and Ireland from around 3000 BC. Such sites were in use for
a period of some fifteen centuries until the influx of the
Bronze Age peoples from northern Europe around 1500 BC.

Inside the first two chambers, Dr O'Riordain discovered
human bones, together with Neolithic artefacts such as
stone tools, flint arrowheads and simple pottery, but the
third chamber was completely different. Surrounded by the
cremated remains of a number of bodies was a pit containing an unburned, intact skeleton crouched in a foetal
position. These remains were clearly later than those in the
other chambers, as they were accompanied by Bronze Age
artefacts such as a dagger and pin.[3]

The discovery of Bronze Age remains in a Stone Age
burial cairn was strange enough, but what Dr O'Riordain
found around the skeleton's neck was truly astonishing: an
exquisite bronze necklace, consisting of an assortment of
amber and jet droplets. Between each segment of amber and
jet was a series of smaller beads, turquoise in colour and
conical in shape.[4] Incredibly, these ancient beads had been
artificially manufactured. Known as faience beads, they
were fashioned from a fired paste made from various
minerals and plant extracts. Although such artefacts were
relatively common in the more advanced civilizations of the
Mediterranean and the Middle East, such as Sumeria and
Minoan Crete, this technology was far beyond the Bronze
Age peoples of Ireland – subsistence farming communities
who still lived in little more than mud huts. Just who was

this mysterious figure, seemingly buried out of time and place?

On forensic examination, the skeleton was identified as an adolescent male, around the age of eighteen, and carbon dated to around 1350 BC. Quickly dubbed the Tara Prince by the Irish media, its accompanying grave goods were rushed to the Department of Archaeology's research laboratory at the National Museum of Antiquities, Scotland, where scientists conducted a round-the-clock spectrochemical analysis of the artefacts.

Faience was the first glazed ceramic to be invented. It was composed of crushed quartz or sand, with small amounts of lime mixed with either natron or plant ash. This was then coated with a soda-lime-silica and copper glaze, generally blue-green in colour. The optical effect of faience, particularly when a fine white quartz layer underlay the glaze, was that of a precious stone, probably intended to resemble turquoise.[5] With such a unique chemical composition, it could be scientifically determined where the raw materials originated. After months of examination, the dating was confirmed. However, the further conclusions were truly staggering. In an article in *Proceedings of the Prehistoric Society* in September 1956, J. F. Stone and L. C. Thomas reported that the beads were of Egyptian origin. In fact, when they were compared with Egyptian faience beads, they were found to be not only of identical manufacture but also of matching design.[6] The famous boy-king Tutankhamun was entombed around the same time as the Tara skeleton and the priceless golden collar around his mummy's neck was inlaid with matching conical, blue-green faience beads.

The ancient Egyptians called faience *thenet*, coming from a word meaning to dazzle or shine. It had been exported to other countries of the Middle East and the

Mediterranean but was unknown anywhere in northern Europe. The findings of the National Museum of Antiquities, Scotland, so challenged the existing thought concerning the extent of contemporary trade routes that the academic community virtually ignored the report. Even the few archaeologists who did respond shrugged off the find as a freak and isolated example: an Egyptian trading with a Minoan, trading with someone on the Greek mainland, then on through a series of European tribes until the necklace somehow, by fluke alone, reached Ireland. We have to consider here that academia is almost like a religion. The majority of scholars would rather 'toe the party line' than question something that could destroy their entire belief system. The question of whether the Tara necklace was a one-off fluke or evidence of trade somehow existing between Egypt and Ireland might have been answered by further excavations around the Mound of Hostages. Tragically, however, Dr O'Riordain died within a few months of his discovery and the excavations ceased.

As an Egyptologist, when I first came upon a reference to the Tara Prince, I was fascinated to discover if further work had revealed more about the site. However, there was so little interest in the find that the excavation had never truly been resumed. I accepted the argument that the necklace could have been a one-off, but decided to surf the Internet to see if this really was the case. Imagine my surprise when I discovered that there was a very similar necklace in the Exeter Museum. It had been found as long ago as 1889 in a Bronze Age burial mound at North Molton in Devon, discovered by a local farmer when his horse had accidentally put its foot through the top of the mound to reveal a chamber containing the skeletal remains of a man with the necklace around his neck. The necklace consists of jet, amber and faience beads, almost identical to the one discovered at Tara. Moreover, it dated from around the same time.[7] Both this and the Tara necklace, now in the National Museum of Ireland in Dublin, had been treated as isolated examples and, as far as I could tell, no one had linked them. To me, the fact that two anomalous necklaces, both similar and contemporary, had been found around the necks of clearly important individuals – probably tribal leaders or religious figures – at two completely different locations, suggested that more than coincidence was involved. I was impelled to ask the question: had deliberate trading somehow occurred between the British Isles and far-away Egypt almost 1500 years before the Romans arrived?

I found it difficult to understand how the potential relevance of the two finds could have been overlooked for so long. I first put it down to an academic oversight. However, as I continued to surf the Internet, I soon discovered that far more direct evidence of trade with Egypt had, it seemed, been deliberately ignored. Compelling evidence had already come to light that indicated not only the possibility of trade routes between Egypt and the British Isles, but that in the fourteenth century BC the Egyptians themselves had actually visited Britain. This remarkable discovery had first been made as long ago as 1937, at North Ferriby in Yorkshire. It began with the preserved remains of an ancient boat, which was first taken to be a Viking longship.

North Ferriby is tucked away under the western side of a chalk escarpment of the Yorkshire and Lincolnshire Wolds, where it is cut by the Humber estuary. On the north bank the area is partially covered by a mantle of glacial till, but at Ferriby itself there is a low tongue of glacial deposits running south-west towards the shore. Long ago, many prehistoric remains were deposited here. In 1937 these deposits attracted the interest of local brothers Edward and

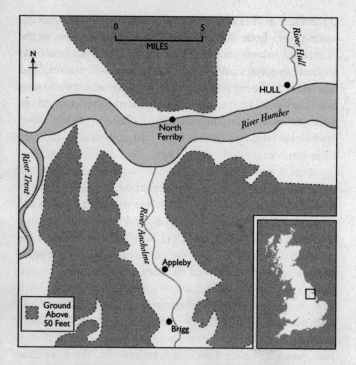

Map illustrating the location of the Ferriby boats

C.W. Wright. As palaeontologists, they easily gained permission to excavate the area from Thomas Sheppard, director of the Hull Museum. For weeks the Wrights scoured the estuary banks of North Ferriby looking for ancient artefacts which erosion had revealed on the surface of the clay. In early September Edward Wright stumbled across something unusual.

> When I saw the ends of three massive wooden planks projecting at a shallow angle from the clay I called across to my brother, who was examining the edge of

the peat a short distance away, that I had found a Viking Ship. His initial scepticism disappeared as he too saw the planks, which could only be part of a larger boat. We were as usual armed with trowels and began to explore the find. We very soon learned that the unexposed part retained its original fastenings, stitches of twisted fibrous material, and that the seams were packed with moss and capped with neatly finished lathes of wood. The outer edges of the planks were found to be furnished with V-shaped grooves into which the bevelled edges of the outer planks fitted closely. Other features observed in the first investigation were a variety of projections on the surface of the planks ... On the next suitable combination of tide and light we undertook a more deliberate investigation of the boat remains and were able to phase our excavation and cleaning.[8]

The pieces did indeed turn out to be part of a boat built from massive planks of oak – a large vessel, some 16 metres long and slightly over 3 metres at its widest point. Paddles had propelled the boat, the remains of several were revealed, and there was room for nine oarsmen on each side. There was even a preserved sail long ago used for downwind travel. Enthusiastically, the Wrights immediately contacted the Hull Geological Society, who visited Ferriby the following spring to see the remains for themselves. In the summer they endorsed a full-scale excavation of the site.[9]

A full team of local archaeologists, led by Maurice Barley, Anthony Congreve and Thomas Romans, joined the Wright brothers. Incredibly, as they dug around the area of the boat, the remains of other, similar boats were found. In these too, timber had been well preserved in the clay, as were fastenings, and often the seams were completely intact.

By the following year they had uncovered three boats in various states of preservation.

In so-called wetland sites, that is lakes, swamps, marshes, etc., the preservation of organic remains such as wood is exceptionally good. Here the organic material is effectively sealed in a wet, airless environment, without oxygen, which favours their preservation as long as the waterlogging is more or less permanent up to the time of excavation. (If a wet site dries out, even only seasonally, decomposition of the organic materials can occur.) Clay will also act as a sealant, binding the ancient wood together and preventing decay. One of the pioneers of wetland archaeology in Britain, Dr John Coles of Cambridge University, estimates that on a wet site like Ferriby, often 75–90 per cent of the finds are organic and will survive relatively intact. Little or none of the material would survive on most dryland sites.[10]

The pieces were carefully lifted from the clay and photographed. Many of the artefacts were taken to the Hull Museum, but the larger planks were taken to be stored in a large wooden shed at the Wrights' home. With each new piece of evidence, it soon became clear that a small flotilla of ships had long ago been wrecked in a storm in what had once been a natural harbour. Unfortunately, however, the excavation was abruptly curtailed, due to the outbreak of the Second World War. Along with other workers at the site, the Wright brothers were drafted into military service.[11]

Owing to the increase in global pollution over the past fifty years, a dramatic rise in sea levels has resulted. The remains still *in situ* were now increasingly at risk from natural erosion of the bank, the process accelerated by the disturbance of the deposits during the unfinished excavation. Even the finds which had been removed to the Hull

Museum were destroyed when the building was hit by a stray bomb during an enemy raid on the shipyards. Luckily, all was not lost, as the larger finds were still preserved at the Wrights' home. Unfortunately, as the war dragged on, these remains gradually dried out, resulting in distortion and cracking.

At the end of hostilities, while the Hull Museum began the process of preserving these surviving pieces, Edward Wright attempted to complete the excavation and record the full extent of the deposits on his own. Support for his work was almost non-existent as the Hull Museum was in total disarray due to its partial destruction in 1941. Nevertheless, Edward Wright managed to uncover the remains of two further boats. He desperately needed help, so in August of 1946 he wrote to archaeologist C. W. Phillips, one of the county's leading authorities on ancient maritime vessels. Phillips had already excavated the famous Sutton Hoo boat, a complete Anglo-Saxon ship discovered buried in a gigantic royal burial mound in Suffolk. On 27 August Phillips visited North Ferriby to see the site and examine the two boats. He was expecting to view the remains of typical Viking longships – not too dissimilar to the Sutton Hoo craft. He just could not believe what he saw. Ecstatic, he immediately wrote to Sir Geoffrey Calendar, Director of the National Maritime Museum at Greenwich:

> I want to present you with a few remarkable facts and learn your reaction to them. In the last two days I have been down at North Ferriby on the north shore of the Humber, five miles upstream from Hull, looking at two boats which C. W. Wright and E.V. Wright of that place began to examine in 1939 [sic] and had to abandon because of the war.
>
> 'Yesterday I . . . exposed some of the most vital parts

of one of the boats as well as studying the conditions in which they rest in the Humber mud ... I can now say that it will be a most unfortunate matter if the better preserved of the two boats is not got out whole, pickled and kept as treasure of the country's archaeology. The wood is in pretty good shape. The technical details of the boat are astounding and are all perfectly preserved.[12]

To Wright's surprise, Phillips told him that these were no Viking longships. To begin with, they were very much smaller. The Viking longship was around 25 metres long and almost 5 metres wide, whereas these ships measured only some 16 by 3 metres. Viking ships had places for around sixteen oarsmen on each side, whereas the Ferriby boats only had room for nine. The basic construction was also very different. The hull planking of a Viking ship overlapped and was fastened in place by iron rivets. The hull planking of these boats, on the other hand, was set end to end, covered by battens and sewn together with strips of yew. The Ferriby boats were of a far more primitive design, very much older than the Wrights or anyone else had suspected. They were ancient vessels of a type previously only found around the Mediterranean. Incredibly, Phillips concluded that they had sunk at least 2000 years before the Viking Age. Just how they got there, or precisely where they came from, however, was a complete mystery.

Because of his academic standing, the response to Phillips's letter was swift and positive: a full-scale excavation of the Ferriby boats would be conducted. The local Ferriby team was thus supported by Phillips himself, H. J. Plenderleith, Keeper of the British Museum Research Laboratory, together with J. W. Brailsford and William Watson, also of the British Museum. It was not long before the entire team agreed with Phillips's initial observations:

the boats dated from around 1350 BC. Nothing like them had ever been found in Britain before.[13]

Scientific confirmation of this dating came with the advent of radiocarbon dating in 1949. In that year the American scientist William Libby invented the revolutionary new dating process of organic materials. All organic matter absorbs the radioactive isotope Carbon-14, which gradually decays once an organism has died. As the rate of decay is constant, the period of time which has elapsed since the organism's death can be gauged by measuring the amount of Carbon-14 which still exists in its remains.[14] By calculating the extent of decay of the Carbon-14 in the wood of the Ferriby boats, it was possible to deduce their age. The problem was that only material uncontaminated by preservatives was eligible for processing and this immediately discounted all the wood discovered so far. Wright had to obtain fresh material from the site and spent the next two years combing the Ferriby shore for any sign of boat remains that could be submitted for dating. At last he came across some oak sealing lathes, and delivered a sufficient quantity to the British Museum Research Laboratory in 1955. This was one of the first institutions in the country to be equipped with the necessary facilities and, due to overwhelming demand, it was three years before the laboratory was able to date the Ferriby material. When the results came back in 1958 they confirmed Phillips's dating – somewhere between 1400 and 1350 BC.

For over ten years many prominent archaeologists had refused to accept that the Ferriby boats could have been so old. The leading sceptic was Sir Lindsay Scott, President of the Prehistoric Society, who had argued strenuously that the boats dated from the post-Roman period and had probably come from Byzantium in what is now Turkey.[15] Like other archaeologists of the time, Scott hailed the invention of radiocarbon dating as heralding a new age of enlightenment for archaeology. Nevertheless, like many of his colleagues, he stubbornly ignored its findings concerning the Ferriby boats. The results had to be wrong, he argued, as no one from the contemporary civilizations of the Mediterranean and the Middle East could, or would, have come to Britain. Such long seafaring voyages outside the Mediterranean were completely beyond their capabilities, he maintained.

As Scott was considered not only the leading authority in his field but also one of the most powerful figures within the establishment, the majority of the archaeological community appears to have quickly forgotten the Ferriby boats. The finds were stored away in the basement of the Hull Museum and the reports and photographs of Edward Wright and his colleagues were left to gather dust in the museum's archives until, by chance, they were examined by archaeologist Professor Sean MacGrail, of Oxford University, when he visited the museum in 1989. He could not believe how such important discoveries could have been hidden away for so long. In a report to a colleague he declared: 'Indeed the Ferriby boats are of world-wide importance, being surpassed in age only by the third millennium, [BC] planked boats from the vicinity of the royal pyramids at Giza in Egypt.'[16]

It was this statement that had me so intrigued. If Phillips's observations were correct and the radiocarbon dating was accurate, then the Ferriby boats dated from the very same period as the Tara and North Molton necklaces. Could the boats actually have been Egyptian?

I had always believed that the Egyptians were more able seafarers than historians had given them credit. However, the general consensus amongst my fellow Egyptologists was that they had not gone far to sea, in the words of one scholar, Alexandria Nibbi, 'because they didn't want to'.[17]

This always seemed to me to be a strange point of view. Not only are we dealing with the nation who invented the sail but, for example, there is a huge Egyptian harbour at Byblos, on the Syrian coast, dating to as far back as the pyramid age, around 2500 BC. Moreover, there is a wealth of literature, dating back to the so-called Middle Kingdom of the seventeenth century BC, solely devoted to tales of seafaring, such as *The Tale of Sinuhe*. This ancient papyrus tells an epic saga of sea voyages that, some have argued, may have been as far afield as the Black Sea and the coast of Spain. As far as I could tell, no Egyptologist had ever studied the Ferriby boats. I was eager to correct this. The first thing I had to do, however, was to reacquaint myself with the style and manufacture of ancient Egyptian boats, in particular those referenced by MacGrail that had been discovered beside the Great Pyramid of Giza.

Described by the ancient Greeks as the First Wonder of the World, the Great Pyramid of Giza, built by the pharaoh Khufu around 2500 BC, was an astonishing 147 metres high and 233 metres wide. Incredibly, its base covered 5 hectares – an area so vast that it could accommodate the cathedrals of Florence, Milan, London's St Paul's, Westminster Abbey and St Peter's in Rome. Remarkable as this structure is, it was merely the centrepiece for a vast funerary complex built for the king's burial. All around the pyramid were temples and shrines where the dead pharaoh could be eternally honoured by the living. Also, buried around the site were sealed pits containing various items: the dead king's possessions that were to aid and enrich him in the afterlife. It was during excavations of one of these by the Egyptian archaeologist Kamal el-Mallakh in 1954 that a spectacular discovery was made. About 18 metres from the south side of the Great Pyramid, el-Mallakh uncovered a pit just over 31 metres long, still covered by 41 limestone blocks cemented together with plaster. Masons' marks on the blocks indicated that it had been sealed with its contents shortly after the death of Khufu.[18]

When the blocks were removed, the planks of a great boat were revealed for the first time in over 4500 years. The planks and all other components of the vessel had been carefully dismantled before being buried, but due to the airtight condition of the chamber, they had been completely preserved. The marvellous 1224 mint-condition pieces of the boat were removed from the pit and, after years of painstaking work, were reassembled like a giant three-dimensional jigsaw. An astonishing 43.63 metres in length, 5.66 metres wide and large enough for a crew of 100 men, it is now housed in its own museum, which stands in the shadow of Khufu's gigantic pyramid.[19]

Egyptologists contend that such boats were only used for trips along the Nile and seldom made voyages out into the Mediterranean Sea. However, such voyages *were* made, as is demonstrated by the harbour at Byblos, in Syrian territory conquered by the Egyptians in Khufu's reign. Although this vessel dated from over a millennium before the Ferriby finds, the Egyptians of that later period were still building boats in very much the same fashion. This is known from various reliefs dating from the fourteenth century BC, such as those at the temple of Queen Hatshepsut in Luxor. Unlike the later Greeks and Romans, the Egyptians did not constantly strive to improve on their technology. Once they had invented something that did the job, they tended to stick with it.

Were such vessels capable of reaching the British Isles? I decided to consult Dr George Simkis of the Maritime Research Unit at the University of Los Angeles, California – one of the world's leading authorities on ancient ship design. As far as he was concerned, there was no reason why such craft could not have made it to the British Isles, providing they went in summer time and did not encounter bad weather. They may not have been capable of trans-atlantic voyages, but they could have left the Mediterranean through the Straits of Gibraltar, hugged the European coastline and crossed the English Channel. In fact, he told me, many of the Greek and Roman vessels that later visited Britain were indeed far less seaworthy.[20] The question, therefore, was not *could* the Egyptians have done it, but *had* they? Were the Ferriby boats Egyptian vessels that had made such a voyage, only to be wrecked within swimming distance of the British mainland?

Thankfully, Phillips's photographs of the Ferriby boats taken in 1946 still survived at the National Maritime Museum in Greenwich, as did drawings reconstructing how the vessels may originally have looked. I contacted the curator, Gillian Hutchinson, who kindly forwarded me copies. These I compared with detailed pictures of the boat at the Giza museum. I was immediately struck by the similarity in design. In fact, to all intents and purposes, the Ferriby craft were simply smaller-scale versions of the Giza vessel.

If the Ferriby boats really were Egyptian, then, taken together with the Tara and North Molton necklaces, the implications for archaeology and ancient history would be immense. Egyptian finds as far afield as Devon, Yorkshire and Ireland: surely this would be more than evidence of a one-off trading voyage that ended tragically in a storm. Had the ancient Egyptians traded directly and regularly with the Bronze Age peoples of the British Isles?

Determining if the Ferriby boats really were Egyptian would need careful study by both Egyptologists and maritime archaeologists. The radiocarbon dating, however, could easily be checked by modern developments in dendrochronology – dating through tree-ring patterns in timber. Trees have annual growth rings, which are wider when the weather is warmer and narrower when it is cooler, and so an accurate year-by-year record of the climate is available from the time a tree began to grow. From the archaeologist's perspective, this can be very useful as the ring patterns for a particular place and period of time are unique. Dendrochronology utilizes wood from datable ancient sites and compares it with wood from undated sites. In this way a reliable dating can often be made. However, before I could instigate any of this, it was imperative that I examine the Ferriby finds first-hand.

I immediately contacted the Hull Museum and waited with bated breath to be invited to study the remains. However, when the weeks passed and I continued to receive an evasive response, I became increasingly frustrated. What was going on? It almost seemed that I was up against the same stubborn adherence to the academic status quo that the Wright brothers and Phillips had faced half a century before. I had assumed that the unreasonably conservative attitude of the 1950s was well and truly a thing of the past, but I could not have been more wrong. I decided to enlist the help of a colleague, a prominent archaeologist from University College, London, to see if he could use his influence to gain me access to the Ferriby boats. He agreed, only to find himself bogged down by excessive red tape. He eventually gave up trying. 'It all seems to be rather embarrassing to them,' he wrote. 'So they would rather leave it alone.'

With what was looking increasingly like a cloak of secrecy surrounding the Ferriby remains, and with archaeologists seemingly determined to block my investigation, I decided to turn my attention to historians. Was there historical evidence, any surviving records that the ancient Egyptians had visited Britain? I could never have dreamt where my research would lead – to uncover what must surely rank as one of the greatest academic conspiracies of modern times.

CHAPTER TWO

~∞~

THE MYSTERY OF SCOTA

Unlike the ancient Egyptians, who had a wealth of hieroglyphic record, the contemporary peoples of the British Isles around 1350 BC had no form of writing. The oldest British texts are in Latin, following the Roman invasion in the first century AD – almost 1500 years after the time of the necklaces and the Ferriby boats. There was, however, a crude form of writing in Scotland that predated Roman times. Known as Pictish script, after the Picts who inhabited the country, its simple pictograms are found inscribed on stone monuments all over Scotland. It is also known from the Romans that the Picts painted such symbols on their bodies before entering battle. In fact, this is how they got their name, Pict coming from the Latin meaning 'painted men'.[1] Although these Pictish inscriptions dated from the Iron Age, at least half a millennium after the relevant period, I was keen to discover if they included any reference to the earlier Bronze Age peoples of northern Britain.

Unfortunately, although it was once understood from

the Firth of Forth to John o' Groats, the Pictish script has defied translation by modern linguists. Nonetheless, I decided to visit the British Library and examine archaeological photographs and reproductions of these simple pictograms. If the ancient Egyptians had visited Britain, it was just possible that some of their hieroglyphics were echoed in Pictish script. However, on examining the Pictish symbols, I found no similarities that could not be explained by coincidence alone. This did not necessarily mean an end to that line of enquiry: the cross-section of Pictish symbols that still survive is extremely limited, as the majority of such inscriptions were long ago eroded away. Unlike Egypt's dry climate which has allowed so many inscriptions to survive, in the British Isles the damp weather has literally washed away much of its history. Maybe, however, I could find further examples of Pictish script preserved in the earliest histories of Scotland. Perhaps they had been copied by scholars of the past.

The British Library had only recently moved to its brand-new building at St Pancras, but thankfully it was business as usual. Gaining access to one of the many computer terminals in Humanities Reading Room One, I began to scan the Library's vast records, seeking out references to the oldest histories of Scotland. After several hours, I noticed an entry entitled the *Scotichronicon* – 'The Chronicles of Scottish History' or ' The Chronicles of the Scots' – compiled in the mid-fifteenth century. As it was by far the oldest book on Scottish history to which I had so far found reference, I decided it was worth examining. Waiting for the librarian to obtain the copy from the vaults, I began to read the biographical information on the author.

Dating from around 1435, the manuscript was written in Latin by one Walter Bower, Abbot of Inchcolm Abbey, a small Augustinian monastery established on a remote island off the north-east coast of Scotland. Bower was born in Haddington in 1385 and entered the seminary of St Andrews in his early teens. Having a passion for learning, he studied theology, philosophy and law. On leaving St Andrews, as both an acclaimed scholar and an ordained priest, he was quick to climb the monastic ladder: he became the abbot of Inchcolm by the age of thirty-three. However, he did not remain forever locked away in this remote corner of Scotland. He frequently travelled to the royal court in Edinburgh, where he served as a leading cleric for King James I. It was while he was at court, in the early spring of 1420, that he obtained a commission from the Scottish Laird, David Stewart of Rosyth, to chronicle the origins of the ancient Scots. Bower was to spend the next fifteen years of his life working on the manuscript, which ultimately extended to ten volumes.[2]

The librarian returned to inform me that the original manuscript was now held in Corpus Christi College, Cambridge University. However, she did have a recent translation made by Professor Donald Watt of the University of St Andrew's. I settled down to read.

Bower's monumental work covered a period from what he believed to have been the time of Abraham to the time of his writing, but there was no reference anywhere in Watt's index to Pictish script. However, my initial disappointment soon turned to exhilaration. As I casually browsed through the first volume, entitled 'The Origins', which dealt with the first settlers in Scotland, I could not believe my eyes. Bower spoke of an ancient time, well before the Romans arrived in southern Britain, when the north had been visited by the ancient Egyptians. In fact, he claimed, they were led by no less a person than an Egyptian princess – a pharaoh's daughter named Scota.

In ancient times Scota, the daughter of pharaoh, left Egypt with her husband Gaythelos by name and a large following. For they had heard of the disasters which were going to come upon Egypt, and so through the instructions of the gods they fled from certain plagues that were to come. They took to the sea, entrusting themselves to the guidance of the gods. After sailing in this way for many days over the sea with troubled minds, they were finally glad to put their boats in at a certain shore because of bad weather.[3]

This shore, Bower tells us, was somewhere in the north of Britain. He went on to relate how a considerable number of Egyptians accompanied Scota: so many, in fact, that they came in a large fleet. They eventually settled in what is now Scotland and, for a while, lived peacefully with the natives. Ultimately, relations deteriorated and the newcomers were forced to leave, setting sail again to land finally in Ireland. Here, they merged with the local population to form a tribe known as the Scotti, named after their founding princess. The Scotti grew in number and power until they dominated much of Ireland and, for a while, their kings became the high kings of the entire country. Many centuries later, after warring with other tribes, they returned to Scotland, defeated the Picts and conquered the Highlands as a whole. Indeed, the very name Scotland, Bower claimed, derived from these people.[4]

I just could not believe it. The finds in Tara and Ferriby implied that the ancient Egyptians had visited northern Britain and Ireland in pre-Roman times and here, in black and white, was a medieval account of just such a voyage. Were the Ferriby boats a part of Scota's fleet, perhaps sunk when it was forced to hold up 'on a certain shore because of bad weather'? Ferriby is in the north of Britain. Was the

Tara necklace a gift to a local chieftain when the Egyptians first arrived in Ireland? Was the Tara prince, perhaps, even an Egyptian himself? In Irish tradition the Hill of Tara was the seat of the high kings of Ireland and, according to Bower, Scota's descendants *were* those high kings. I found it hard to resist the urge to dash over to the person sitting at the terminal next to me and cry '*Eureka*!' But I calmed myself down. I had to step back and weigh the evidence. After all, it might all be coincidence: Bower might simply have made the whole thing up.

Scota was certainly not an Egyptian name. Although the people of Ireland were called the Scotti in Roman times, they were not named after an Egyptian princess. The word came from a Latin word meaning 'raiders', a term the Romans used for the unconquered Irish because of their daring raids of plunder across the Celtic Sea.[5] Nevertheless, this term could have been confused with the princess's real name at some stage as the story was recounted down the ages. On the positive side, Bower's account was certainly feasible in one respect: his Irish invasion of Scotland did fit within the framework of known historical events.

In the mid-first century, when the Romans had conquered Britain they found it impossible to control the Scottish Highlands. The fierce Pictish tribes were thus left free to raid the new Roman towns established in the north of England. At the beginning of the second century, when the Picts sacked the city of York, defeating a legion of around 5000 men, the Emperor Hadrian ordered that a great defensive wall be built across the entire country, effectively isolating Scotland from what is now England. After this, the Romans abandoned plans for further conquest in the British Isles and Ireland was left alone. In fact, it was the Irish who eventually tried to invade Britain.

When Rome was sacked by the barbarian Visigoths in

AD 410 and the Roman legions withdrew from Britain, central administration collapsed and virtual anarchy ensued. Across the Irish Sea, the Irish seized the initiative and mounted an offensive, quickly gaining a foothold in many parts of western Britain. However, the Britons eventually organized a successful counter-attack and by the sixth century the invaders were largely driven out. It was then that the Irish turned their attention to the Picts north of Hadrian's Wall. Here they succeeded where the Romans failed and by the eighth century had control of the entire region. The Irish tribes who now ruled the Highlands became the great clans, and the peoples of the south – now called the English – still referred to them by their Latin name, Scotti – the Scots.

So Bower was right about the Scotti of Ireland conquering the Picts and lending their name to Scotland – land of the Scots. But what about the story of Scota and her people? If the Tara, North Molton and Ferriby finds in any way reflected Bower's account, then the Egyptians arrived around 1350 BC, over 2500 years before Bower's time. Could such a story have survived for so long?

In 1350 BC, the Bronze Age peoples of mainland Britain were virtually indistinguishable from their counterparts in Ireland and close ties existed between the two. Around 700 BC, however, both were joined by the Celts from continental Europe. The Bronze Age weapons of the native inhabitants were no match for the superior Iron Age weapons of the Celts. Soon, in Britain, the Celts overran the native population. However, in Ireland the two cultures seem to have coexisted peacefully.

As the Bronze Age peoples of Ireland harmoniously merged with the Iron Age Celts, it is reasonable to assume that their oral traditions survived. Also, as they were unconquered by the Romans, such traditions may well have survived until the Irish invaded Scotland in the eighth century AD. The story of an Egyptian presence in Ireland around 1350 BC could, therefore, have been preserved in either Scottish or Irish folklore to endure until the time of Walter Bower. Does historical evidence of any such folklore still exist today?

Owing to the nation's turbulent history, much of Ireland's literary heritage has been lost. Luckily, however, some of it was preserved by monks in the Middle Ages. I therefore decided to consult the earliest surviving manuscript to contain these remnants of old Irish literature. Known as the *Book of Leinster*, it dates from around AD 1150 and is now in the care of the Irish Texts Society in Dublin. I was in luck. The opening section of the manuscript deals with the origins of the Irish people and seems to have been compiled from an amalgamation of recorded history and oral tradition. Here, in the '*Lebor Gabala*', the 'Taking of Ireland', Scota was indeed referenced. It was only a passing mention and amounted to just a couple of lines, but it did refer to Scota, the daughter of an Egyptian pharaoh, landing with her fleet on the shores of Ireland.[6]

It was not, however, only in Ireland that the story of Scota existed before Bower's time. I later discovered reference to the same tradition in Scottish folklore. Around 1050 Reimann, Abbot of Metz in Moselle, France, wrote a biography of the tenth-century Scottish saint Cadroe. He begins the biography with a brief history of Scotland where he explains that the Scots claimed descent from 'a certain Scota, the daughter of a pharaoh of Egypt'.[7] Although neither of these sources included more than a passing mention of Scota, the former, dating from the twelfth century, and the latter, dating from the eleventh, it showed that Bower had not made the story up.

Interestingly, as it turned out, Bower himself seems to

have taken his account from a Welsh source. A few times in his work Bower mentions the *Historia Brittonum* ('History of the Britons') by the ninth-century monk Nennius, from the abbey of Bangor in Gwynedd. Now preserved in the British Library, in a manuscript catalogued as Harley 3859, is an early twelfth century copy. However, the style of writing, together with older fragments of the work which still survive, indicate a much earlier date for its original compilation, sometime around AD 830.[8]

When I returned to the British Library to examine the Nennius manuscript, I did indeed find the Scota legend, almost word for word as it appeared in Bower's account. So the story of Scota not only existed well before the Middle Ages, it was widely spread throughout the British Isles. This alone implied that it was a well-established tradition. But just how old was the story? What was Nennius's source?

Nennius lived during the so-called Dark Ages, a time after the collapse of the Roman Empire, when England had been invaded by the Anglo-Saxons from Denmark and Germany and the native Celts were driven into what is now Wales. Here, the ravages of civil strife and continual hardship meant that much of Britain's history was being lost. Books were either burnt by raiders or perished as civilization continued to collapse. For this reason, Nennius attempted to preserve what was known of the history of the British Celts. He introduces his work by claiming to have compiled his history of the Britons by making 'a heap' of what he could find amongst old documents at his disposal. He tells us: 'I have heaped together all that I found, from the annals of the Romans, the chronicles of the Holy Fathers, the writings of the Irish and the Saxons and the traditions of our own wise men.' The result is disorderly, but certainly appears to be a genuine attempt by the writer to reconstruct a history.[9]

From his work we can gather that the opening verses, those that include the story of Scota, were taken from the *World Chronicle* compiled by the Roman writer Eusebius of Caesarea in around AD 320. Eusebius was the leading bishop at the time of the first Christian emperor Constantine the Great and many of his works were preserved in the Vatican. Unfortunately, the *World Chronicle* was lost when Rome was sacked by the Visigoths in AD 410.[10] Thankfully, however, the work is referenced by the Christian scholar St Jerome, who wrote in Palestine around AD 400. Although his surviving works do not make direct reference to the Scota story, Jerome does recount how Eusebius's Egyptian source was the Greek historian Euhemerus, who visited Egypt and compiled a definitive history of the country around 300 BC.[11] As it seems most unlikely that the wealthy and influential Eusebius consulted colloquial traditions from the remote province of Britain, it was quite possible that his account originated with Euhemerus and so from ancient Egypt. Infuriatingly, this was as far back as I could trace the story, as Euhemerus's work no longer survives.

If Bower's story of Scota's voyage to Britain originated in ancient Egypt, it seems to have been long forgotten, or at least any surviving references must have been pretty obscure. In all my years as an Egyptologist, I had never come across such an account. My best hope was therefore to attempt to identify the mysterious princess. Who exactly was Scota thought to have been?

I had already reasoned that her real name was not Scota: this name was probably due to confusion made in Nennius's day when the Irish were still called the Scotti. By this time it was a common practice to ascribe a people's national name to some specific founder. The mythical hero Romulus was said to have founded Rome, the goddess Athena founded

Athens; even the Britons were said to have derived from a Trojan hero called Britu. If the princess's true name had been forgotten, for Nennius and his contemporaries it would have been quite natural to assume that the founder of the Scotti had been called Scota. Nonetheless, if she existed then her true name must have been preserved in Egyptian records. After all, she was supposed to be the daughter of a pharaoh.

This was, in fact, my best lead. Bower actually names the pharaoh in question. He calls him Achencres.[12] However, like Scota, this is no Egyptian name. Actually, it sounds Greek. Perhaps it originated with Euhemerus. The ancient Greeks often coined Greek sounding names for historical figures. The name Jesus, for example, is a Greek version of the Hebrew name Yeshua. This was particularly true with the Egyptians. Euhemerus's contemporary historian was a man named Manetho, who also wrote in Egypt, and provided a lengthy list of the pharaohs, in which he uses the Greek versions of their names. Manetho was an Egyptian priest who lived at the Temple of Sebennytos in the Delta of Egypt. He had first-hand experience of Egyptian religious beliefs and customs as well as a knowledge of both Greek and Egyptian hieroglyphs. This gave him a background to write eight books, of which the most important was called *Aegyptiaca*. Manetho calls Khufu, for whom the Great Pyramid was built, Cheops; Tutmosis III, the Napoleon of ancient Egypt, he calls Thuthmosis; and Ahmose I, the founder of the Eighteenth Dynasty, he calls Amosis. Indeed, it was in Manetho's work that I found a king by the name Achencres.[13] This was the Greek rendering of the name Akhenaten, a pharaoh who reigned for seventeen years during the middle of the fourteenth century BC – around 1350 BC. Surely this was no coincidence. In all the 3000 years of ancient Egyptian history, this was the only pharaoh to bear that name, and he just so happened to reign at the precise time that the necklaces and the Ferriby boats suggest that the Scota story was set.

Was the mysterious Scota really a daughter of Akhenaten? It would certainly seem appropriate that this enigmatic voyage should have taken place during Akhenaten's reign. It was by far the most mystifying period in Egyptian history. Assuming, for argument's sake, that an Egyptian princess really did lead an expedition to Britain around 1350 BC, the question is why? Mere trading visits would seem most unlikely, in view of the prosperity of the existing commercial networks throughout the Mediterranean. Why else would people risk their lives on these uncharted waters? There would have been no commercial need for the Egyptians to undertake such a long-distance voyage into unknown and hostile territory. Trade alone would certainly discount the pharaoh's own daughter embarking on such a trip, never to return. Bower tells us that the voyagers 'had heard of the disasters which were going to come upon Egypt, and so through the instructions of the gods they fled from certain plagues that were to come'. Akhenaten's reign saw more than its fair share of disasters and it ended with an epidemic that killed off half the royal family. The problems originated at the beginning of the so-called New Kingdom, in the early sixteenth century BC.

From about 1567 BC, the god Amun became the chief deity of all Egypt and his temple at Karnak, in the capital city of Thebes, was expanded to an unprecedented size. This huge temple consisted of a gigantic complex of shrines, courts, halls and processional ways covering hundreds of acres. It is estimated that at the height of the kingdom's power an astonishing 86,000 people staffed the temple of Karnak alone: a multitude of priests, scribes, servants and religious officials, whose essential purpose was to conduct the intricate daily rituals deemed necessary to assure the blessing of Amun and the continued prosperity of Egypt.[14]

The reign of Amenhotep III, in the early fourteenth century BC, was the most prosperous and stable period in Egypt's history. International trade flourished, tributes flooded in from foreign lands and the god Amun was venerated like no other god before. When Amenhotep's son, Akhenaten, succeeded to the throne, everything changed. Trade trickled to a standstill, the empire disintegrated and the god Amun was abandoned. At the beginning of Akhenaten's reign he suddenly, and for no apparent reason, decreed that a new god, a minor solar deity called the Aten, should replace Amun as the chief god of Egypt. Akhenaten outlawed the Amun priesthood, desecrated their temples and seized their great wealth to build a new religious centre to the Aten at Amarna in Middle Egypt.

From palace and tomb reliefs at Amarna we know that Akhenaten's queen was Nefertiti and that the royal couple had no sons. However, they did have six daughters. The first relief to show all six daughters alive is from the private chambers of the royal palace. Dating from the eighth year of Akhenaten's reign, this wall decoration shows the king and queen seated on stools with their six daughters before them, the youngest a babe in her mother's lap. The six princesses were, in descending order of age, Meritaten, Meketaten, Ankhesenpaaten, Neferneferuaten-ta-sherit, Neferneferure and Sotepenre. Which of these might have been the mysterious Scota?

Two of these princesses died and were buried in Amarna by the fourteenth year of Akhenaten's reign. A chamber in the royal tomb complex is decorated with a death-bed scene of a princess lying on a couch. She is mourned by her weeping parents and two distraught attendants, while standing nearby is a nursemaid holding a baby. The inference appears to be that this princess died in childbirth.[15] A companion scene on the opposite wall identifies the deceased as the princess Meketaten, Akhenaten's second eldest daughter. As there are only four princesses in the funerary procession, it appears that one of Meketaten's sisters had also died by this time. This princess was evidently interred in a separate chamber in the royal tomb, but who she was is unclear from the inscriptions alone. Two long scenes in the chamber show the king and queen accompanied by five daughters making offerings in a temple court. Other scenes show the king grieving for the princess, who lies prostrate on a bier. A similar scene above shows the king and queen mourning at her death-bed. Once more, a nursemaid is seen outside the room holding a baby, suggesting that this princess also died in childbirth. As there are five living daughters illustrated here, this cannot be a further representation of Meketaten's funeral, at which only four daughters were present. The name of the deceased has crumbled from the walls, but it would seem to have been the princess Neferneferure, as in 1984 a fragment of a funerary vessel bearing her name was discovered amongst rubble in the area by the Egyptian archaeologist Dr Aly el Kouly.[16]

Two other daughters appear to have died from a plague that decimated the capital towards the end of Akhenaten's reign. A series of inscribed clay tablets, despatches to Akhenaten from foreign dignitaries in the East, found in the ruins of Amarna in the nineteenth century, actually make reference to an unspecified plague which swept the entire Egyptian Empire. After the fifteenth year of Akhenaten's reign, a great many Egyptian nobles disappear from record, including Nefertiti and the queen mother, Tiye. They had evidently all died of the plague.[17] As Neferneferuaten-ta-sherit and Sotepenre are amongst those who are absent from all royal scenes after this time, it seems that they too had died in the epidemic.

The third-eldest daughter, Ankhesenpaaten, survived the plague, but she is accounted for in Egypt well after this time. In fact, she married one of Akhenaten's successors, the famous Tutankhamun, and is depicted in scenes from his tomb. Tutankhamun is thought to have been the son of Akhenaten by a secondary wife named Kiya. Upon his death Ankhesenpaaten went on to marry his successor, the pharaoh Ay, and died in Egypt some years later.

So the only daughter unaccounted for is Meritaten. After the death of her mother Nefertiti, Meritaten is referred to in diplomatic dispatches sent to Akhenaten by various correspondents. One such person is Burnaburiash II, King of Babylon, who calls her by the affectionate nickname 'Mayati', and refers to her as 'the mistress of your house', implying that, as the eldest surviving daughter, she assumed the duties of the dead queen.[18] Strangely, Meritaten disappears around the time of Akhenaten's death. As the eldest princess, she should have been married to the boy-king Tutankhamun, effectively her half-brother, but instead it is her younger sister who has that honour. Nevertheless, there is no record of Meritaten's death and her tomb has so far never been found. What became of her is a complete mystery. As all the other daughters are accounted for, if Scota was a daughter of Akhenaten, as Bower and his sources maintain, she has to have been the enigmatic Meritaten.

Everything seems to fit with the story of Scota coming to Britain. The Ferriby boats appear to place the Egyptians in northern Britain around 1350 BC and the Tara necklace further places them in Ireland. The pharaoh Achencres – Akhenaten – did have a daughter who vanished from Egyptian records at this time. In fact, she disappeared at the very time that the Amun priesthood reasserted their authority and the Aten religion was itself outlawed and its practitioners persecuted. There was indeed a viable motive for the princess and her entourage to flee the Egyptian Empire in a fleet of boats.

It was now time for me to return to Egypt and search for direct evidence of such a voyage.

CHAPTER THREE

—◦◦◦—

THE THEBAN SUPREMACY

It could be argued that the history of Thebes, and its patron god Amun, is the history of Egypt itself. Located approximately 600 kilometres south of Cairo, it is known today by its Arabic name, Luxor, and is one of the most popular tourist sites in the world. In millennia gone by, however, its influence and notoriety spread throughout the known world. In Homer's famous work it was referred to as the 'fabled city of a hundred gates',[1] and, as such, the Greeks named it Thebes, after their own great city, whilst the Egyptians called it Waset, meaning 'dominion'. Thebes was, in effect, the sacred city of Egypt and poetry celebrated its importance. The Papyrus Leiden, dating to the New Kingdom, *circa* 1550–1050 BC, states: 'Thebes is the pattern for every city. Both water and earth were within her from the beginning of time. There came the sands to furnish land, to create her ground as a mound where the earth came into being. And so mankind also came into being within her, with the purpose of founding every city in her proper name. For all are called City after the example of Thebes.'[2]

Consequently, the rise of Thebes would provide the backdrop to my investigation. To understand Akhenaten and what he did, we must examine closely three fundamental issues. Only then will the truth about Scota be revealed. They are as follows: first, the supremacy of Thebes and the phenomenon of the cult of its god, Amun; secondly, the rise of its associated priesthood, the object of Akhenaten's particular vilification; and finally, the character of Akhenaten himself. With the trail now leading into the desert regions of Egypt, it is only fair to prepare the reader for the journey ahead.

During the Renaissance in Europe, interest in ancient Egypt was rekindled. However, unlike the languages of the Greeks and the Romans, the language of ancient Egypt had not been spoken for many years. The land of the Nile was filled with temples, tombs, palaces etc, but to the European visitors, no one could understand the accompanying inscriptions.

Egyptian is first attested in written form around 3300 BC, and survived as a spoken language until the fifteenth century AD. Initially the writing resembled a form of simple pictograms, which was soon developed into a system of decorative hieroglyphs used to decorate the monuments, together with the administrative hieratic script, which was used for writing on papyrus. For years the translation of these mysterious symbols defied all attempts, and it was not until the end of the eighteenth century that it was at last made possible by the discovery of the Rosetta Stone. Housed in the British Museum, this slab of black basalt, measuring nearly 1.2 metres in length and 0.6 metres wide, was originally discovered in August 1799 near the town of Rosetta at the mouth of the River Nile.[3]

Inscribed with fourteen lines of hieroglyphs, thirty-two lines of demotic symbols and fifty-four lines of Greek, the

Stone was apparently written by the priests of Memphis in the reign of Ptolemy V Epihanes in about 179 BC. The importance of the stone was immediately recognized because the Greek inscriptions provided a key to the translation of the Egyptian hieroglyphs. Their decipherment was accomplished by an Englishman, Thomas Young and by the more famous Jean Francois Champollion of France. Young identified the names of Ptolemy and Cleopatra and recognized in which direction the texts should be read whilst, in 1821, Champollion succeeded in the complete decipherment of both the hieroglyphic and demotic script upon the Stone.[4]

When the Greek historian Herodotus first visited Egypt some four and a half centuries before the birth of Christ, he was mesmerized. 'The wonders were greater than those of any other land,' he remarked.[5] Herodotus was born in Halicarnassus around 485 BC and his extensive travels took him to Egypt in about 450 BC, during a period when the country was ruled by the Persian Empire. His book *The Histories* was mainly an account of the country's history and geography, but he made a habit of recording the many strange things he encountered. There were two things that intrigued him more than any other: Egypt's immense antiquity and the River Nile. No one who visits Egypt can fail to be amazed at the effect the Nile has on the country. For nearly 3000 years, its valley sustained a spectacular civilization, dependent entirely on the river. The Egyptians themselves referred to it as *iteru aa*, 'the great river',[6] but it was the invading Greeks who named the river 'Neilos', the Nile. Carrying the waters of Lake Victoria more than 3000 miles, every year vast torrents, full of rich sediment, sweep across the plains of Africa, flooding the banks of the river. It is this silt that gave the valley its astonishing fertility. Abundant in minerals, it transformed one of the largest arid deserts in the world, and allowed Egyptian civilization to develop into the power-base it became. Without it, it would have been a desolate waste. The contrast between the desert and the cultivation could not have been more apparent. Whereas the desert was referred to as Deshret, the 'Red Land', the Egyptians called their country Kemet, the 'Black Land', after the colour of the soil.[7]

The River Nile had a profound effect on all aspects of Egyptian life. Their calendar of twelve months, each of thirty days, was based upon it. This ancient calendar is the model we use for our own one today. They divided the year into three seasons: the time of the summer flood was called the 'inundation'. 'Emergence' was the phase when the water receded and the crops could then be planted, and the 'dry time', during the spring, was the time of the harvest.[8] Compared to any other of the world's great rivers, the Nile was more constant than most. But life on the Nile could still be precarious.

As you look at a map of Egypt, the Nile flows from south to north and the narrow valley in the southern part of the country is thus called Upper Egypt. The flat alluvial plain of the Delta region in the north was referred to as Lower Egypt. Together they combined to form the sacred 'Two Lands'. The two kingdoms were integrated under one ruler in around 3100 BC, but each had its own individual regalia. The low Red Crown, called the *deshret*, represented Lower Egypt, and its emblem was the papyrus plant. Upper Egypt was represented by the tall White Crown, called the *hedjet*, its symbol being the flowering lotus. The combined Red and White Crowns became the *shmty*, the Double Crown of Egypt.

The history of Egypt rests upon a number of sources. Five inscribed monuments have so far been uncovered that give the names and order of the succession of many of

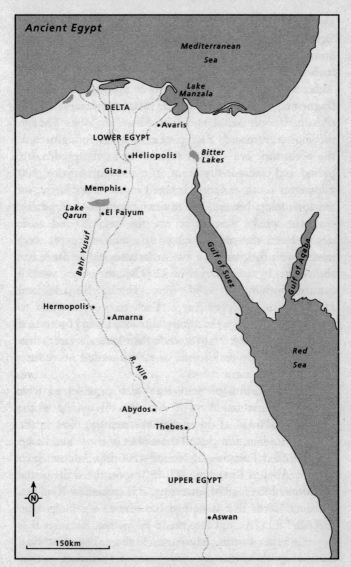

Map of ancient Egypt

Egypt's pharaohs. Of the earlier annals kept by the ancient Egyptian scribes, only one survives. Called the Palermo Stone, it consists of a black diorite slab, originally thought to be over 2 metres long, dating from around 2470 BC. Although the slab has obviously been broken up into small fragments, it is quite plausible that many more pieces remain, if only scholars knew where to look. Though incomplete, it records a series of early kings dating back to the prehistoric era. This is referred to as the predynastic period and traditionally began at the site of Abydos, 300 kilometres south of Cairo. It was here in Upper Egypt, on the low desert beneath the towering western escarpment, that the predynastic rulers of the region, and their descendants, the earliest kings of a united Egypt, were buried with their possessions. Archaeological evidence has shown that by the end of *circa* 3200 BC, the most powerful centres within the land were Thinis, Naqada and Hierkonpolis in Upper Egypt. Each territory appears to have been ruled by a hereditary elite exercising power on a regional basis. Regrettably, while their status is clear, they are quite literally prehistoric, as they have left no written records of their time.[9]

The application of 'king lists' also provides us with further information. A royal list was discovered in the Temple of Karnak at the turn of the century. Now in the Louvre Museum, it included the names of those kings who had preceded Tutmosis III around 1500 BC. Another such list, the Abydos King List, still in situ on the walls of the corridors of the Hall of Ancestors, was erected by King Seti I around 1290 BC. It named the seventy-six kings who preceded him. A duplicate made by his son Rameses II is now in the British Museum. Sadly, as a historical chronology these lists are inadequate on their own as they fail to provide the length of each individual pharaoh's reign.

Luckily, however, one ancient text has survived: a list of some 300 kings, written on a long sheet of papyrus dating from around 1200 BC. Though damaged and now incomplete, it is the finest record of the chronology of the Egyptian kings. Originally in the possession of the King of Sardinia, it was sent to Turin in a box without any packing for protection. Consequently, it arrived at its destination broken into innumerable fragments.[10] Called the Royal Canon of Turin after the museum in which it is housed, it not only gives the order of succession, but also provides the exact period of each reign, right down to the months and days. Other dating checks are provided by the biographies on tomb inscriptions.

Today, historians ascribe the foundation of Egyptian civilization to approximately 3100 BC. According to Manetho's work, this culminated with the unification of the kingdoms of Upper and Lower Egypt. Tradition attributes this unification to King Menes, although whether he truly existed or was simply a symbolic figure is open to question. Egyptologists divide the history of Egypt into thirty-one separate dynasties, grouped into three major periods when stable and unified government presided over the land. These periods are usually termed the Old, Middle and New Kingdoms. On occasions they are interrupted by intervals of social and political upheaval. These are called the First, Second and Third Intermediate Periods. For example, Akhenaten reigned at the end of the Eighteenth Dynasty during the New Kingdom period. Regnal dates are also used, such as Akhenaten's Year 12, which is applied not for confusion but to ensure the greatest possible accuracy.

Unlike a modern day monarch, the King of Egypt was seen as a semi-divine figure by the people, the sole go-between connecting the world of the heavenly and the world of men. He was a necessity. In some ways, you could say, he acted as an agent for the gods. He occupied the highest position in Egyptian society, like the capstone of a pyramid; his role was pivotal to Egyptian culture. In theory he was Commander-in-Chief of the Egyptian armed forces, the high priest of every temple in the land, the head of the administration and treasury and also the chief judge, responsible for administering justice.[11] Every strand of life ultimately came together in the person of the king. He was accepted without question as an absolute ruler who owned both the land as well as the people within.

The modern word 'pharaoh' evolved from the Egyptian word per-a'a meaning 'great house'. As a rule there was only one male native-born king on the throne of Egypt at any given time, although some chose to share their power with a co-regent, usually the designated son and heir. However, during the so-called Intermediate Periods there were, more often than not, two or three kings claiming to rule over a disjointed country. Surprisingly, in nearly 3000 years of continuous history, there were only four women who had sat upon the throne of Egypt. This may be due to the simple fact that the King of Egypt was viewed by the people as the living incarnation of the *male* falcon god Horus, the son of the sun god Ra.[12] When the king died, he was thought to become Osiris, God of the Underworld. Central to this view of kingship was the concept of *maat*. A complex notion, it has been roughly translated by scholars as 'truth' or 'justice'. It was personified by a goddess, also called Maat, who was regarded as the daughter of the sun god Ra and who would preside over the judgement of the dead. From an early age, the kings of Egypt were taught to uphold the principles of *maat* and be a 'good king'. Each new king claimed to have restored the spirit of *maat* upon his accession to the throne, no matter how benevolent the rule of his predecessor.[13]

By Akhenaten's reign, a well-defined social pyramid had evolved. The king was supported in his tasks by an elite band of nobles, all of whom were male and, more often than not, close family relations. Next there were the prominent local families, who gave their undying support to the king and were employed at the highest levels of local government. This upper tier of society, it has been argued, numbered no more than 2000–3000 people, whilst the total population of Egypt during the New Kingdom has been estimated at somewhere between 3 and 4 million. This group was followed by the middle classes including administrators, minor priests and artisans, whilst the lower middle classes included such people as foot soldiers and peasants who worked the land for the king and the temple estates. The lowest on the social scale were the farmers.[14]

The Eighteenth Dynasty was a period when Egypt was experiencing its greatest era of prosperity. The country's success lay in the activities of its first ruler and founder, the great military leader Ahmose who, in around 1550 BC, successfully rid the land of the loathed Hyksos rulers, and united Egypt once more. He was revered for his talent as a mighty warrior king and succeeding Eighteenth-Dynasty monarchs therefore deemed it necessary to place great emphasis on their military strength. Nowhere is this better illustrated then during the reign of the so-called 'warrior king', Tutmosis III, *circa* 1479–1425 BC. In less than five months in power, he had travelled from Thebes right up the Syrian coast, fought a number of decisive battles, captured three cities and returned to his capital to celebrate his victories. He captured the eldest sons of the various foreign kings and princes as hostages and deported them to Thebes. The spoils of victory included 900 chariots and over 200 coats of mail.[15] Remarkably, a campaign was launched against Syria every summer for the next eighteen years, as well as the customary expeditions deep into Nubian territory. With such increasing military activity in the Near East, it was time for Egypt to maintain an efficient fighting force. For the first time in its history there was now a full-time army that soon became a focus of national honour and pride. In addition, it was viewed as an excellent piece of propaganda for the king to be seen defending his territory and smiting his enemies before him.

The early Eighteenth-Dynasty rulers broke with tradition when they established their capital at their home city of Thebes. During the Old Kingdom period, Thebes had apparently been an unimportant provincial town and it was not until the civil unrest of the First Intermediate Period that the name Thebes was firmly placed on the Egyptian map. Previous to that, the city of Memphis, in the Delta region, was the site of the main royal residence and the country's administrative centre. Situated at the crossroads between the two traditional regions of Upper and Lower Egypt, Memphis enjoyed excellent communications with both north and south. Accordingly, during the Eighteenth Dynasty, both Thebes and Memphis became sites of royal residence. The latter is particularly associated with the young princes, who were often sent to Memphis to be educated in the affairs of state. Even so, Thebes was still regarded as the undisputed state capital and, more importantly, the religious centre of Egypt. It was this supremacy that Akhenaten was later to try and take on to create his own power centre.

Another innovative feature of the Eighteenth Dynasty was the brand new location selected by the kings for their burial. It appears they abandoned the earlier custom of pyramid building and opted for deep rock-cut tombs instead. It has to be said, however, that the geological formations of the Theban cliffs do look like a natural pyramid, both in shape and in colour and, this may have encouraged the Egyptians to choose such a site in the first place. Isolated and relatively easy to guard, but also close by the city, these inhospitable valleys were regarded as an ideal location to develop as the royal necropolis. Today, this windswept, narrow gorge is called the Valley of the Kings.

But perhaps the most defining characteristic of the Eighteenth Dynasty was the improvement in the status of women, without which the tale of Scota would probably not have been recognized, let alone recorded. Ancient Egyptian society maintained a distinction between the roles of the sexes, and since the beginning of Egyptian history, women, not even royal women, were rarely depicted. But now, for the very first time, the prominence of the queens is apparent in the monumental art. From the beginning of the Eighteenth Dynasty, wives, mothers and daughters were frequently shown accompanying the king, whereas the royal men were now generally unseen.[16] In defiance of previous royal tradition, the Theban rulers of the Eighteenth Dynasty accepted that their womenfolk were quite capable of assuming a prominent role in state affairs and, most importantly, a unique significance was attached to the positions of King's Wife and King's Mother. As we shall see (see Chapter 6), this is no better illustrated than during the time of Scota's grandfather, Amenhotep III, and beyond, including the extraordinary status awarded to her mother Nefertiti and even the eminent rank bestowed upon Scota herself.

Another common feature of the royal family was the prominence of brother-sister relationships. The reasons behind such unions are unclear. They were unique and it appears that during the Eighteenth Dynasty the royal family had no desire either to increase its numbers or to unite with any other families. Incestuous marriages were therefore a suitable means of ensuring the purity of the royal line. Perhaps by restricting the size of the royal family, 'royalness' could be maintained within a close but small group of individuals. In addition, incestuous marriages ensured that a suitable husband could always be found for the highest-ranking princess.[17] As we shall shortly see, Scota eventually married her own father, Akhenaten, and became the King's Chief Wife. For those like Akhenaten who believed that royal blood made them profoundly different from other mortals, a sister or daughter made the logical choice of spouse. After all, surely an Egyptian princess was the best possible mother for the future king of Egypt.

By the middle of the Eighteenth Dynasty, Egypt ruled a great Empire, stretching northwards into the Near East as far as the Euphrates River and southwards deep into present-day Sudan. It was an empire forged initially by military might but sustained in the end by diplomacy and the gift of gold.[18] The most beautiful and precious of all materials, gold was universally sought after throughout the Near East, and Egypt was its main source. From the mines of Nubia enormous quantities of gold poured into the treasuries of the pharaohs. Inscriptions dating from the time of Tutmosis III record that during three years of his reign an aggregate of 9277 deben of gold was received from these sources. A deben was a basic unit of weight, equivalent to 91 grains. The total gold recorded is therefore equivalent to 794 kilograms, and would be worth many millions of dollars at today's prices.[19] A succession of strong figureheads now turned Egypt into the most powerful state in the world and Thebes became the most influential city. Wealth poured in from client kingdoms in the form of gold, luxury goods and slaves. International diplomacy developed and the architecture was as ambitious as any foreign policy, reaching its zenith with the construction of the great Temple of Amun at Karnak.

From the beginning of Thebes's meteoric ascent, the god Amun had been directly at its side. His great temple and priesthood at Karnak would, in time, wield unprecedented power. They ensured that Amun had no other rival. When Egypt's imperial conquests had reached their peak, the Theban priesthood promoted Amun as a 'ruler of all peoples'.[20] A major cult site was even established deep within Nubian territory at a sacred place called Gebel Barkal. But where Amun had stemmed from has puzzled Egyptologists for centuries.

The images that appear on the temple and tomb walls paint an idyllic picture of life along the banks of the Nile, but in truth it was a life full of uncertainty. To understand the world around them, the Egyptians created a vast assortment of deities. The role of religion in the life of ancient Egypt can be difficult for the modern mind to appreciate. Nowadays, religion generally encompasses an individual's relationship with those aspects of life that cannot be explained 'scientifically'. In ancient Egypt, as in other ancient societies, religion and science were regarded as one.[21] Where modern science explains the universe in terms of a set of physical laws, ancient minds saw the phenomena as the manifested forces of sentient, godly beings. In Egyptian thought, there were as many such beings as there are forces in the universe: the sun (Ra), the earth and sky (Geb and Nut), the atmosphere (Shu), the annual inundation (Hapy), order (Maat), disorder (Seth) and kingship (Horus). Accordingly, religion was a way of life, yet for most people the concept of organized religion, such as communal worship, had no meaning. Since the gods were completely integrated into Egyptian society, they simply lived among their supporters, tending to the needy, answering the prayers of the troubled and governing every aspect of daily life. The gods not only belonged to Egypt, they were considered to be Egyptians![22] Their multitude fell into three main categories:

1. Local gods, which were inanimate objects, or animals, birds and other living creatures with a particular locality.
2. Universal gods, the cosmic deities who represented the forces of nature – the sun, the moon, the stars, wind and storm.
3. Personal gods, the objects or creatures chosen by individuals to receive their allegiance.[23]

Our knowledge of Egyptian deities derives mainly from the numerous inscriptions and carvings upon the tombs and temple walls, whereas specific myths were, more often than not, written down on papyrus by the royal scribes. Few Egyptian myths are as well known, or had such an impact on Western culture, as the cycle of tales regarding Isis and Osiris at Heliopolis, or the great god Ptah centred at Memphis. But despite a proliferation of powerful gods which had dominated Egyptian thought for centuries, it was Amun, a little-known god of the wind, who, in a short space of time, took Egyptian religion by storm. From humble beginnings, in around 1991 BC, this insignificant deity rose to become the supreme state god of Egypt and his influence spread rapidly right the way through the ancient world. Temples and shrines were erected throughout Nubia and the Near East in his honour. In later years, making his way to the Siwa Oasis, in the Eastern Desert, Alexander the Great visited the Great Oracle of Amun. After Amun had acknowledged him as the god's son and pharaoh incarnate, Alexander then declared, 'I have spoken to the one true God.'[24]

Amun's rise to pre-eminence was as a direct result of the

Eleventh and Twelfth Dynasty Theban rulers. The original local god of Thebes had been Monthu, a warrior god, known as the Lord of Thebes. Yet, through the activities of the newly crowned Theban kings, in particular Amenemhat, *circa* 1990–1962 BC, Amun ultimately became both King of the Gods and Lord of the Two Lands.[25] The ram became his most sacred symbol and he was depicted as a man, painted blue-black, and wearing the characteristic crown of two tall plumes. His name translates as 'the hidden one' and his creation is shrouded in ambiguity. Around him was woven an intricate web of Egyptian beliefs and myths, each embracing the idea of a heavenly king, a supreme all-powerful god.[26]

His consort was the ancient goddess Mut, who was usually depicted with a vulture headdress or wearing a crown, either the White Crown of Upper Egypt or the Double Crown of Upper and Lower Egypt. The name Mut, which is written using the hieroglyph of a vulture, is actually thought to have been the old Egyptian term for vulture. However, her name also signifies 'mother' and she is sometimes identified with the protector goddess Apet. Like other mother goddesses, such as Isis, she was regarded as the Great Mother who gave birth to all that exists.

Their son was Khonsu, a moon god who was depicted wearing a crescent moon upon his head. In addition, he was also portrayed as a mummiform figure, with a side-lock of hair, the traditional representation of Egyptian youth. As a moon deity, Khonsu caused the crops to grow and ripen, yet he was also the ancient Egyptian god of healing. Together they formed the Theban triad, the most powerful conglomerate of deities the ancient world had ever known.

Around 2000 BC Egypt entered a new phase of religious development, with Amun at the helm. Whether to increase his grip over the Egyptian state or to appease the traditional elements within the higher echelons of society, the Theban kings quickly amalgamated the archaic sun god Ra with their own, to form a new composite god, called Amun-Ra. Such composite gods were common in Egyptian mythology and the combining of two powerful deities was not unique.

Dating to somewhere in the prehistoric era, the cult of Ra had developed primarily at Heliopolis in the north. He was effectively the god of the king and was embraced for the most part by the Royal family and the higher echelons of Egyptian society. Accordingly, he had no appeal to the general masses. Nevertheless, by openly uniting the two gods, the Middle Kingdom rulers hoped to spark a move towards a more personal piety. In Amun, the people of Egypt had discovered a deity that was sympathetic to all levels whilst the Ra element appeased the higher nobility. It was a shrewd move by the newly installed Theban kings.

For the majority of the population, the most direct encounter with Amun occurred when his cult statue came out of its sanctuary on the occasion of major festivals. The most important of these was the beautiful Feast of Opet, when the statues of Amun, his wife Mut and their son Khonsu were escorted in a great and joyous procession down an avenue of sphinxes, 3 kilometres long, to the temple of Luxor. It was an event eagerly awaited by the Egyptian people. On the fifteenth or the nineteenth day of the Akhet season, a riot of activity would erupt as the triad appeared at the door of the temple in their ceremonial travelling barques, hoisted on the shoulders of the priests. Soldiers and citizens chanted hymns of praise, others kneeled in adoration and kissed the ground. Musicians, dancers and acrobats performed for the gods, priests clapped their hands and women shook their rattles. Along the route, specially built chapels with offerings provided rest stops for the gods and the priests, while vendors lined the way supplying food for the masses.[27]

Just as the Old Kingdom had become obsessed with the pyramids and the dead, the New Kingdom became obsessed with the worship of Amun. No longer would he be regarded as a mere religious icon, he was now a major political figure. In the role of protector god of the pharaoh, he was regarded as directly responsible for Egypt's military success in the Near East during the Eighteenth Dynasty. The kings openly acknowledged that their prosperity was due to the patronage of their local god Amun of Thebes. His banner, or standard, in the shape of a golden container, an ark, was paraded at the head of the army as they prepared to attack Egypt's enemies. For instance, in an inscription on the walls of Karnak Temple at Thebes, Tutmosis III thanks Amun for his military conquests:

> I come to thee, lord of gods; I do obeisance before thee in return for this thou has given to me the kingdom of every land in the presence of the two lands. I am satisfied with victories, thou hast placed every rebellious land under my sandals which thy serpent-diadem has bound, bearing their gifts. I have seized them in victory according to thy command; they are made my subjects.[28]

Such campaigns brought considerable wealth into Egypt, a large quantity of which ended up in the hands of the priesthood of Amun. In return for their loyalty, Amun was considered to have rewarded the pharaoh with supreme power throughout Egypt. The balance of power between the two prominent deities, Amun and Ra, was no longer level, as it had been during the Middle Kingdom period. The sun god Ra would now play a far smaller role in Egyptian political affairs. Kings were no longer regarded as the 'Son of Ra'; a new title was introduced and they now became 'the son of his Father Amun'.[29] Emphasis was now placed on Amun as the creator god of all mankind, absorbing all the qualities and features of Egypt's more ancient and traditional gods. His priesthood began to promote a new cosmogony, whereby Thebes replaced Egypt's long-established religious centre, Heliopolis, as the new 'place of Egypt's creation'.[30] All earlier creation myths, including those of the sun god Ra, were now ousted by Amun's cult centre at Thebes. It surely can be no surprise then that the time-honoured priesthood of Ra did not take kindly to the affront afforded to them. In next to no time, it had effectively been ousted from having any influence on the crown, let alone Egypt's political and religious organization. For the time being, the Heliopolitan priesthood remained powerless to oppose the new religious order. Biding its time, it sat back and watched as the Theban kings, in gratitude to their patron god Amun, erected one of the greatest sanctuaries the world has ever seen – Karnak Temple.

CHAPTER FOUR

———————

PIETY AND POWER

Unlike churches, the temples of ancient Egypt were not places of communal worship. Carefully designed to mirror the universe, they functioned more like well-oiled machines, maintaining the status quo.[1] They possessed huge estates and employed a large number of people to do the deity's bidding. They were, to all intents and purposes, big business, and as such they played a vital role in the social, economic and administrative life of the country. The ancient Egyptian term for temple was *hwt ntr*, which means 'mansion of the gods'. The latter was originally the term for the royal residence but eventually designated both the residence and the ruler in the name 'pharaoh'. The god's temple was, in fact, his house, his earthly home.

Since each temple was the god's official residence, it is not surprising that the services performed within them reflected daily life. Every morning, the priests would slide back the bolt on the doors of the shrine, opening them to reveal the sacred image of the god and performing the necessary offerings. The accompanying temple choir would greet the awakening god with a hymn. An example exists in the Chester Beatty papyri, which are now in the British Museum and date to the reign of Rameses II (*circa* 1279–1212 BC):

What is sung by the two river-banks to Amun in the morning:
The doors are opened at the sanctuary, the shrine is thrown
    open in the mansion,
Thebes is in festivity, Heliopolis in joy, Karnak is rejoicing.
Jubilation fills heaven and earth . . .
Song is made for this noble god Amun-Ra, Lord of the Thrones
    of the Two Lands,
And Amun, Lord of Luxor.
His fragrance has encompassed the circuit of the Great Green
    [Sea],
He has bathed them in gold with his rays.[2]

After this, the god, represented by his cult statue, was washed, dressed for the day and given his breakfast. Early each day with the dawn, the workshops and stores were busy with people preparing the offerings for this morning service; a fresh supply of bread, cakes and beer, fresh fruit and vegetables and so on. The food would then revert to the priests of the temple. During the evening service the god was given his evening meal and prepared for bed, after which he would be locked away in his own shrine. The average Egyptian was strictly forbidden to enter temple ground. This was the sole domain of the god's servitors, the priests. Only during 'feast days' were the people allowed to pay homage. It has been shown, for example, that at Luxor Temple members of the local populace were allowed inside and indeed possibly encouraged to enter parts of the temple, in order that they could witness some of the rites of the Opet Festival. However, the areas they could visit there seem to have been limited to only one side of the two open courtyards.[3]

At the height of Egypt's greatness, during the New Kingdom, temples were built on a large scale. Nowhere is this better illustrated then the great Temple of Amun at Karnak. Its sheer majesty cannot fail to impress. Compared to the Pyramids at Giza, which appear cold and lifeless, it represents the true life-blood of ancient Egyptian religious and political beliefs. It once led the pioneering Egyptologist Amelia Edwards to remark: 'How often has it been written and how often has it been repeated that the great hall of Karnak is the noblest architectural work ever designed and executed by human hands. There is in truth no building in the world to compare to it.'[4]

The first drawings of Karnak Temple were made by the explorer Captain L. Norden, who rediscovered it in the early eighteenth century. He was soon followed by the English traveller Reverend Richard Pococke, who was responsible for creating the first site plan. Pococke first visited Egypt in 1737 when, on his Nile journey, he viewed the temples at Denderah, Armant and Thebes. His *Travels in Egypt* was published in 1743, and the account already comments on the damage to the monuments: 'They are every day destroying these fine morsels of Egyptian antiquity, and I saw some of the pillars being hewn into mill-stones.' It was Napoleon's expedition to Egypt, in 1798, which provided the first real scientific exploration of Karnak. Napoleon established a special Scientific and Artistic Commission to obtain both cultural and technological information on ancient Egypt.[5] The Commission undertook their research with the aid of a library and scientific apparatus imported from France. The team consisted of 167 scientists and technicians, including mathematicians, astronomers, chemists, engineers, mineral-

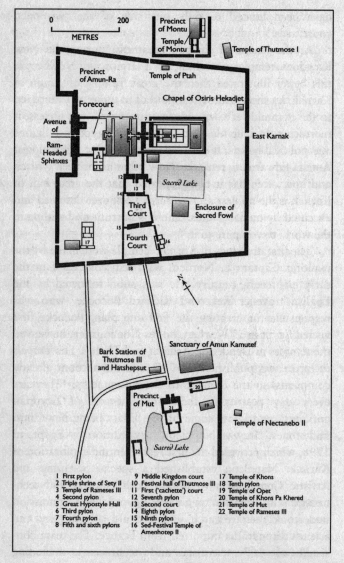

0   200
METRES

Precinct
of Montu
Temple
of Montu

Temple of Thutmose I

Precinct
of Amun-Ra

Temple of Ptah

Chapel of Osiris Hekadjet

Forecourt

Avenue
of

Ram-
Headed
Sphinxes

East Karnak

Sacred Lake

Enclosure of
Sacred Fowl

Third
Court

Fourth
Court

N

Bark Station of
Thutmose III
and Hatshepsut

Sanctuary of Amun Kamutef

Precinct
of Mut

Temple of Nectanebo II

Sacred Lake

1 First pylon
2 Triple shrine of Sety II
3 Temple of Rameses III
4 Second pylon
5 Great Hypostyle Hall
6 Third pylon
7 Fourth pylon
8 Fifth and sixth pylons

9   Middle Kingdom court
10 Festival hall of Thutmose III
11 First ('cachette') court
12 Seventh pylon
13 Second court
14 Eighth pylon
15 Ninth pylon
16 Sed-Festival Temple of
    Amenhotep II

17 Temple of Khons
18 Tenth pylon
19 Temple of Oper
20 Temple of Khons Pa Khered
21 Temple of Mut
22 Temple of Rameses III

Site Plan of Karnak Temple

ogists, naturalists, botanists, surgeons, physicians, artists, writers and antiquarians. The various members worked for three years, mapping and gathering information, and produced nineteen volumes of the *Description de l'Egypte* (1809–1828).

The modernization of Egypt's economy and the need for stone for the ever-growing construction industry meant that the ancient temples were frequently used as quarries. It was thought that the original Middle Kingdom temple of Karnak was destroyed in this way, piece by piece. For their own part, the Egyptian people also used the temple mud brick as fertilizer for their crops, destroying the monuments and archaeological evidence in the process. Faced with such pillaging, in which numerous self-appointed Egyptologists participated, the likes of Jean Francois Champollion, who is more famous for his decipherment of Egyptian hieroglyphs, raised the alarm. Regrettably, economic interests prevailed and their efforts went unheeded. In 1835 the Viceroy of Egypt, Muhammad Ali, issued a decree protecting the ancient monuments of Egypt, but despite his pronouncement, even five years afterwards the pylons (gateways) in the processional way were still being used as stone quarries. The obelisk guarding the entrance to Karnak's sister temple at Luxor was carried off to Paris and then, in 1843, the Hall of Ancestors was transported to the Louvre. It was not until 1858 that the Egyptian Antiquities Service was founded and under the direction of the late, great French archaeologist Auguste Mariette, the quarrying was stopped and the temples cleared. In 1875 Mariette published two volumes entitled *Karnak: étude topographique et archeologique*. It was the very first historical outline of the development of Karnak Temple.[6]

The central temple at Karnak was dedicated to the god Amun and it forms one of the largest religious complexes in the world. Inside the main sanctuary there were a number of other smaller temples dedicated to the god Ptah and the moon god Khonsu, as well as a number of minor shrines. The ancient Egyptians called Karnak Iput-Isut, meaning 'the most esteemed of places', and there is possibly evidence to suggest that a temple may have stood there as early as the Old Kingdom. Regrettably, due to the pillaging, little archaeological evidence remains. Nonetheless, there is certainly evidence for the existence of the Karnak Temple in the reign of Inyotef II (*circa* 2117–2069 BC), when it was called the 'abode of Amun'. The core of these Middle Kingdom buildings now lies in the heart of the current temple.

The extent, scale and quality of the remains at Karnak are quite astonishing. From its central core, dating to the Twelfth Dynasty, Amun's great temple expanded along two axes, towards the river Nile and the corresponding Temple of Mut, whilst its enclosure wall approached the precinct of Monthu in the north. Covering an area of 150 hectares, it is larger than the modern Vatican City. Ten massive gates, each reaching a height of 75 metres, divided the temple into three huge precincts, housing over twenty individual temples. Extensive courtyards were filled with an array of statues, shrines and gigantic gold-tipped obelisks: endowments from a succession of appreciative pharaohs. At the heart of the temple was the most sacred sanctuary of all: a dark, windowless chamber known as the 'Holy of Holies'. Here, a golden statue of the god Amun was protected, securely in his ark (barque) shrine.

Since the main channel of communication in ancient Egypt was the Nile, and the boat was the most obvious means of transport, it was perhaps inevitable that the barque, or ark, should have been established as the vehicle in which the Egyptian gods were transported from one shrine to another. These divine barques were similar in design and shape to Nile boats, except that their prows and sterns were adorned with the symbol of the god in question. The cabin contained the cult image of the deity. These barques were usually kept in the inner sanctuary of the temple.[7]

Many ancient documents have survived which record Karnak's splendour. One such is kept in the vaults of the British Museum. Called the *Great Harris Papyrus*, after its finder, and dated to the day that Rameses III died, in around 1151 BC, it informs us that the temple complex was so huge that it was staffed by an astonishing 86,000 people. As a result, it was by far the largest ecclesiastically-controlled economic unit in the country. The papyrus also lists an inventory of Amun's possessions. In total the holdings of the temple of Amun comprised 2393 kilometres of arable land, almost a quarter of the cultivated land in Egypt, 433 orchards, 421,362 head of livestock, 65 villages, 83 ships and 46 workshops or building sites. It owned two-thirds of all the temple land in Egypt, 90 per cent of all ships and 80 per cent of all factories. To top it all off, the Karnak granaries had a total income of nearly 2 million sacks of grain each year.[8] But what is important to appreciate here is that the *Great Harris Papyrus* dates from an era when Egypt was in decline. The true extent of Karnak's power and economic stranglehold over the country during its high point, namely the Eighteenth Dynasty, can only be guessed at. It is thought that throughout this era, the Amun precinct employed over 20 per cent of Egypt's total population.

What is abundantly clear is that from the figures quoted above, the temple's domination would have been immense. From this position of ultimate supremacy, did they threaten the one position that was held most sacred in the land of Egypt – the king? Considering the king's crucial role in

Egyptian society, would the Amun priesthood have posed such a threat? Could it have mustered enough political weight to challenge the widely held belief of a divine sovereign? As we have seen, the king was pivotal to the orderly functioning of the state. There was no alternative: I had to see for myself the true extent of Amun's might and influence. It was time to travel to Thebes.

The sun had just risen above the banks of the Nile as I finally reached my destination on 8 July 1998. Even so, the temperature was well above 100 degrees Fahrenheit. Ironically, Egypt was in the throes of a heatwave! I paid the taxi driver and purchased my ticket from the booth. Passing the remains of the ancient dock, I made my way to the entrance of Karnak Temple – the home of the god Amun.

Approaching this most sacred of places via an avenue of ram-headed sphinxes, the imposing First Pylon, or gateway, loomed above me, casting a huge shadow over the nearby causeway and providing welcome relief from the sun for tourists and residents alike. It is impossible to express the vast magnitude of this imposing gateway – 130 metres wide and 43 metres high. Dynasty after dynasty added to it and one might speculate about which ruler oversaw each of the various sections. I passed through and entered into the Great Forecourt, which consists of a wide open expanse covering a total area of 8919 square metres. I ignored the throng of tourists assembled upon the path, and turning to my immediate right, I headed towards one of the most surreptitious and enigmatic temple structures in the complex.

Situated in the far south-west of the Karnak precinct, today the Temple of Khonsu is surrounded on all sides by a heap of bricks, rubble and sand, some reaching a height of over 2 metres in places. Gateway construction on the neighbouring Tenth Pylon has transformed this particular area into what can only be described as a building site. Consequently, tourists are forbidden to enter the temple confines. Mercifully, the previous evening, after many long hours of negotiation, I was privileged to obtain a special permit from Mr Raschid, a representative of the Supreme Council of Antiquities, allowing me access. So, ignoring the Arabic 'Keep Out' signs, I clambered over the rope barricade. No sooner had my feet touched the ground than I was accosted by the habitual temple guardian. Reaching into my bag, I pulled out my precious permit and explained that I had been given permission to visit this forbidden area. The guard eyed the piece of paper suspiciously and stated that my permit would need to be authenticated. This could set me back hours! Finally, I gave in to the customary 'donation' of 10 Egyptian pounds, whereby the guard smiled, moved aside, and let me pass.

Thought to have been built by a succession of kings named Rameses (*circa* 1186–1069 BC), although some Egyptologists believe that it may have originally been constructed by Amenhotep III, the Temple of Khonsu stands on the left of the main road. It is parallel to the River Nile, and the great gateway which rises before it forms the terminus of the famous avenue of sphinxes. Erected by Ptolemy III Euergetes, walls originally ran from the right and left of the gate enclosing the entire temple complex. Unfortunately, these have been entirely destroyed. Entering the temple via the east wall, I was shocked at what lay before my eyes. Khonsu was in a pitiful condition and a very dangerous state. Carefully crossing the ruins, I made my way into a dark and gloomy hypostyle hall. Relatively small in size, four large and four small columns support the roof, all covered with an array of crudely inscribed reliefs. Alas, many had now been damaged by bird-droppings or blackened by time. It was therefore impossible for me to make any sense out of the accompanying inscriptions.

Passing through into the open forecourt, I went in search of my final objective.

Assembled around 1080 BC, the forecourt hides one of Egypt's greatest secrets. Little known outside the realms of Egyptology and very poorly documented, the temple walls recount the life and times of one Herihor who, for a short time, held the office of High Priest of Amun. I began a detailed exploration of the vicinity. At the south end of the west wall, above the doorway, two galleys are depicted being rowed upstream to Luxor. Behind them they tow the sacred barque of the god Amun, now somewhat difficult to distinguish. Between the second and third columns, Herihor is shown aboard the galley upon which the portable barque has been placed. At the end of the wall other galleys are shown in full sail. This procession formed a part of the great annual festival of Amun, during which the image of the god was conveyed from the Holy of Holies at Karnak and travelled down the Nile to its sister temple at Luxor.

Turning towards the east wall, I discovered another representation of Herihor, this time kneeling before the god Khonsu. At the end of the wall, an additional row of priests is shown carrying upon their shoulders a standing figure of the god Khonsu, to whom Herihor offers flowers. Immediately opposite, Herihor can been seen receiving gifts from Khonsu. To my dismay, however, many of the associated hieroglyphs appeared to have been hacked away. Whether it was deliberate or not, it was almost impossible to tell, and precisely when the damage was inflicted was also difficult to say. There are no textual references that document any desecration to the Temple of Khonsu. I began a painstaking examination of the surrounding area. It was soon apparent that, underneath the grime, many carvings had also been attacked and gouged away.

Brushing away some loose debris, I sat down to ponder

what I had just witnessed. A number of things were apparent. First, throughout the forecourt, in many of the religious scenes, Herihor was depicted carrying out the specific duties that were traditionally the sole responsibility of the king. Even though the appointed priests were allowed to carry out those particular functions, they were never depicted as doing so. Every need of the god was always shown attended to by the king. The fact that in the Temple of Khonsu it is Herihor who is the one shown as being attending to the needs of the god could easily have been construed as a defiant act, punishable by death in Egyptian law. In addition Herihor is the one who also openly receives offerings from the god! Moreover, in many of the wall reliefs, the traditional insignia of kingship, the cobra, rested proudly upon Herihor's brow. Never before had a mere priest defied the authority of kingship and in such an unashamed manner. The best, however, was yet to come. As the sun's rays bounced off an adjacent column, I noticed an inscription that had thankfully eluded the desecrators – a single inscription deeply embedded in the stonework. It read: 'Herihor – First Prophet of Amun, King of Upper and Lower Egypt'!

Here was the evidence I had been searching for – confirmation of many hours of research in the libraries at home. For the first time in nearly 2000 years of Egyptian history, the High Priest of Amun had openly declared himself as king. Considering the supremacy of the king and the accepted structure of Egyptian society, how was this possible? Even though it was nearly 300 years after the reign of Akhenaten, could there be some connection? After all, we have already seen the particular loathing Akhenaten had for the Theban priesthood (see Chapter 2). Could there be some consequential link between the Amun priesthood and the flight of Scota from Egypt? I needed to examine everything about the Theban priesthood.

As we have seen, in historical terms all the religious functions and the political ones were united within one person, the king. But as Egypt grew in power and might, the pharaoh would find it increasingly difficult to administer an ever-growing government, let alone journey to every temple throughout the land making the necessary offerings and reciting the prayers to sustain the daily needs of every god. Someone was needed who could stand in for the pharaoh at the numerous shrines throughout Egypt, someone who could make the necessary offerings and who could recite the obligatory prayers. So the priesthood of Egypt was born. But before we tackle the complexities of the development of the Amun priesthood at Thebes, it would be wise to give a general overview of what being an Egyptian priest entailed.

It is essential to underline the differences between the functions of the Egyptian priesthood and those of religious leaders such as a Christian cleric or a Jewish rabbi. The primary objective of the latter is to minister to the religious well-being of their community. However, for an Egyptian priest, his role in society was very different. His main function was to minister to the needs of the god. In effect, the priest was the servant of the god. The Egyptian temple was not a church. There was no congregation or mass worship. In fact, the only time the general public had an opportunity to participate in the temple rituals, especially at Thebes, was, as we know, at the great Festival of Opet, which took place every year during the flooding of the Nile. Here the statue of Amun at Karnak was clothed in gold and jewels and taken from his holy sanctuary to be mounted upon his sacred barque. Borne by a party of shaven-headed priests, the barque was then carried to the side of the Nile. Together with his consort Mut, they were placed on a barge, which sailed down to visit Karnak's sister temple at Luxor to pay homage. This was the only time the Egyptian public ever got to see their saviour god Amun.

In ancient Egypt, purity was considered to be essential in all persons and things associated in any way with the cult of the gods. For that reason, before a priest could enter the innermost parts of the sanctuary, where the god resided, a complex purification procedure was necessary. This was not a spiritual act, as in Christianity, but a succession of physical undertakings. Accordingly, the Sacred Lake, at the heart of any Egyptian temple, was an important place. It was here that the priests underwent their ritual purification. Several days before entering the temple, they had to purify themselves by chewing natron, salt, and fumigating themselves with incense. Another basic precondition was circumcision. If this had not been done in youth, then the novice had to undergo the operation before he could be accepted into temple society. Bodies also had to be clean, so as to avoid lice and disease. Consequently, priests are always depicted in tomb paintings, and reliefs, with shaven heads and with their eyebrows and eyelashes also shaved off. Interestingly, as Egyptian civilization fell into decline, any foreigner who wanted to know more about the secret sciences studied within the temple confines had to have his or her hair and eyebrows shaved off too! Priests would also be required to abstain from certain foodstuffs such as beef, pork and mutton. It was strictly forbidden to eat the meat seen as an incarnation of a god.[9]

> Egyptian priests were considered also as philosophers among the Egyptians, that they chose the temples as the place to philosophise. For to live close to their shrines was fitting and it gave them security because of the reverence for the divine, since all the people honoured the philosophers as sacred animals. And they could live

a quiet life, as contact with other people only happened at assemblies and festivals, whereas for the rest the temples were inaccessible to others.[10]

The number of priests serving in a temple would naturally depend on its size and importance. The majority of Egyptian deities, such as the god Ptah, based at Memphis, or Ra at Heliopolis, would have their own hierarchy of priests. In particular Karnak Temple would have had a vast number of priests serving within its sacred grounds. Surprisingly, a high percentage of priests were actually part-time laymen who, after a period of service within the temple community, returned home to carry on with their normal life, whether they be carpenters, teachers or doctors. These priests were divided into 'gangs', with four gangs to each temple, and each served one lunar month in four during their years of service in the temple.[11]

Each temple would be designated its own hierarchy of priests, and each group had a series of specific duties which were rewarded with their own list of privileges. Certain categories of priests were permanent members of the staff. For example, the priesthood of Amun, headed by the First Prophet or High Priest, was composed of an upper clergy, often referred to as the Fathers of the God, which included the Second, Third and Fourth Prophets of Amun. The position of the high priest in a temple was usually hereditary and various autobiographies have survived in which they state that they held the very same office as their grandfathers and fathers and so on.

The ordinary priests were simply called the Purified Ones, and there were a series of specialized priests such as Lector-Priests who were responsible for saying the morning and evening prayer. The Stolists were priests who attended specifically to the statue of the god. They anointed it on a daily basis with a series of fragrant oils and incense, and wrapped it in a strip of the finest white linen. Ladies of rank frequently served as musicians in the temple of Amun and, as members of a company of priestesses, were described collectively as the Harim of the God.[12] The advantages of being a priest were many. Each received a share of the income from the temple estates and of the offerings that came into the temple each day. The wives and daughters of priests were entitled to certain allowances from temple revenue. And according to the Decree of Canopus, an allotment from the temple revenue was due to the daughters of priests from the day of their birth. The priests themselves were exempt from certain taxes.[13]

I have always been convinced that historians have underestimated the role played by the priesthood of Amun at Karnak during the late Eighteenth Dynasty. Aided and abetted by the Tutmoside pharaohs during the formative years of the New Kingdom, the Theban priesthood succeeded in consolidating Amun's supremacy over his fellow divinities. Consequently, the Temple of Karnak and its servitors played an important role within the economic and political life of this period. The priesthood benefited directly from foreign campaigns as an endless stream of prisoners of war and slaves were presented to the temples to be used in the service of the god. The temple of Amun also owned mines where materials were excavated for the finest temple equipment. It owned estates, often of the best land, where livestock was reared, crops were grown and gardens and vineyards tended to supply the temple needs. For instance, the revenue produced by the lands belonging to the temple of Amun at Teuzoi was divided into 100 equal portions. A remarkable twenty portions, a fifth of the entire revenue, went to the high priest himself, whilst one portion was assigned to each of the priests who served under him. These so-called stipends seem to have been paid annually.[14]

Such vast landholdings required an ever-increasing workforce which would come directly under the control of the high priest. Other areas of the country also paid a form of levy to Karnak, to labour in various ways for the King of the Gods. This was more often than not paid in kind, as Egypt did not have a uniform monetary system, and it was collected by the fleet of ships owned by the temple of Amun and stored in the Karnak repositories. Karnak Temple was protected by royal decree from the extortion of the crown's agents and never had to pay any tax on any of its considerable assets. But the key factor in their advancement, of course, was the generosity of the king to the god. We have already noted the immense bounty bestowed upon Amun in gratitude for his part in Egyptian conquests abroad. But with Thebes now the official royal residence, and the capital of the Egyptian Empire, it was far easier for the priesthood to exert their influence, not only throughout the country, but also directly upon the crown. All along the Nile, from the Delta in the north to the southernmost realms of Nubia, new cult places to Amun were swiftly established and fresh temples erected in his honour, frequently replacing or overshadowing the shrines of the old local deities.

It was by no means rare for members of the priesthood of Amun, especially the High Priest, to acquire additional titles, and the responsibilities that came with them. For instance, during the reign of Amenhotep II (*circa* 1453–1419 BC), the High Priest Mery also held the official titles of Steward of Amun, Overseer of the Treasuries of Amun, Overseer of the Fields of Amun, Overseer of the Cattle of Amun and so on.[15] Before long, the high priest began to take an active part in the temple administration, and in some instances even held the prominent title of Southern Vizier. There were also the added responsibility of Mayor of

Thebes. Apart from the king himself, the office of vizier, or *djat* in Egyptian, was one of the most important and powerful positions in society. They served as the chief justices of the courts, hearing all domestic territorial disputes. They maintained a herd census, controlled the reservoirs and the food supply, and supervised industries and conservation programmes, and they were required to repair all dykes. All government documents used in ancient Egypt had to have the seal of the vizier in order to be considered authentic and binding. Tax records, storehouse receipts, crop assessments and other necessary agricultural statistics were also held by the office of the vizier.[16]

The dead, as well as the living, also came under the jurisdiction of the Amun priesthood, for it governed not only the east bank at Thebes but also the west bank, where the great necropolis of the dead lay. This was a highly important task, for as we know, Egypt's well-being was dependent upon the king achieving the afterlife. The priesthood was not only in charge of the royal tombs belonging to the kings but those of the queens and nobles too. The extensive mortuary temples that stretched along the western bank of the Nile were also directly in their care.

During the Eighteenth Dynasty, all Egyptian-held territory in the southern regions came under the direct control of the High Priest of Amun for the first time. This included the important gold- and mineral-producing regions in Nubia, on which Egypt's 'superpower' status was dependent. In a short space of time, not only had the pharaoh bequeathed to the high priest his religious standing but, more significantly, he had also given the Amun priesthood direct responsibility for the day-to-day running of the country, and, more importantly still, total control of Egypt's immense wealth. Although the estates of Amun were established primarily as a 'god offering', there can be no doubt that a sizeable portion of the vast income from these estates reverted directly to the priesthood. It was a system that was wide open to corruption and the priesthood rapidly became one of the country's wealthiest and most envied classes. Taking matters into their own hands, it would not be long before they began to exert their immense influence directly upon the royal succession.

The power of the Amun priesthood over the ruling family was further strengthened by the events surrounding the reign of Tutmosis II. He came to the throne of Egypt in around 1518 BC and reigned for fourteen years. Upon his death, apparently of ill health, whilst still in his early thirties, a power struggle ensued for control of the throne. The two main contenders were his younger son, also called Tutmosis, and the reigning first lady, the dead king's wife, Hatshepsut. The king must have realized the overwhelming ambition of his wife and, with the direct intervention of the Amun priesthood, attempted to curtail it by declaring his son his successor before he died.[17] During a religious ceremony at Karnak Temple, in front of his father, the religious leaders and the royal court, the Amun priesthood proclaimed the young prince the future Lord of the Two Lands. The future Tutmosis III was a devout follower of the god Amun, and with good reason, as he had served in the Karnak Temple community. In an inscription on the Seventh Pylon at Karnak Temple, Tutmosis III relates the events whereby the great god himself selected him as a future king:

My Father Amun-Ra-Harakhti granted to me that I might appear upon the Horus Throne of the Living . . . I having been appointed by him, within the temple, there having been ordained for me the rulership of the Two Lands, the thrones of Geb and the offices of Khephri at the side of my father, the Good God, the King of Upper and Lower Egypt, Aakheperenre, given life forever.[18]

The accepted chain of events appears to have involved a secret pact between the High Priest of Amun and the king himself, Tutmosis II. As the festival procession progressed, inside the inner sanctum of Karnak Temple, the high priest had 'arranged' for the image of Amun to 'seek out' the young prince. Carrying the image of the god upon his sacred ark shrine, the group of accompanying priests was told to stop directly in front of the prince. Amun was then seen to bow down to the prince, thereby designating him the next pharaoh of Egypt. At the time of his father's death it is thought that Tutmosis was but a child and his exact age at the time of his accession is unrecorded. Consequently, the reins of power were left in the capable hands of his step-mother, Queen Hatshepsut, who acted as regent for the young king.

Within two years the unthinkable happened. Hatshepsut assumed the throne for herself and, in front of assembled dignitaries, was crowned king. The exact date of her elevation is uncertain because she always used the same regnal years as Tutmosis III, effectively dating her own reign to the young prince's accession to the throne. How did she achieve this? For one thing is blatantly obvious: a female on the throne of Egypt did not conform to the proper order of things. After all, as we have seen, as the embodiment of Horus, on earth, the king had always to be a man. In assuming the throne as the undisputed king of Upper and Lower Egypt, Hatshepsut had dared to do something that her female predecessors had not: to put on the kilt and crown of the king.[19]

Hatshepsut was a cunning ruler and she knew her position was precarious. Accordingly, she bolstered it with a combination of propaganda and influential allies, but more importantly, she courted the support of the Amun priesthood. Stealing the crown from the young prince was a bold step and she knew that she had to justify such a move – and quickly. The fact that she was a woman may also have caused quite some resentment among the higher nobles and officials. To counteract any opposition, she resorted to using the divine oracles. In an inscription carved upon her famous Red Chapel at Karnak Temple, the god Amun-Ra is shown to have prophesied the ascent of Hatshepsut to the throne through 'a very great oracle proclaiming for me the kingship of the Two Lands, Upper and Lower Egypt'.[20] A series of scenes follow in which Amun-Ra is depicted crowning her a king – an iconographic programme designed to confirm her legitimacy.

One of the most influential of Hatshepsut's supporters was a man named Habusoneb, who held the titles of Vizier and the High Priest of Amun. He had effectively secured the two most powerful positions in the kingdom. Related to the royal family through his mother, Ahhotep, he was descended from a very high-ranking family indeed. Even though his father, Hapu, had served in the Temple of Karnak as a lector-priest, his grandfather had been the vizier during the reign of Tutmosis I. A shrewd man, Habusoneb later installed his own son as Scribe to the Treasury of Amun, directly responsible for Amun's vast wealth.[21] Clearly, one is tempted to see him as the true power behind the throne and certainly Hatshepsut needed all the help she could get. Her alliance with the High Priest of Amun was one of political practicality.

Embracing the guidance of Habusoneb, she quickly proposed the magnificent notion that she was, in fact, the physical daughter of Amun-Ra, the god. The aim of this was to legitimize her right to rule; in effect, to demonstrate openly to the world that she had deliberately been chosen by Amun to wear the sacred Double Crown. Thus, forever more, she would be known as 'She Who Embraces Amun, the Foremost of Women.'[22] In gratitude, she built an impressive mortuary temple dedicated to Amun at Deir-el-Bahari, on the west bank of the Nile. One of the most striking monuments to have survived from ancient Egypt, the temple is strategically placed, directly opposite Karnak Temple on the opposing bank.

Through the authority of Amun, Hatshepsut had successfully disposed of her young co-regent, Tutmosis III, and subsequently fabricated a co-regency with her father, Tutmosis I. Whatever the combination of propaganda and influence involved, Amun had played an important and significant role. Capitalizing on his benevolence, Hatshepsut succeeded in not only gaining the throne of Egypt but holding it for a further twenty years.

A new religious mood swept through the land and was reflected in reliefs and inscriptions throughout the length and breadth of Egypt. A two-fold religious policy was quickly instigated whereby the entire temporal estate of Amun was united under a single authority, the high priest, together with all other priesthoods and their accompanying estates. The revenue from all the other gods' temples now came under the authority of the High Priest of Amun. The Theban priesthood, who now claimed jurisdiction over them all, quickly usurped the ancient titles of High Priest of Ra at Heliopolis and High Priest of Ptah at Memphis.[23] The High Priest of Amun was now *the* high priest throughout the land.

As the priesthood of Amun became so huge after only a few hundred years, it is not surprising that many capable and ambitious men quickly rose to the top. Throughout Egyptian history the different branches of the priesthood, such as those of Amun and Ra, were fiercely competitive, each claiming priority for their own god, seeking the pharaoh's special patronage and in turn reaping the rewards it would bring. Thrusting your patron god to the forefront did not just earn you theological 'brownie points'; it was a struggle for wealth and status, something the priests of Egypt knew very well. The Theban priesthood had risen to the top and it is hardly necessary to add that the High Priest of Amun was now one of Egypt's richest and most influential people. Some may argue that, next to the pharaoh, he had become the most powerful man in Egypt itself. So, was he a real threat to the throne of Egypt? Could his influence truly challenge the long-held belief in a divine kingship, a belief that held Egypt united through times of discontent? The priesthood may have thought so, but their good fortune was about to change. It was time for the pharaohs to fight back.

So far we have recounted the facts behind the Amun priesthood and their rise to power. Those very same reasons that catapulted them to the top position in the Egyptian state were to bring about their ultimate downfall during Scota's lifetime. The fact that we have to travel so far back in Egyptian history is fundamental to our understanding of the cataclysmic events that were to follow and which would explain why Scota and her followers had to flee Egypt. The stage is now set to introduce the two men, her great-grandfather Tutmosis IV and her grandfather Amenhotep III, whose actions upon the throne eventually turned a princess into a refugee.

CHAPTER FIVE

⟨⟨⟨⟨⟨⟩⟩⟩⟩⟩

THE SUN KINGS

In about 1419 BC, the son of Amenhotep II came to the throne of Egypt. Named Tutmosis IV, meaning 'Thoth is born', his reign not only signalled a marked transformation in the fortunes of Amun, it also set into motion the very religious principles to which Akhenaten adhered. Although he lived some fifty years before the birth of Scota, his activities would, in due course, force her to flee Egypt for her life. We have seen how the cult of the ancient sun god Ra had suffered at the hands of its rival at Thebes throughout the Eighteenth Dynasty. In New-Kingdom Egypt, for the ordinary person in the street Amun still reigned supreme. However, during the later stages of the Eighteenth Dynasty, the priesthood of Ra slowly began to exert what little influence they had remaining directly upon the country's pharaohs.

Based at Heliopolis, this priesthood had for centuries endured the indignity of having the High Priest of Amun directly responsible for its well-being. Their heritage was as old as Egypt itself, but they now found themselves being

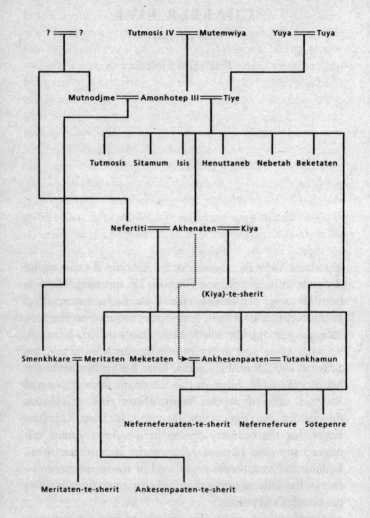

The Amarna family tree

treated as second-class citizens in both the theological and the secular state. There can be no denying that Heliopolis was a great centre of learning, known throughout the ancient world. The Greek historian Herodotus, writing in the fifth century BC, visited it and subsequently recorded that, in his opinion, its priests had 'the reputation of being the best skilled in history of all the Egyptians'.[1] Not only were they versed in geometry, medicine, philosophy and mythology, they were also looked upon as 'masters of astronomy'.[2] The priests also informed him that the Egyptians were the first to use the 'names of the twelve gods, which the Greeks adopted from them'.[3]

The battle for supremacy between the two great religious centres, Heliopolis and Thebes, had been going on for centuries. At times it seemed almost to border on pettiness. For instance, just because Heliopolis had a high priest called Great of Seers, so Thebes also had to name its high priest 'Great of Seers' and even, on occasion, called itself 'Heliopolis of the South'.[4] Since Heliopolis had its sacred stone, called the benben, in the form of a pyramid, Thebes had to have an obelisk with its summit in the shape of a pyramid. Because Thebes had its Great Hymn to Amun, Heliopolis had to follow suit and adopt their own Hymn to Ra-Horakhty, and so on.[5] With the accession of Tutmosis IV, the situation was about to change dramatically. The ancient sun god of Heliopolis, far from being forgotten, was almost overnight elevated to the status of 'supreme deity', worshipped in a specific form of the sun god called Ra-Horakhty, meaning 'Horus of the horizon'. A red granite stela, called the Dream Stela, was erected between the paws of the Great Sphinx at Giza to commemorate Tutmosis's unusual act of piety.

One day it happened that the royal son Tutmosis went

for a walk at midday. He sat down in the shadow of the great god; sleep and dreaming came upon him when the sun was at its height. He discovered the majesty of this venerable god who spoke to him as a father speaks to his son; Look at me, behold me, my son, Tutmosis, for I am your father Harmakhet-Khepri-Ra-Atum – the one who shall give you kingship upon the earth before the living peoples. You shall wear the White Crown and the Red Crown on the throne of Geb, the rightful heir. Yours is the earth and its length and its breadth, that which the eye of the Lord-of-All lights up. All the produce of the interior of the Twin Lands is set before you, and the great tribute of every foreign land, and a life span of a great period of years. My concern is yours, my desire is yours, and you belong to me. But look, my condition is that of someone in distress for all my limbs are covered up, and the sands of the desert – that which I used to be upon – has come over me. I have waited to let you do what is in your heart, knowing that you are my son and champion. Come close then, for I am with you and I am your guide.[6]

The sphinx is a mythical beast usually portrayed with the body of a lion and the head of a man, and usually wearing the royal *nemes* headcloth. Although the ancient Greek term meant 'strangler', it has been suggested that the origin of the word may have been the Egyptian phrase *'shesep ankh'*, meaning 'living image'.[7] The Egyptian sphinx was closely associated with both the king and the sun god, and the largest known monument is the Great Sphinx at Giza. Measuring a full 73 metres long and a maximum 20 metres in height, it was carved from a knoll of rock left behind after quarrying. The three daily forms of the sun god were deemed present in the figure: the sun is Khepri in the morning, Ra-Horakhty in the middle of the day and Atum at the coming of the night.[8]

If the inscription upon the Dream Stela is to be believed, then it would appear that the Sphinx was in a very poor condition indeed. Neglected for centuries, its body lay entirely covered by sand. It seems that some form of arrangement was made between Ra-Horakhty and Tutmosis; in essence, in return for clearing away the sand from its body, the Sphinx would grant Tutmosis the throne. This was an audacious shift in policy considering that his predecessors were, as a rule, granted the throne of Egypt by the god Amun. In truth, the statement concealed an increasingly complicated political situation. So let us examine it a little more closely.

That the young prince should have been active at Memphis is not surprising, as his father, Amenhotep II, was born there. Although Thebes was still the state capital, we have seen how the ancient city of Memphis continued to remain at the heart of the administration. In addition, according to tradition, young princes were sent to Memphis to gain knowledge of the affairs of state before they ascended the throne. However, what is most remarkable in this instance is the diligence with which Tutmosis IV venerated the Memphite sun god Ra. The reason behind his sudden change in allegiance is unclear. Perhaps the fact that the heart of Amun territory and dominance was some 600 kilometres away to the south gave the priesthood of Ra the perfect opportunity to influence the young prince without any interference. Whatever the realities of the Dream Stela, it confirms three crucial things. First, it would seem that the young prince was not the designate heir to the throne. As with so many other Eighteenth-Dynasty kings, he needed the approval of the gods to legitimize his claim. Secondly, unlike his predecessors, Tutmosis IV appears to have patronized the Heliopolitan cult of Ra, at the expense of the god Amun. Previous kings of the Eighteenth Dynasty had, after all, revered the god Amun to rather extreme lengths. Finally, it cannot be denied that the hard-done-by priesthood of Ra must have supported the young prince in his aspirations. If he was not the designated heir to the throne he would need the support of one priesthood or another to legitimize his claim. His choice of the god Ra-Horakhty led to the establishment of a new alliance between the royal family and the Heliopolitan priesthood. Could this new political state of affairs have something to do with a desire to counteract the dominant priesthood at Thebes? Taking into account Tutmosis's next steps, it would appear so.

No sooner had the Double Crown of Upper and Lower Egypt been placed upon his head, than he began a radical shake up of the Amun priesthood at Thebes. Sacking the reigning high priest, he replaced him with a man of his own choice. Called Amenemhat, he was the son of a woman of lowly birth, and just one of many simple priests serving within the temple community. How he even came to be noticed by the king is a matter of conjecture. Nevertheless, whatever the reasons behind his astounding promotion, he was the preferred choice of Tutmosis IV. Accordingly, at the age of 54, Amenemhat became the new High Priest of Amun and Overseer of All the Prophets of Upper and Lower Egypt. But unlike the previous high priest, his civil offices seem to have been few indeed.[9] Clearly, Tutmosis IV was attempting to remove the reins of authority from the priests at Thebes. By choosing Amenemhat, was he consciously making a statement to the Theban powerbase? Or was he just simply asserting a royal prerogative that had been disregarded by his predecessors? Regrettably, there are no surviving documents which explain his intentions. What is apparent, however, is that he was deliberately bypassing more senior candidates with a vested interest in order to insist on his own right to appoint a 'king's man'. Furthermore, to the office of Second Prophet of Amun he also appointed another loyal follower, a man named Amenophis.[10]

With his own men now strategically positioned within the higher ranks of the Theban priesthood, Tutmosis IV seemed to be less concerned than his predecessors with Theban affairs and with promoting the wealth of its god. After many years of being overshadowed at the hands of Amun, Lower Egypt was now to play an increasing role in the government of the country, with officials from the Delta region, in particular Memphis, becoming important throughout the region. Tutmosis continued the construction of a temple, dedicated by his father Amenhotep II, in the vicinity of the Sphinx, and he also left foundation deposits containing his cartouche in the temple of Ptah at Memphis.[11]

As we have seen, the pharaohs of the Eighteenth Dynasty had traditionally always bequeathed the spoils from their victorious campaigns abroad to the service of the estates of Amun. We have documents from the reign of Tutmosis III that record the donation of 588 Syrian prisoners to the temple of Amun at Karnak.[12] But Tutmosis IV chose to ignore this precedent. Though there is little evidence of military action during his reign compared to those of his predecessors, our knowledge may be marred by lack of texts. A definite Nubian campaign is recorded in his Year 8, which was highly successful. There also appear to have been some Syrian campaigns, as the king is also referred to as the Conqueror of Syria.[13] Even with this limited military activity, however, in what would appear to be a direct snub towards the priesthood at Thebes Tutmosis dedicated all his spoils of war to his own mortuary temple.

Another departure was the introduction of a different burial site. Ignoring his predecessors' tombs, Tutmosis IV selected a brand new and impressive branch of the Valley of the Kings, located in the east, for future burials. He also took the unprecedented step of erecting a single obelisk that honoured his benefactor god Ra-Horakhty on the east–west axis line of the Amun precinct at Karnak. Today the obelisk stands in St John Lateran, Rome. Another example of the burgeoning influence of the Heliopolitan sun cult is the discovery of a large stone scarab beetle issued during his reign. Inscribed upon the beetle was a dedication to a new form of the sun god, the Aten, spoken of as a 'god of battles' who makes the pharaoh 'mighty in his dominion and brings all his subjects under the sway of the sun disc'.[14] This is the first notable mention of an innovative and universal aspect of the sun, which was to receive supreme position under his grandson, Akhenaten.

The reign of Tutmosis IV also marks a turning point in the fortunes of the Eighteenth Dynasty in a wider context. The relentless military action in western Asia, which was pursued by his predecessors to extend the boundaries of Egypt, was now finally over. So-called police actions on the unpredictable frontiers were the only foreign adventures that were now called for. The rulers of the great powers in the Near East had agreed to stabilize their relations by numerous treaties cemented with marriage alliances with the pharaoh of Egypt. In particular, the rival king of the Mitannian Empire, whose forces were dominant in northern Syria at this time, entered into even more cordial relations with the pharaoh, whom he now referred to as his brother. This understanding was further cemented by the entry of the daughter of Artatama, King of Mitanni, into the harem of Tutmosis IV, doubtless with a magnificent dowry, corresponding to the wealth and status of her father. Egypt now embarked upon nearly half a century of peace and prosperity.[15]

Tutmosis IV appears to have died at an early age, probably from some illness in about 1386 BC. His mummy was found in 1898 in the tomb of Amenhotep II. During the 21st Dynasty (c. 1050 BC) this particular tomb was used by the High Priests of Amun to store all the mummies of the Pharaohs of Egypt. Upon examination, the mummy of Tutmosis IV revealed a slightly balding, extremely emaciated man. Howard Carter discovered his tomb in 1902 on Thebes's western shore. It was a great complex of underground passages, stairways and chambers. The burial hall was designed with pillars and a sunken crypt with a huge granite sarchophagus.

On his death, his son Amenhotep III (meaning 'Amun is content') ascended the throne. Unusually for Eighteenth-Dynasty kings, he was Tutmosis's first son and chosen successor, his mother being a secondary wife called Mutemwiya who, some argue, was possibly a Syrian princess. His reign of thirty-eight years was peaceful and brilliant, and he earned his title 'magnificent' rather by his wealth and splendour than his qualities as a statesman.[16] Egypt's prosperity was by now the envy of the world and it was perhaps the most trouble-free time in the country's history. Amenhotep had little to concern himself with politically, due to the conquests of his enterprising predecessors, and the only uncertainty was a Nubian revolt that was quickly quashed. He was rather proud of this campaign, arguably because it was his only one, and he boasted of his excellence above any other Egyptian king. Consequently, the records were exaggerated out of all proportion. They report how the Egyptian host passed the southern border town of Aswan, going north on the return voyage. On their way three large and bombastic Steles of Victory were carved on the rocks. Upon one of them it was inscribed the god Amun had said: Welcome in peace, O my beloved son! My heart is glad to see thy victories and the power of thy fame overwhelming foreign lands. I give thee southerners as thy serfs, and the northerners abjectly submitting to thy fame.[17]

Amenhotep continued the Egyptian policy of 'defending commercial interests assertively but with the minimum of direct military intervention'.[18] His supremacy in the Near East remained unchallenged, but in the tradition of his forefathers he did not hesitate to project himself as an all-conquering king. He flaunted his prowess as a 'fierce-eyed lion' and a 'raging fire' when smiting Egypt's traditional enemies.[19] The Egyptian Empire was expansive and, by this time, comprised almost all of western Asia, Syria, Palestine, Phoenicia and the western part of the Euphrates, Nubia and certain areas of Libya. Trade flourished as wealth poured in from the various client states. Extravagant caravans brought endless supplies of gold and silverware as well as various metalwares, spices, ivory and timber and an entire procession of exotic animals to titillate the royal court. The temples were bursting with tribute and the columns were encrusted with richness and colour. Feasts and festivals were bountiful and the general mood was one of contentment.

The reign of Amenhotep marked an extraordinary rise in the status of royal women. He seemed to have been sur-rounded by powerful women, which would no doubt have had a profound effect on his son, Akhenaten. His chief wife was Queen Tiye. The king seems to have married at quite a young age and his chosen wife would appear to have been a woman of non-royal rank. In choosing her, Amenhotep III seems to have broken with tradition. This may have been a deliberate attempt to prevent the priests of Amun from interfering in the royal succession, as they had done during the Hatshepsut era. A series of 'marriage scarabs' were issued to commemorate this happy but unusual union. On the base was the inscription:

> The king's great wife, Tiye, may she live,
> The name of her father is Yuya
> The name of her mother is Tuya
> She is the wife of a mighty king.[20]

Anybody reading between the lines would get the message: Tiye is a commoner, but you had better accept her as my wife or else! She was the daughter of a nobleman called Yuya, whose titles included God's Father and Commander of the Chariotry, a powerful military leader during his time. Even though it was not of the royal line, the family was an important one, and he and his wife Tuya, a priestess of the god Min, held much land in the Delta region.[21] For the first time in Egyptian history, the queen's name frequently accompanies that of her husband in ceremonial inscriptions. She is shown at the king's side on statues and in numerous royal monuments and private tombs. Her figure, sometimes on a huge scale, often appeared in equal proportion to that of the king. Her titles proclaimed her might and status, and signalled the central importance that women of the later Eighteenth Dynasty were now to occupy within society. Remarkably, her position in the Egyptian government was recognized by foreign kings and officials, and it was not unheard of her to correspond with them as an equal. Her significance in the general scheme of things is therefore clear and unquestioned: 'The Heiress, greatly Favoured, Mistress of All Countries, Lady of Delight, who Fills the Palace with Love, Lady of the Two Lands, Mistress of Upper and Lower Egypt.'[22]

Queen Tiye bore the king six children – four daughters

and two sons. The eldest girl, Sitamun, seems to have been her father's favourite and was in her later years elevated to the position of king's wife. She is attested by inscriptions on the monuments of her parents and by objects found in the tombs of her grandparents, Tuya and Yuya, although relatively few of her own monuments survive. The eldest son, the heir to the throne, was the prince Tutmosis, named after his grandfather, who was stationed at Memphis as the High Priest of Ptah. The second son was named Amenhotep after his father, but came to be known in later years as the heretic king, Akhenaten.

With peace and prosperity ensured, the king now dedicated himself to the arts. Temple sites were refurbished and enlarged on an unprecedented scale, whilst monuments were erected to honour his patron deities. The high quality of artistic skills during this time is exhibited in the tombs of endless high officials. Amenhotep III erected the enormous Third Pylon at Karnak, now largely ruined, but his principal cult buildings within the Karnak sanctuary were the temple to the local god Monthu, just outside the North Gate, and an entire precinct to Amun's consort, Mut. During his reign, Amenhotep for some reason commissioned over 600 black granite statues of the lion goddess Sekhmet and stationed them in the precinct of Mut. Today the British Museum has the largest number, in various states of preservation. His greatest architectural triumph, however, was Luxor Temple, approximately 3 kilometres to the south of Karnak. Built as a sister temple to Karnak, the Luxor precinct was dedicated to the Theban triad, but in particular it came to be regarded as the home of the wife and son of Amun; that is, Mut and Khonsu. An impressive sphinx-lined avenue was built, linking the two temples.

One may be led to think that all this adoration of the Theban gods would have forced Amenhotep III to stray from the path that his father, Tutmosis IV, had initiated. On the contrary, however, he now venerated the sun god, in the form of Ra-Horakhty, and later the Aten, with a passion never before witnessed. Although he may have been born at Thebes, Amenhotep had resided, like his father before him, at the ancient capital of Memphis. There is still evidence of his residence in his twentieth regnal year. However, as his reign entered its third decade, he took the unusual decision to move the entire royal court back to the 'Southern City', Thebes. In doing so, his first priority was to build an immense palace, called Malkata, directly across the river from his newly constructed Luxor Temple. It was here that Scota was most probably born. It was a huge estate, incorporating vast parade grounds, a series of small chapels, large decorated halls, and villas for all his loyal officials. Sadly, little remains of the palace complex and only a few solitary walls have survived. Egyptian palaces were only intended to last the lifetime of one pharaoh and were therefore usually built out of plain mud brick.

The reason behind Amenhotep's sudden move to Thebes remains a mystery. Nevertheless, considering the turn of events instigated by his father, Tutmosis IV, it is surely not beyond the bounds of possibility that such a move may have been a direct attempt to exert some sort of control over the powerful Theban priesthood. Unable to restrain them effectively from Memphis, in the Delta, perhaps Amenhotep decided it would be better to return to Thebes.

Consequently, as soon as he had settled the royal court at Thebes he continued with his father's persecution of the Theban priesthood, a somewhat aggressive, and perhaps some may argue a foolish, move considering that he now resided in the priesthood's sphere of control and influence. Once again the reigning High Priest of Amun, Ptahmose, felt the full brunt of the king's 'reforms'. Ptahmose was a very powerful individual indeed. Examining his titles, it is apparent that he not only held the office of High Priest and Overseer of All Prophets of Upper and Lower Egypt; in addition, he was also the Great Vizier and Mayor of the Southern City.[23] We saw, in Chapter 3, what a potent combination these titles were. Effectively, in one man, Ptahmose, you had an archbishop and a prime minister. To Amenhotep III, this must have seemed an unacceptable union of temporal and secular power. But who was Ptahmose and where did he come from? His name suggests a Delta origin, though this is not definite. Perhaps he was given the position early on in Amenhotep's reign, although a man from the north would surely have no allegiance to the priesthood of the south.

Whatever the reasons behind his appointment, during the later years of Amenhotep's reign it is clear that Ptahmose must have been the most influential man in the realm. Is this the reason why Amenhotep III decided to move the royal court back to Thebes? Did Amenhotep believe that Ptahmose might pose a real threat to his authority? It is impossible to be certain. It is noticeable, however, that Amenhotep's first action was to strip Ptahmose of the vizierate and confine him to religious duties only. A few years later he replaced him altogether and appointed a new High Priest of Amun, an obscure official called Meryptah.[24] The high priest was then stripped of the title Overseer of All Prophets, which was handed on to the vizier, Ramose. It would appear that both Meryptah and Ramose were of Memphite origin; in fact their associated inscriptions say as much. Consequently, they had no loyalty to Thebes whatsoever, or to its god Amun. Even so, by replacing Theban officials with Memphite men, Amemhotep III could not guarantee full and unquestioning support. To counteract this problem, he began to install his own family in key positions throughout the land. As we have seen, the young heir to the throne, Tutmosis, was given the important position of High Priest of Ptah at Memphis. This was a shrewd move by Amenhotep, as he now had a loyal family member inside this powerful Delta priesthood.

After disposing of what he viewed as a potential threat to his crown, Amenhotep took upon himself a new title, 'Dazzling Sun Disc of All The Land'.[25] This new aspect of the sun disc was called the Aten and the royal court now devoted itself entirely to the worship of the Aten in all its glory. People in the highest of places were paying far more attention to religion and it is noticeable that reverence to the god Amun was conspicuous by its absence.

Amenhotep spent the last decade of his life preparing for his jubilee or *sed* festival. In fact his reign witnessed the celebration of no less than three *sed* festivals in years 30, 34 and 37. The first king's jubilee or *sed* festival was celebrated way back in predynastic times, but remained popular throughout Egypt's history. It takes its name from the jackal god, called Sed, and is closely linked with the Egyptian perception of kingship.[26] The festival itself was a symbolic renewal of the king's physical and magical powers and it was usually celebrated in the thirtieth regnal year. However, the surviving inscriptions and monuments associated with this festival seem to show that the many kings whose reigns were shorter then thirty years also celebrated their jubilee rites before the required time. The reasons for this are unclear.

The two essential elements of the ceremony were paying of homage to the enthroned king and the ritual of territorial claim. Both are beautifully depicted on a small label, now in the collection of the British Museum. Dating to as far back as Egypt's very first dynasty, the ceremony is intricately carved on a small piece of ebony wood, a mere 5.5 centimetres in height. Belonging to King Den, and discovered at Abydos, in the right-hand corner of the label the king can first be seen seated on one of the special festival pavilions wearing the Double Crown of Upper and Lower Egypt upon his head. In a later scene, the king is depicted as running between two sets of cairns or boundary markers, which Egyptologists believe symbolized the physical borders of Egypt itself.[27]

Although there is a remarkable continuity throughout Egyptian history with regard to the specific jubilee rites, it would appear that Amenhotep adapted the symbolism of the *sed* festival to suit his own political agenda. To judge by the number of contemporary reliefs and paintings devoted to the commemoration of these celebrations, they must have been regarded as the most important events of his reign. Each one took place at Thebes and was witnessed by a series of invited foreign officials from Syria, Libya and Nubia, and also, of course, the Amun priesthood. The huge lake excavated to the east of the palace of Malkata appears to have functioned as the setting for his reinvented *sed* festival, 'in his palace, the House of Rejoicing'.[28] In a dated scene commemorating his first jubilee, now preserved in the Theban tomb of Kheruf, there exists one of the most remarkable scenes in Egyptian dynastic history. Amenhotep III is actually depicted seated in the distinctive ark of the sun god, thus identifying himself as the god while he was still alive! Furthermore, the following carvings depict the king and the divine statuary of Amun both being carried along on sacred arks. This was a truly remarkable statement. No longer was Amenhotep III to be regarded as just a mere agent of the gods. Without prevarication, he was announcing to all those present that he was now to be regarded as a living god. Under normal circumstances, only upon death could a pharaoh thus become deified. This was a step never before taken by any reigning Egyptian pharaoh.

It is also interesting to note that even though the festival was celebrated deep within Theban territory, the entire ceremony had an undeniable Memphite feel to it. Even the officiate was the High Priest of Ptah and not the customary delegate of the Theban state god. Could this have been yet another snub to the Theban priesthood? The exceptional nature of the event is underscored in the accompanying text, where it is stated that these particular jubilee rites had not been celebrated 'since the time of the ancestors',[29] and that the king decreed they be enacted 'in accordance with the writings of old'.[30] There can be no denying Amenhotep's intentions. By openly declaring himself a god, he was now on an equal standing with Amun himself.

Additional new material pertaining to Amenhotep's deification whilst alive has emerged over the past few years. Astonishingly, they depict scenes of him worshipping figures of himself. The autobiography of the High Steward of Memphis records that an enormous temple was constructed at Memphis. Here, it states, Amenhotep III was worshipped as the embodiment of the god Ptah.[31] Other reliefs, preserved in the temple of Soleb in Nubia, also show Amenhotep worshipping himself as the living god Nebmaatre – Lord of Nubia.[32]

After his first jubilee in Year 30, Amenhotep initiated a series of reforms, increasing his control over the Egyptian state. A new robust writing of his prenomen – his throne name – appears but, unlike his predecessors, a figure of himself, the king, now represents the traditional depiction of *nb*, meaning lord. The feather in his hand represents Maat and the disc on his head spells out Ra.[33] Amazingly, this newly deified king was commemorated by the inauguration of a new complex at Karnak Temple. Forgoing the veneration of the Theban triad, the new temple was dedicated to Amenhotep's new god, the Aten. Queen Tiye also participated in the deification ritual of her husband and she also became a living goddess. She became the manifestation of 'all Egyptian goddesses throughout the land' and was represented thereafter as the sun god's consort, Hathor.[34]

Inscribed clay dockets from the palace of Malkata record dates to at least Year 38 of Amenhotep's reign, implying that he may have died in his thirty-ninth regnal year. His robbed tomb was unearthed by a French expedition in 1799 in the isolated western half of the Valley of the Kings. Amongst the debris they found a large number of figures of the king, some complete but the majority broken. Why he chose not to be buried near his Eighteenth-Dynasty ancestors we will never know. His mummy was also discovered in the tomb of Amenhotep II in 1898 by the French Egyptologist Victor Loret. The anatomy expert Elliot Smith subsequently removed the wrappings on 23 September 1905. It revealed a severely damaged mummy, perhaps the worst of all the royal mummies that have been found so far. The head had been broken off, the front part of the body is missing and all the limbs were damaged.[35]

What does this all this mean? Well, we know that the reign of Scota's grandfather, Amenhotep III, was an era of prosperity such as Egypt had never previously enjoyed. The wealth of the temple of Amun and the city of Thebes must have been enormous. We also know that the power of the priesthood had been increasing steadily throughout the Eighteenth Dynasty and that the later pharaohs began to apply various methods to strip the Amun priesthood of its influence upon the state. The accumulating evidence also indicates that during his last decade, Amenhotep III was officially considered to be a living manifestation of the creator god Ra, particularly in his manifestation of the sun god's disc, the Aten. Hence he had now become the living embodiment of all the gods of Egypt and their 'living image' on earth.

The actions of both Tutmosis IV and Amenhotep III must have made a tremendous impression on Akhenaten before he came to the throne. The crucial role that they played in the initial impetus of Akhenaten's religious revolution cannot be underestimated. Akhenaten's devotion to and preoccupation with the sun disc, the Aten, certainly had its origins in the eventful last decade of his father's rule. Accordingly, his obsession with his new solar cult, it could be argued, was not only rooted in the deification programme of his fathers, but, to all intents and purposes, was probably the culmination of that deification programme.[36] As we shall now see, Akhenaten just took it one step further. The Theban nobles could not have been aware of the storm that was so soon to break over their beloved homes and to wreak havoc in their most cherished ideals and beliefs. They were about to enter the dark days of the man dubbed the heretic king.

CHAPTER SIX

HERESY

We come at last to the reign of Akhenaten. In the middle of the fourteenth century BC, Egypt experienced a revolution 'from above', which for a brief period affected almost every sphere of life. For centuries, the religious institutions had remained virtually unchanged. As we have seen, the gods were an integral part of Egyptian culture and, therefore, had always been a necessary feature of Egypt as a whole. But, with the country apparently in the most powerful and stable period of its history, the pharaoh named Akhenaten transformed everything.

As we have seen, Akhenaten was the second son of Amenhotep III and Queen Tiye. He was crowned Amenhotep IV in around 1353 BC. He took the new name, Akhenaten, early on in his reign. Nothing is known of his childhood; even the date and place of his birth are also unknown, which may only be due to an accident of the archaeological record, but may also point to the fact that he was unimportant before his accession. Interestingly, Akhenaten does not appear on any monuments during his father's reign. It appears that he was not the heir apparent. Tomb 226 at Thebes, which belonged to a royal scribe and palace steward of his father Amenhotep III, shows the tomb owner sitting with four boys upon his lap. The boys are of varying sizes and ages. The caption by the eldest boy reads 'the king's true son, beloved of him, Akheprure'.[1] This is not one of the titles bequeathed to Akhenaten, and must have belonged to another son. This suggestion is supported by an inscription on a whip found in the tomb of Tutankhamun, which reads: 'the son of the king, captain of the troops, Tutmosis'.[2] This name also occurs on a monument at Memphis, where, as we saw in the last chapter, he was the High Priest of Ptah, and this refers to him as the eldest son of Amenhotep III. Unfortunately, the reasons for his mysterious disappearance have yet to be explained.

The only assured reference to Akhenaten seems to have been on a wine-seal from the palace of Malkata, where it states: 'the estate of the king's son Amenhotep'.[3] He was then old enough to have his own establishments during the last decade of his father's reign, and was probably residing with the rest of the royal court at Thebes. Despite the fact that there is some evidence to suggest a co-regency with his father, Akhenaten probably ascended to the throne at the age of sixteen. His installation is clearly illustrated in the tomb of his vizier, Ramose, an unfinished tomb at the foot of the Sheikh-Abd el-Qurna hill on the west bank of the Nile at Thebes. Here the king is shown as a normal young man seated upon the throne of Upper Egypt. He is described as 'the image of Ra who loves him more than any other'.[4] Wearing the customary coronation crown, and holding the sceptres of kingly power, the crook and the flail, he receives his officials who are acting in the function of the Theban gods.

His chief wife was a woman called Nefertiti, whose

name means 'the beautiful one has come'. Little is known
about her background and the debate still continues, but her
looks alone made her a remarkable woman. Her reputation
as a great beauty is based upon one single statue, the famous
Nefertiti Bust now on display in the Agyphtes Museum in
Berlin.

The beginning of Akhenaten's reign marked no great
discontinuity with that of his predecessors. He was raised in
the traditional manner and observed the religious rituals of
the god Amun. He was crowned in the temple of Amun at
Karnak and continued very much in the same vein as a
traditional pharaoh of Egypt. For a few months into the
new reign, or perhaps for as much as a year, he persisted
with the architectural decoration of the temple in much the
same way as pharaohs past. The two pylons belonging to his
father were mostly left undecorated at the death of
Amenhotep III, and work was continued by Akhenaten. The
southern gate was decorated with a series of reliefs, each
showing Akhenaten in the traditional guise of a pharaoh,
offering to the falcon-headed sun god Ra-Horakhty. On the
Third Pylon, there is even a traditional head-smiting scene,
in which the cartouche or name-ring of the pharaoh reads
Amenhotep IV. The latter's representation is unexceptional,
save for his ubiquitous epithet, written upon the columns,
which calls him 'he who rejoices in the horizon in his name
Sunlight that is in the Disc'.[5] The gate was named after
Amenhotep IV, his original throne name, and the adjacent
towers were decorated with traditional scenes. As was
consistent with the very notion of kingship, Akhenaten is
seen to be the only one who makes the necessary offerings
to the gods, or is depicted riding in his customary chariot,
the wheels crushing Egypt's traditional enemies beneath
him.

Traditional though the form looks, it seems Akhenaten

was already beginning to question both the norms of art and the cult with which he had been brought up. Within two years of his father's death, he announced the decision to celebrate his jubilee or *sed* festival early in his reign. What motivated him to even entertain the prospect is as much a mystery to us today as it probably was to his contemporaries. As we saw in the last chapter, jubilees were not celebrated until the thirtieth regnal year. Nevertheless, it was a deliberate move and some time early in his second year, at the latest, Akhenaten took the unprecedented step of celebrating a jubilee as his father had done in his last decade.[6] The time was set to coincide with the third anniversary of his ascension to the throne.

Unbeknown to the royal officiates, this was to be no ordinary jubilee. For the first time in Egyptian history, there were to be no statues of Amun, Osiris, Mut, Isis or any of the other gods of Egypt's time-honoured pantheon. Although the festival continued on the same lines of old, with the priests in the procession carrying the standards of the gods, the famous deities themselves do not appear to have been present. Controversially, all the shrines now held statues of the king, and the king only.[7] Akhenaten had succeeded in banishing the entire Egyptian pantheon. This deliberate exclusion of the major state gods should have served as a warning to the priests of Amun.

Akhenaten's next move was to gather his chief sculptors around him and issue new orders: the king's form was now to be portrayed in such a way as to emphasize the attributes that differentiated it from a traditional royal subject. As a result, the iconography of the pharaoh underwent a transformation that must have shocked even his most loyal subjects. Akhenaten was determined that he was not to be represented in an idealized way. In doing so, he went to the other extreme. In a newly built temple at Karnak, colossal sculptures of the king, about 5 metres high, were erected against a series of massive pillars that surrounded the temple court. Unlike the pharaohs of the past, he appears strangely, almost grotesquely, distorted. His enormous thighs are tightly drawn together by a knee-length kilt whose upper edge, supported by a heavy, angular belt, droops below a protruding belly. Long, sinewy arms are crossed across a narrow waist while the hands are placed across rather effeminate breasts.[8] Never before had a pharaoh of Egypt ever been depicted in such a manner, and what he expected to achieve is unknown. But it certainly set him apart from other mere mortals. It was a sign of things to come.

As we have seen, his grandfather Tutmosis IV and his father Amenhotep III had recognized the growing power and influence of the Amun priesthood and had sought to curb it. Throughout each of their reigns, the divine position of the Aten, the sun-disc, as a form of the sun god Ra, had been somewhat ill defined. Akhenaten was to take the matter one step further. After his jubilee, in a few short years he introduced what has often been called a new monotheistic cult of sun worship. Such veneration would now be directed at the sun-disc itself. It has to be said this was not a new idea, as the disc was a relatively minor aspect of the sun god Ra-Horakhty and had first appeared during the Old Kingdom. To be more precise, Akhenaten's innovation was to worship the Aten in its own right. No other gods existed in his official scheme of things. The old iconography of the falcon-headed Ra-Horakhty was abandoned and replaced by the Aten, which took the form of a faceless sun disc, whose protective rays terminated in hands holding the ankh hieroglyph for life. The Aten was only accessible to Akhenaten, and therefore avoided the need for an intermediary priesthood. The elevation of the

Aten allowed the king to become the most prominent figure in any religious scene: all eyes were now focused on Akhenaten himself. The king had become the Son of the Disc whilst the latter had become his father. The Disc is said to have been the one that 'created his beauty'.[9] Unlike his predecessors, who had been granted their kingship by the state god Amun, Akhenaten had been granted his kingship and dominion by his father, Ra. On his temple walls at Karnak it states:

> May the good god live who delights in truth, lord of heaven and lord of earth, the Aten, the living, the great, illuminating the Two Lands. May the father live, divine and royal, Ra-Horakhty, rejoicing in the horizon in his aspect of light which is in the sun-disc, who lives for ever and ever, the Aten, the great, who in jubilee with the temple of the Aten.[10]

The Aten, however, was not an innovative concept. The revolutionary aspect was how Akhenaten chose to perceive this god. Apart from the odd passing allusions, there are only a handful of references predating Akhenaten's reign which refer to the Aten with any real significance.[11]

From the point of few of the Egyptian imperialists, the reign of Akhenaten was a distinct misfortune. With such a flagrant disregard for the state god, Amun, it would not be long before he was on a direct confrontational path with the priesthood. As we have seen, Amun's high priests had been accustomed to occupying the most prominent and influential positions in society. By openly allying himself with this new god, the Aten, Akhenaten was, quite literally, threatening the cult of Amun with political extinction. What action the priesthood took to curb his unfavourable policies is unclear, but something was done, or attempted, that aroused the anger of the king to such an extent that he began to wage a war of bitter persecution against both the god Amun and Thebes.

In the fourth year of his reign Akhenaten made one of the most daring moves yet. During the decisive opening phase of his revolution, the High Priest of Amun, up to then arguably the most powerful man in the land, was sent on a quarrying mission, quite literally 'into the wilderness'.[12] Such expeditions were commonplace, but were definitely beneath a man of his stature. At this point in the late Eighteenth Dynasty a high priest would never have been sent simply to find lumps of rock to be carved into statues; it would have been quite literally an insult. The exact circumstances of the matter are never fully explained, and whether the high priest ever returned to Egypt or was replaced by some underling is not known. However, what is apparent is that Akhenetan had succeeded in ridding himself of the biggest thorn in his side. With the high priest kept far away from events at Thebes, Akhenaten could pursue his ambitions without any opposition.

The 'banishment' of the High Priest of Amun sparked the beginning of an energetic building programme. To coincide with Akhenaten's new directives, the Aten was promoted as the new state god, immediately replacing Amun. In addition, a series of temples devoted entirely to the Aten, in which Akhenaten for the first time incorporated his new artistic ideas, were rapidly built at the sacred site of Karnak. His new construction was very different in form from the traditional temple design in that the emphasis was on open-air worship rather than the dark seclusion of rooms in the heart of the temple. The choice of east Karnak for the site of his new temple was bold, if not challenging. It is perhaps significant that this location received the life-giving rays of the newborn sun each morning before the temple of Amun was brought to life. Called the Temple to the Aten, it consisted of four major structures: the Sun-Disc is Found; the Mansion of the Benben Stone; Sturdy are the Monuments of the Sun-Disc Forever; and Exalted are the Monuments of the Sun-Disc Forever.[13]

The temple was constructed around a rectangular court about 130 metres wide by around 200 metres deep. An ambulatory ran around the perimeter and consisted of a roofed colonnade of square piers facing inwards and rising to a height of more than 7 metres. Against each pier was stationed a painted sandstone colossus of the king holding the traditional symbols of kingship, the crook and flail sceptres, across his chest. But the most outstanding feature of every relief or inscription is that all allusions to the old god Amun had now ceased to exist entirely.[14]

For the very first time, Scota is depicted with her mother, Nefertiti, upon the temple walls. It has been argued that she was probably no more than five years old at the time. In the earliest reliefs she stands directly behind her mother, dressed in the same garb, and shaking the sistrum, a stick-like instrument made of wood or metal containing a series of small metal discs that rattled when it was shaken. It was popular in the cult of the goddess Hathor but it was also the favoured instrument in the cultic rites in Egypt's temples and shrines and was used frequently in religious processions. Considering Akhenaten's abhorrence of all other gods, the latter is perhaps the most plausible explanation why Scota would be holding such an item. The stereotyped caption text never changes: she is identified as 'the king's bodily daughter whom he loves, Meritaten, born of the great King's Wife Nefertiti, may she live'.[15]

Owing to the destruction of the temple by Akhenaten's immediate successors, not one of the four Theban monuments has survived. Smashed into smithereens, instead of a series of impressive temples the remains consist simply of a vast number of inscribed and painted sandstone building blocks that are today simply known as the Karnak Talatat. Used as building filling for later structures, over 45,000 disjointed blocks have so far been collected from within the walls and the gateways of Karnak Temple. Nearly all of them came from the Aten Temple and many are sculpted in sunken relief, showing scenes from Akhenaten's early years as king. Owing to their complexity, many scholars believed that the lost Aten scenes would never be restored. That was until the advent of computer science.[16]

In 1965 Ray Winfield Smith, an American businessman, conceived a plan to recreate on paper what could not be done in stone. He wanted to rebuild the Temple to the Aten that Akhenaten had built at Thebes. Hence the Akhenaten Temple Project was born and, under the directorship of Professor Donald Redford of Toronto University, the mission has been dedicated to the recovery of the lost images. By employing a combination of photography and space-age computer graphics, it has so far been possible to reconstruct over 2000 individual scenes of Akhenaten's early reign.[17]

Some time in his fifth regnal year, Akhenaten's burning zeal seems to have made it impossible to keep up any pretence of traditional kingship or links with the Theban god Amun. He dropped the name Amenhotep IV and adopted his more familiar name, Akhenaten, a name evoking the shining, exalted state in which the king perpetually walked during his lifetime on earth. He is an *akh*, a 'transfigured one', who stands in the horizon between heaven and earth, mediating the radiance and the power of the eternal sun god through his effective deeds on earth.[18] Henceforth his official titles were as follows:

The Living Horus:
Mighty Bull, beloved of Aten:
Two Ladies:
Great of Kingship in the Light-land-of-Aten:
Horus of Gold, who exalts the name of Aten:
The King of Upper and Lower Egypt
Who lives by Maat,
The Lord of the Two Lands:
Beautiful-of-transformations-is-Ra
Sole-One-of-Ra:
The Son of the Sun who lives by Maat:
Lord of Diadems: Akhenaten
Great in his lifetime, given life forever.[19]

The career of Amenhotep IV was now over, and the reign of Akhenaten had begun. With the decoration of his new temples complete, the king could now openly break with Amun without fear of reprisal. The 'king of the gods' had been tolerated to this point, but now Egypt witnessed the formal expunging of his name and the closing of all his temples, including Karnak. The programme of defacement which followed was so thorough that we must postulate that either a small army of hatchet men were dispatched throughout the realm or parties of inspectors were charged with seeing that local officials did the job. Everywhere, in the temples, the tombs, on statuary and even upon casual inscriptions, the hieroglyph for Amun and the representation of the god were chiselled out. Even the tallest obelisks and highest architraves at Thebes were scaled to hammer out the name and figure of Amun. Throughout the land objects sacred to him were likewise defaced or destroyed. His statues were smashed; even small scarabs that bore his name were defaced. What is more, people who bore names compounded with 'Amun' were obliged to change them.

Even the Amun element in his father's name, Amenhotep III, was obliterated from the smallest toilet vessel that once belonged to his mother, Queen Tiye.[20]

The god of the underworld, Osiris, and his cycle of mortuary gods were not immune to Akhenaten's hatred, and subsequently suffered the same fate as Amun. This was a daring and controversial move. By officially ridding Egypt of the concept of a god of the underworld, Akhenaten succeeded in casting out one of the country's oldest traditions and placing himself at its head. Only through adherence to Akhenaten and his intercession on their behalf could the people of Egypt now hope to live beyond the grave. The ancient mortuary practices might be retained, but only if they were purged of any polytheistic elements. Traditional canopic equipment, the containers used in the funerary rituals to preserve the viscera of the deceased after embalming, maintained the usual iconography, but the atypical goddess figures at the corners were now replaced by the sun god Ra-Horakhty. *Ushabtis*, the little servant figures that accompanied the dead to the next world, might be retained, but without the standard inscription of the chapter of the *Book of the Dead*.[21]

The *Book of the Dead* was a loose collection of magical spells and incantations that were written on papyrus, normally illustrated, and was popular throughout the New Kingdom. The purpose of the book was to instruct the deceased on how to overcome the dangers of the afterlife, by enabling them to assume the form of several mythical creatures, and to give them the necessary passwords for admission to certain stages in the underworld. But with the abolition of the underworld, only the names of the deceased could be written on the *ushabtis*. Heart scarabs, which in the old Osirian order prevented the heart from witnessing against the deceased at the last judgement, continued to occur, but only inscribed with a simple offering formula to the Aten disc. All the gods of Ancient Egypt and the denizens of the underworld are pointedly ignored in all funerary literature, and the Underworld itself is merely referred too as 'the place from which the deceased comes forth to view the sun'.[22]

One traditional religious concept, however, was retained and even emphasized by Akhenaten. This was the concept of *maat* which, as we have seen, can be translated as 'truth' or 'justice'. Represented by the goddess Maat, daughter of Ra, it now had to be spelt phonetically and not represented by the glyph of a woman squatting with a feather on her head. Similarly, the word *mut,* meaning mother, was also spelt out in glyphs and not characterized by the vulture goddess Mut. The common title of the king, 'the Good God', was also avoided and Akhenaten introduced a new version, 'the Good Ruler', instead.[23]

Following the precedent set by his father, Amenhotep III, from early in his reign Akhenaten also increased the power of his queen, Nefertiti. Women in ancient Egypt had enjoyed equality under the law and many had high positions, riches and privileges. The Great Wife was even accorded her own palace. However, Akhenaten went much further. From her depictions, it is quite apparent that Nefertiti enjoyed far more influence than almost any other Egyptian queen. Remarkably, she was recorded with regnant qualities throughout this revolutionary period and often seems to have pharaonic authority equal to that of her husband.[24] Akhenaten probably felt it was necessary to emphasize to the rich and entrenched priesthood of Amun the unequivocal nature of the position that she held. Here was not a goddess but a regnant queen. From the very first Temple of the Aten, Nefertiti was shown as equal to her husband. Accordingly, her prominence in the main temple cult was a cause for astonishment, even shock, to contemporary Egyptians. After all, in the great state cults, the king was the sole representation of mankind before the gods. The determined and powerful purpose is obvious behind these numerous carvings. Not only was Akhenaten demonstrating to the people the new social and religious development but, also, his wife's equality.[25] In Thebes this policy was instigated as soon as the High Priest of Amun had been banished to the eastern desert. The idea of a ruling queen, however, did not come easily to the Egyptians. Hatshepsut had overcome this problem by collaborating with the Amun priesthood. With no priesthood left, how would the regnant pair resolve this? Before long Nefertiti would have to be seen wearing the king's crowns whenever she was depicted with her husband.

What could be deemed the final seal of Nefertiti's regality was carved upon the walls of the Aten temples at Thebes. Here, for the world to see, she is depicted in the traditional pharaonic role of a warrior king subduing the enemies of Egypt. With a mace in her hand, she gets ready to smite those in front of her. It was the custom in Egypt that only the kings were ever depicted in this symbolic stance of a sovereign towering above enemy captives. So such militaristic postures were normal for Egyptian kings, but most unusual for queens. Akhenaten had, yet again, dispensed with convention. In another depiction Nefertiti is even shown as a sphinx, another kingly image, trampling across the enemy. She inherited the title 'Lady of the Two Lands' from earlier queens of the Eighteenth Dynasty, However, no queen before her had been denoted solely by this term, and only for her does the designation appear directly in front of the cartouche, the name-ring, with her name. Since 'Lord of the Two Lands' was a common description of the Egyptian king, the title 'Lady of the Two

Lands' emphasized Nefertiti's strong position as a counterpart to the pharaoh.[26]

The peculiar depictions of the king and the royal family really hurt no one. Even the elevation of his new god, the Aten, to a place of prominence at Thebes might just have been acceptable. But when Akhenaten declared that the Aten was now the sole god of Egypt, the battle lines were drawn. If any further proof is required of what Akhenaten was trying to do, let this one significant omission suffice: the plural word 'gods' is never attested to after Year 5 of his reign.[27] If we believe the rhetoric of this megalomaniac king, seven years after Akhenaten came to the throne, the integrated system of politics, economics, and cult that Egypt had known for 1700 years had been drastically modified, if not turned upside down. Consequently, it would appear that the once thriving administrative centres of Thebes and Memphis stood idle. According to his proclamations, the temples and government offices had been virtually shut down and the sons of distinguished houses, who had served pharaoh well, suddenly found themselves bereft of function and court connection. A new epoch had descended upon the land of Egypt. In Year 5, having experienced events that were 'worse than those heard by any kings who had assumed the White Crown,'[28] the king decided to move the royal residence and seat of government to a new site.

Opposite Mallawi, in Middle Egypt, the eastern bank of the Nile presents the appearance of a gorge with sheer limestone cliffs plunging into the river and affording no space for a continuous highway or cultivation at the water's edge. This rocky escarpment extends south for some 65 kilometres. The notable exception is an abrupt curve from the bank for a distance of 12 kilometres, where the sandy plain of Amarna appears. This was the site to which Akhenaten was supposedly directed by divine inspiration, in his fifth

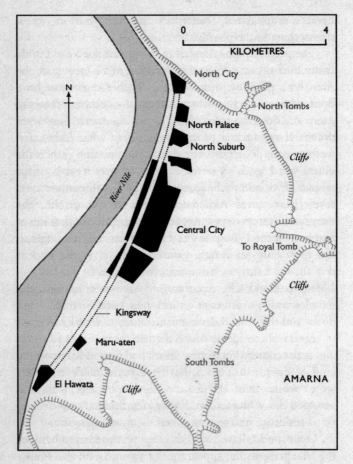

The royal city of Amarna

regnal year, as the place where his sole god had manifested himself at the Creation of the World.[29] Here it was that the king founded a great capital on virgin ground, which was built, occupied, and extended during the remaining twelve years of his reign. He called his new city Akhetaten, 'the horizon of the Aten'. Today it is better known by its Arabic name, Amarna. From the boundary stela surrounding the city it states: 'Behold Akhetaten which the Aten desires me to make unto him as a monument in his name forever. It was the Aten my father that brought me to Akhetaten. Not a noble directed me to it saying, "It is fitting for his majesty to make Akhetaten in this place." It was the Aten my father that directed me to it, to make it for him as Akhetaten.'[30]

How and why he was directed to this site is not made clear. However, his visionary intentions are inscribed upon a series of Boundary Stela surrounding his new sacred city. Carved at intervals into the cliffs on both sides of the Nile, they state that it was the Aten that selected it and led him to the site. Within these limits the temples and the palaces would be built. Each stela contained an oath of the king:

My oath of truth, which is my desire to pronounce, and of which I will not say: 'it is false', for ever and ever: Akhetaten extends from the southern tablet as far as the northern tablet, measured between the tablet and tablet in the eastern mountain, likewise from the south-west tablet to the north-west tablet in the western mountain of Akhetaten. The area within these four tablets is Akhetaten itself; it belongs to Aten my father: mountains, deserts, meadows, islands, high ground and low ground, water, villages, men, animals and all things which the Aten, my father, shall bring into existence eternally and forever. I will not neglect this oath which I have made to the Aten my father eternally and forever.[31]

The British explorer John Gardner Wilkinson made the first proper account of Amarna in the late 1800s. He was the son of a minister, who attended Oxford University but left before obtaining his degree for a career in the army. While he was stationed in Italy, word filtered through to him about the attempts by Egyptologists to decipher hieroglyphs. Wilkinson had been fascinated by the land of the pharaohs since boyhood. Excited, he headed straight for Egypt, where he remained for the next twelve years. Together with the antiquary, geologist and draughtsman James Burton, more famous for his work in the tomb of Tutankhamun, he explored the rock-cut tombs to the east of the Amarna village, copying the scenes of ancient priests and nobles on the walls. Though many of the accompanying inscriptions had been damaged, Wilkinson realized that their decoration was different from any that had previously been found in Egypt. Unlike the stark traditional religious and military iconography, the decoration was concerned with that of the royal family. Sadly for Wilkinson, he could not decipher the hieroglyphs, but he was the first to observe what would later become a crucial clue to the fate of Amarna. The city had not just been deserted in antiquity; it had, quite literally, been taken apart.[32]

Shortly after Wilkinson's initial outing, the great Prussian expedition to Egypt also decided to make two visits to Amarna, one in 1843, the other in 1845. Under the auspices of Richard Lepsius, a disciple of Jean Francois Champollion and the foremost Egyptologist of his day, they spent a total of twelve days studying the tombs and making drawings. The massive twelve volumes entitled *Denkmaler* were based on these engravings.[33] Housed in Berlin, the records were invaluable and were to provide the definitive text for scholars throughout the remainder of the nineteenth century, as regrettably many of the inscriptions and illustrations no longer exist. The Amarna tombs had lain open on the northern hills for thousands of years since the final desertion of the city below, and most of them were badly damaged and polluted by generations of squatters in early Christian times. Nowadays, colonies of bats inhabit the tombs of the dead. The local population also began to resent the intrusion of these eminent explorers and soon took it upon themselves to destroy all the carvings and reliefs. So, without the work of these first explorers, the relics from Amarna would have been lost forever. What foresight they had to copy the magnificence they witnessed.

The last scholar to work at Amarna before the wanton destruction was Norman de Garis Davies, the surveyor for the British-based Egypt Exploration Fund. In the 1890s, over a period of six years, he painstakingly copied all the decorations that still survived in the cliff tombs and published them in his six-volume *The Rock Cut Tombs of Amarna*. They were almost the only means by which later scholars could piece together the life and times of Akhenaten.

The earliest archaeological excavation of Amarna was carried out by one Flinders Petrie, a young British archaeologist, in the 1890s, and for the first time the colossal scale and splendour of the city became apparent. Akhetaten was a straggling metropolis built along a 10-kilometre stretch of the Nile: a northern town with its royal palace and suburbs, a central city with its sacred temple, and a southern town with its mansions for the upper classes. The whole city was constructed around a 40-metre wide processional way which swept down from the northern palace and on through the central city, where it was flanked by a series of official buildings, a ceremonial palace and the new, open-air temple to the Aten.[34] There must have been a mass exodus from other Egyptian cities in order to build such a place from scratch – artists, sculptors, craftsmen, brewers, bakers and so on. The same fervour and energy that built the cathedrals in the Middle Ages seem to have flowed at Amarna. For in an incredibly short space of time a city, complete with sun temples, mud-brick palaces, villas, gardens, military barracks and living quarters for the workforce, sprang up out of nowhere as miraculously as the dawning of the Aten. In admiration, Petrie said: 'No king of Egypt, nor of any part of the world, has ever carried out his honesty of expression so openly. Thus in every line Akhenaten stands out as perhaps the most original thinker that ever lived in Egypt, and one of the greatest idealists of the world. No man appears to have made a greater stride to a new standpoint than he did.'[35]

The records of who actually went with Akhenaten to his new city are limited. We definitely know that the great royal wife Nefertiti was present and that Scota was also by his side, as the king was already planning their tombs high in the mountainous areas of the city's boundaries. It is perhaps interesting to note that one of his many proclamations upon the Boundary Stela surrounding the city stated that if any of these three were to die elsewhere in Egypt, their bodies should be brought back for burial at Amarna.[36]

Akhenaten had also persuaded his own personal staff of friends and family to take up office at Amarna with him. One of the most influential, and the one destined to play a major role in the flight of Scota, was Ay, 'the favoured one of the good god, fan-bearer on the king's right hand, true king's scribe and god's father, trusted throughout the entire land, commander of chariotry'. Brother of Queen Tiye, he was curiously absent at Thebes but comes into the picture at Amarna. There was also Parennefer, 'the pure-handed royal butler of his majesty', who was present at Thebes and also now turns up at Amarna; Tutu, 'the chamberlain of the Lord of the Two Lands, and treasurer'; Khay, 'the table-scribe of the Lord of the Two Lands', and Ranefer, 'the king's personal charioteer'. Last but not least there was Ahmose, the king's steward and 'sole friend'.[37]

In addition, there would have been a vast array of cabinet ministers and civil servants, including the vizier Nakht, the scribe of recruits Ramose and numerous officials from the armed forces. From the information provided, it appears that none of the old guard of Theban priests and officials followed Akhenaten to his new city. Not surprisingly, they appeared to shun the king and his new religion.

The city of Amarna, of course, contained several temples to the Aten. As his physical form was the sun, his worship had to take place in the open. The huge Great Temple to the Aten, almost 731 metres in length and around 229 metres wide, catered for this.[38] The worshipper, after entering through the formal gateway, passed through a columned hall and came into an open court filled with offering tables, at the back of which lay a separate area called The Aten is Found. The Mansion of the Aten had a similar layout. Another site devoted to the worship of the Aten lay at the eastern end of the city, where two separate areas were enclosed by walls. Inside the walls lay lakes surrounded by gardens, within which were set pavilions and shrines, and altars to the sun stood on small islands. This was Maru-Aten and, in the words of one scholar, it exemplified the 'spirit of sun worship, providing an idyllic landscape of greenery and water presided over by the sun.'[39]

The limits of the god Aten's new territory were defined in a series of massive inscriptions carved upon huge granite stela at strategic points into the limestone cliffs. Eleven were erected in the east and three were raised in the west. It could be argued that Akhenaten was providing his god with a self-contained kingdom which not only allowed plenty of room for internal growth but which, the king swore, would never be expanded beyond its stated boundaries. It is difficult to calculate how much of this area was fertile land, but it has been suggested that the cultivation would have been capable of supporting a population of up to 45,000 people.[40]

What made Akhenaten choose this site? Why did he go to such lengths to build a new city? There is not enough evidence to reconstruct what actually happened, but forces at Thebes, both political and religious, must have created a situation that could only be resolved by separation. Many historians believe that Akhenaten built his new city simply to give the Aten a cult centre of its own. But if this assumption is correct, then why could he not base himself at Heliopolis in the north, the designated city of the sun god since the beginning of time? Probably because he was too radical even for Heliopolis as he strove to provide an entirely different basis for Egyptian kingship.[41] Clearly the increasing emphasis being placed on the Aten had brought Akhenaten into conflict with the priesthood of Amun. But had he successfully rid himself of that particular hindrance? And where did he get the revenue required to build all the new temples, let alone a new city? And if there was no apparent threat from the Amun priesthood, why did he choose to uproot the entire Egyptian state and move it to a patch of desert in the wilderness? One possibility has been put forward by the late Cyril Aldred, an expert in the Amarna period. In *Akhenaten – King of Egypt*, he points out that the gap in the eastern hills, where the sun is seen to rise from the city of Akhetaten, appears to resemble a saddle-back indentation similar to the hieroglyph used to denote the word *akhet*, meaning horizon. If Akhenaten had witnessed such a scene, perhaps on a visit to the region, it may have sealed his decision to build a city here and name it Akhetaten, 'the horizon of the Aten'.[42] Maybe, in the end, the site of Amarna was simply the ideal place to create a new religious power base.

Nothing shows the true driving force behind such

innovations better than the position Akhenaten assigned himself in the new scheme of things. The decoration of the tombs of the nobles depicts the royal court bowing in uniform obeisance to the king; there is no room here for a direct relation between the individual and the god, all divine contact was now solely reserved for the king only. Prayer also had to be channelled through the king, and shrines at home had to replace the old gods with images of the royal family under the rays of the Aten.[43] To a degree far greater than any of his immediate predecessors, he set about establishing the paternity of the sun, the unity of sun and pharaoh, and the individuality of the god itself. Nowhere is this better illustrated then the graphic offering scenes on his temple walls, where Akhenaten is 'said to be shone on by the sunlight which emanates from his father'.[44] Akhenaten's image completely dominated the city, and in life the man himself ensured that his subjects were continually aware of his physical presence.

By maintaining a distinction between himself and his father, Akhenaten also heightened the awareness of his own individuality. The sunlight was deemed to be the source of the king's being. If Akhenaten had declared himself a god outright, like his father before him, it would have placed the embodiment of the ideal before men's eyes, where its imperfections would be plain for everyone to see. Akhenaten was too shrewd for that. If things went wrong, there would be only one person that the Egyptian people would blame and that would be the king. But in maintaining that he was a little lower than a god, the distinction gave Akhenaten a freedom of action that absolute identification as a god would have rendered impossible.[45]

Akhenaten saw the Aten as the universal creator of all life, and celebrated this form in several hymns that have survived on the carvings in the Amarna tombs. Their sentiments were not themselves new in Egypt. A well-known hymn on a papyrus in the Cairo Museum, dated to before Akhenaten's reign, addressed the Theban god Amun in similar terms of universal power and solar imagery. However, where Akhenaten's hymns differ is in the absence of reference to any other god but his own. In the older hymns, the gods were seen as a complementary aspect of Amun. Here, the Aten, devoid of human features, became the only divine image, as Akhenaten could tolerate no rivals upon earth. Akhenaten and the disc were alone and supreme in the universe, over all men; there were no other gods. He was the 'living Disc – there is no other than him'.[46] Nowhere is this better illustrated than in the so-called 'Great Hymn to the Aten'. Some say Akhenaten wrote it himself, though this hypothesis has no grounding in fact. Inscribed on the tomb walls of the Grand Vizier Ay, it is a stunning piece of ancient literature. It sums up the whole ethos of the Aten cult, in particular the concept that only Akhenaten had access to the god.

Akhenaten frequently emphasized that he, and he alone, was the go-between for this new divine life for Egypt. The sole god of Egypt was now mediated through Akhenaten. At the close of the 'Great Hymn to the Aten' it says, 'There is no one who knows you, except your son, Akhenaten.'[47] By channelling all such worship through himself, perhaps he hoped to avoid the creation of a strong and dominant priesthood such as that of Amun. Together the Aten and the king shared in the divine rulership of heaven and earth, a fact symbolized by the inscription of the Aten's name in the two royal cartouches exactly like the king's. In respect of the divine union, all monuments of the time are ascribed jointly to Akhenaten and the Aten.

The ultimate sign of Akhenaten's determination to break with the past was a promise to site tombs for himself and his family in the eastern hills, in a new Valley of the Kings. Consequently, his courtiers were expected to do the same. The new burial site was in a peculiar, remote location. From the city, a trek of 5 kilometres takes one to the entrance to the wadi which leads to the Royal Valley, although another 6 kilometres lie ahead before the site of the royal necropolis is reached. The Royal Valley has been called a savage place, devoid of vegetation and shade but of an awesome beauty in the morning and evening light. Occasionally, sudden storms break over the entire area, discharging torrents of water that scour the valley. In this way fragments and debris from the tombs have been carried far beyond its mouth, a fact well known to the local inhabitants, who must have combed the region many times in the hope of finding antiquities that others have overlooked.[48]

Of the various tombs planned, only one was brought anywhere near to completion, and that was Akhenaten's own. The site of the royal tomb had been disclosed to the French mission, who were operating at the time in the southern tombs at Amarna, by local villagers, in the early nineteenth century. The reason why the tomb of Akhenaten had escaped detection for so long was because it was situated in the eastern hills, not among the private tombs, but in a remote side valley.[49] Most of the decoration has been lost, but a few fragments which survive show pictures of the royal family and the Aten. No remains of a body have ever been found within the tomb, but tiny fragments of what is considered to be the sarcophagus of Akhenaten were discovered. Traces of inscriptions, in a very fragile state near the line of the ceiling, give the titles and name of the Aten, Akhenaten and his wife Nefertiti. Akhenaten's preparation of a tomb at Akhetaten at least illustrates that he had faith in the city and expected his ideas to last for ever.[50]

There was a rigid official adherence to the cult of the

Aten among the elite at Amarna, many of whom built shrines dedicated to the new royal family and the Aten in the gardens of their villas. In all scenes one theme is stressed, the bounty of the king and of his father the sun. The prosperity of Egypt depended upon them alone. The king was 'the Nile which fills the entire land'. He was the one who gave to those whom he loved, who ordained burial for one who put him in his heart. 'Adore the king who is unique like the Disc, for there is no other beside him! Then he will grant you a lifetime in happiness of heart, with the sustenance he is wont to give'.[51]

Up to now we have concentrated mainly on Akhenaten and his religious revolution. Let us return to Scota for one moment. What part, if any, did she play in her father's reforms? We saw in Chapter 2 how important she appears to have been, because of her unparalleled representations in religious reliefs at Thebes. And after her arrival in Amarna, at approximately six years of age, her role certainly did not diminish; if anything it appears to have increased.

During the early German excavations at Amarna, a series of workshops and compounds were discovered in the centre of the city. They belonged to the Chief of Works, the sculptor Thutmose. Only a few metres away from the famous bust of her mother, Nefertiti, a brown quartzite figurehead of Scota, sculpted to size, was uncovered at the southern enclosure wall of the compound. It can now be viewed in the Berlin Museum. It has a distinct front profile and back views. In traditional Egyptian art a back pillar usually decorated such sculptures. Not so here: no slab of stone encumbers the elegantly carved back of Scota's thin neck. All the more striking is the peculiar shape of her head, elongated, with a shaved skull.[52]

Initially, the shaved head was just a fashion suited to the hot climate of Egypt, aiding cleanliness and the wearing of courtly wigs. However, at least from the Middle Kingdom onwards, it was also associated with the purification rites prescribed for those persons performing a range of priestly tasks. It is difficult to determine why Thutmose chose to represent Scota with an entirely shaved head. Earlier representations of royal children were always shown with a characteristic side lock of hair. It must have been a deliberate decision.[53] As Akhenaten had used Scota as an icon at Thebes, was Thutmose now emphasizing her importance in a similar religious context at Amarna?

The day-to-day scenes in Amarna regularly depicted Akhenaten and his wife Nefertiti relaxing in the company of their six daughters. At that time, it would appear that Scota had a charmed childhood. The first picture to show all six daughters alive is the one in the so-called King's House, a series of private chambers that had been joined to the ceremonial palace by a bridge. Here the outstanding wall paintings depict the king and queen on stools with all their daughters before them. The three eldest stand before their parents' knees, the youngest Sotepenre, is a babe in her mother's lap, and the other pair are shown at her feet.[54]

Furthermore, in the tombs of the high steward Huya and the harem overseer Meryre, the wall paintings show the royal family attending an event which is dated to Year 12 of Akhenaten's reign. It was a magnificent reception graced by a procession of foreign ambassadors with tribute for the king. Gold, silver and precious jewels were placed on the ground in the royal presence. Here the royal pair are shown seated upon the gilded thrones whilst the six daughters, three of them holding hands whilst the others play with their pet gazelles, are shown on either side.[55]

Nine 'beloved king's daughters of his flesh' are documented at Amarna, and six of them are specified as 'born of the king's Chief Wife Nefertiti'.[56] Who were the other three? From the end of the Amarna period there are a number of mysterious princesses whose names are attested in texts on blocks dismantled from various temples and palaces. One such daughter is Meritaten the Younger, whose mother has been identified as Scota herself. Damaged and altered texts also refer to a king's daughter named Ankhesenpaaten the Younger. This possibility has led to the suggestion that Akhenaten not only married Scota, but also his third daughter Ankhesenpaaten, and that he had children by both of them.[57]

Although she was scarcely as prominent as Nefertiti, or the royal daughters, there was a secondary wife, named Kiya. She appears to have been Akhenaten's 'favourite' and was honoured at Amarna with her own sanctuaries and chapels. Kiya seems to have borne at least one child to Akhenaten, a daughter whose name is not known. In addition, it is thought that Kiya was also the mother of Tutankhamun.

From very early on at Amarna it is apparent that Scota is singled out from her sisters by being nearest to her father. Why this is so is unclear. On a domestic stela, now in the Berlin Museum, her father has lifted her up and is kissing her on the cheek. On another stela and a wall relief she receives an earring from his hand, and in an unfinished group sculpture she is probably the young woman whom Akhenaten kisses.[58] Unexpectedly, as the reign draws to a close, Scota gains in power. In the final years of her father's life she continues to be referred to on wine-jar dockets and reliefs alike as 'the king's beloved daughter'. Moreover, between the years 14 and 15, Scota is referred to in the Amarna Letters, correspondence sent to Akhenaten by various people including Burnaburiash of Babylon and Abi-Milku of Tyre. As we saw in Chapter 2, they call her by her affectionate nickname, Mayati, and refer to her as the

'Mistress of your House', implying that she had now assumed the duties of the 'Great Royal Wife' or 'Chief Queen'.[59] In fact Burnaburiash complains in one passage that she had not sent presents or condolences when he was ill.[60] Comforting correspondence would be expected from the king and his consort, not from a mere princess.

Obviously Scota had achieved an exalted station, by reasons unknown, and she now appeared in relief scenes cut over those of other royal ladies, including Akhenaten's favoured second wife, Kiya. A typical example of an image of Kiya changed into Scota exists in the Copenhagen Museum. In the two columns there is a clear superimposed inscription, which now reads: 'daughter of the king of his flesh, his beloved Meritaten'. But the faint remains of the original inscription show that it once said 'the wife and beloved of the King of Upper and Lower Egypt who lives on'.[61] Sometimes Scota even usurped the monuments of her mother, Nefertiti. Eventually, however, she was designated the king's Chief Wife and her name was appropriately written in a cartouche. Whether Nefertiti was dead or not at this time is a matter of conjecture.

In a few short years Akhenaten had succeeded in eliminating all the traditional characteristics of the Egyptian state, the priesthood, the gods, the temples and so on. With the vast majority of Egyptian people worshipping a highly personal mixture of regional deities and family-based cults, the gods would almost certainly be missed. The shift from visual gods to an abstract concept like the Aten was perhaps a fundamental error on Akhenaten's part, and his faith was misplaced. He was rejected by later generations as not having been a legitimate king, and came to be referred to in terms such as 'that enemy Akhenaten'.[62] The rapid abandonment of his ideas also meant that the city of Amarna had little future. It was a tumultuous time and one in which

Scota was born and raised. From an impressionable young child, as we first see her in the scenes from the Temple of the Aten at Karnak, she had now become a willing participant in her father's heretical doctrine.

CHAPTER SEVEN

~~~

SCOTA'S DARKEST HOUR

Since Scota was now effectively the most powerful woman in Egypt, why was she forced to leave? What went so horribly wrong? From the information available, we know that her father's revolt against the Amun priesthood was not a spur-of-the-moment thing. Akhenaten's religious changes were carefully implemented as soon as the necessary political conditions had been created, manipulating the power of the institutions at his command. It was a calculated risk, and apart from his spiritual qualities and creative ruthlessness, there must have been an outside body which provided him with unquestioning support. After all, getting rid of traditions that have been established for over 2000 years is not an easy task by any means. How did Akhenaten achieve his aims?

It is obvious that if Akhenaten were to totally desecrate the old religion he would have to use the heavy-handed tactics of a military coup. To drive his message home he would not only have to destroy all representations of the old gods but also instil a reign of fear over their followers. Is it then possible to conceive that Akhenaten used his armed forces to bring forth an era of religious totalitarianism? Examining the army's role in this ancient drama will hopefully reveal the truth about Scota's sudden downfall.

Surprisingly, there was no permanent armed force in Egypt until the New Kingdom period. A royal bodyguard would naturally have existed to protect the monarch, but when the king required a force to repel a possible invasion or even mount his own strike against raiders or bandits, the bulk of his army would consist of young conscripts, taken from the fields to serve their pharaoh. Apart from their military duties, these conscripts were also involved with trading and mining expeditions. One such text, recorded on a papyrus and now in the British Museum, describes conscription as follows: 'All the king's subjects are mustered and the best will be taken. The man is made into a soldier and the youth into a recruit. The boy is born only to be torn from his mother's arms and he reaches manhood only to have his bones battered.'[1]

During the New Kingdom, the officers were the only career soldiers. Life for the ordinary soldier was hard and, it would appear, extremely unpleasant. A similar text taken from a pottery shard now in Florence describes the lot of the downtrodden soldier:

> His superiors are numerous. There are the general, the commander auxiliaries, and the officer who leads the host, the standard-bearer, the lieutenant, the recruiting officer, and the captain of fifty and the leader of the squad. They come and go in their quarters saying, 'Get the men to work!' The soldier is awakened after only an hour of sleep and he is worked like an ass until sunset . . . He is always hungry. He is like a dead man and yet he lives.[2]

It is significant that, during the later periods of the New Kingdom, from the beginning of the Nineteenth Dynasty onwards, men with military backgrounds soon began to rise to the throne. This was as a direct result of the death of Akhenaten and his only son and heir, Tutankhamun, who were the final true Egyptian bloodline.

The army was now, more often than not, led by one of the king's own sons; it consisted of both northern and southern corps, each commanded by a so-called 'chief deputy'. When campaigns were unleashed to expand Egypt's frontiers into the lands of western Asia, Libya or Nubia, there were usually four of five large divisions, each comprising of about 5000 professional soldiers and conscripts. Each division would be named after a god, such as Amun or Horus, and those unlucky enough to be captured by the Egyptian forces were incorporated into the army with the promise of being able to gain their freedom if they served the pharaoh. The alternative was torture and death.[3]

With the need to control the conquered lands, and the necessity for rapid military action in external emergencies, a permanent military administration was developed, headed by a 'great army general'. Divided into various units, each with its own hierarchy of officers, the military administration supervised local areas, carried out mining and trading expeditions for the king, organized local commercial networks using their agricultural surplus and acted as recruitment officers for both the army and the workforce.[4] With garrisons now needed abroad, the army general was directly responsible for a continuous levying and training programme. This created an experienced reserve that could be called upon and rapidly mobilized.[5] This was increasingly enhanced by the new chariot contingents, which also came into being at the beginning of the New Kingdom, and which quickly formed the most prestigious and glamorous section of the army. In next to no time, they constituted the new elite. Some of the tomb autobiographies suggest that it was considered a special honour to grow up in the 'stable of the king' – i.e. the royal chariotry. The special status accorded the drivers is reflected in the fact that they were sometimes used as royal emissaries on diplomatic missions. The evidence implies that in the Eighteenth Dynasty soldiers, and particularly members of the chariot corps, received some of the most influential court appointments.[6]

From the information available it is apparent that during the Eighteenth Dynasty the personnel surrounding the king included a significant number of high-ranking army officers. They were highly organized and, with the potential for great coercive force, it is not surprising that they could directly influence Egyptian policy. Its functional and ideological links with the kingship were also strong. After all, we have seen how the king was frequently depicted as an almighty warrior, smiting the traditional enemies of Egypt. It was these particular elements that Akhenaten exploited for his own aims.[7]

A central feature of Akhenaten's government is that his immediate entourage was drawn directly from the military. Scenes of soldiers and military activity flourish in both the private and royal art of Amarna. If we take the reliefs at face value, then it could be argued that the city of Akhetaten was virtually an armed camp! Everywhere we see parades and processions of soldiers, infantry and chariotry with their massed standards. Large platoons march at double speed, or stand at ease, and it is noticeable that these forces are never very far away from the figure of Akhenaten. There are soldiers under arms standing in front of the palaces and the temples, and in the watchtowers which border the city. There are scenes of troops, unarmed or equipped with staves, carrying out combat exercise in the presence of the king whilst bound and fettered prisoners of war from Asia and Nubia are ushered in before him.[8]

A glance at the records proves that the military officers enjoyed a particularly high station. For instance, the verbose and bombastic Maya held the title 'General of the Army of the Lord of the Two Lands', undoubtedly because he was greatly trusted by his lord . . . The only competent one in the presence of the Lord of the Two Lands, who filled the ears of the king with the truth . . . one whom the king has made great because of his fine qualities'. Nevertheless, if ever Maya were not in charge for one reason or another, the king could doubtless call on many others, such as Ramose or the battalion commander Neha-em-pa-aten or Ranefer or Ay.[9]

The military ethos of the city is also implicitly emphasized in the official art. In the so-called Royal Tomb, both Akhenaten and Nefertiti are constantly shown worshipping the Aten protected by the massed flags of the infantry and the standards of the chariot brigades. Fragments of relief from the numerous temples and palaces also depict similar scenes. In one, a charioteer rides up in his vehicle brandishing his shield to all comers. In another a battle had obviously taken place, for in the lower part we see the tassled helmets and bow-tips of Egyptian chariot crews, whilst in the upper carving the wheel of an Egyptian chariot and the hooves of its accompanying horse team run over the prostrate body of the enemy.[10]

Perhaps the most telling example of the military 'feel' to the Amarna period is in the images of the king himself. It is striking that in the vast majority of his representations in both the official royal art and in the private depictions, Akhenaten is shown wearing either the Blue Crown or the short Nubian wig rather than the traditional ceremonial crowns of Upper and Lower Egypt. Both items of headgear were, in ancient Egypt, regarded as war crowns. Akhenaten's use of these two items of military headgear on almost every public occasion may have been intended to identify himself constantly as a military leader in the minds of the people.[11] It is certainly feasible, indeed almost certain, that Akhenaten's strength arose partly from his skilful manipulation of the traditional resources of kingship but predominantly from his image as a war leader, backed by his military commanders.

One of Akhenaten's closest adherents was the military commander Paatenemheb. His tomb, numbered 24 by Egyptologists, is located in the hills at Amarna. A fierce ally of the pharaoh, he is referred to as the 'Royal Scribe, Overseer of all works in Akhetaten, Army Commander of the King of Upper and Lower Egypt'.[12] These titles are reminiscent of another strong military commander who appears in the later years of Akhenaten's reign. His name is Horemheb, and he not only became 'General of the Army' under the reign of Tutankhamun but later gained the throne of Egypt upon the young boy's death. Could Paatenemhet and Horemheb be one and the same?

In January 1975 a joint team of the Egypt Exploration Society and the Leiden Museum set out for Egypt. Under the directorship of Professor Geoffrey Martin, they had been given permission by the Egyptian authorities to relocate the tomb of May, overseer of the Treasury during the reign of Tutankhamun. Only a few days after they had opened the excavation, the team stumbled upon a column bearing the representation and name of the army commander, Horemheb. By a miracle, the lost tomb of one of the most famous men in Egypt began to emerge from the sand. Horemheb, whose deeds were already well known to scholars from the many surviving monuments and sources, had at last been found. Their project had clearly got off to an auspicious start.[13] Not only did the inscriptions depict Horemheb at the height of his powers, but Dr Martin was also able to ascertain the exact titles he was accorded during the years at Amarna.

It has to be said that the titles of the two generals are very similar. And by replacing 'Paaten' with Hor (Egyptian for Horus), 'Paatenemheb' becomes 'Horemheb'. Nothing is known about the career of Horemheb before the reign of Tutankhamun, but he can hardly have sprung into prominence overnight as the chief army commander and regent of the boy king. Like many people who have attained high rank and influence in Egypt, he may have come from peasant stock. One thing is blatantly clear, though: there was no love lost between Horemheb and the pharaoh. On a statue of Horemheb and his wife Mutnodjemet, now in the Turin Museum, a long inscription on the back pillar reads: 'The heart of the King was pleased with his work, agreeing with his decisions. He made him Lord of the land in order to maintain the law of the land as hereditary prince. He was unique, without an equal. All the plans for the Two Lands came from his hands. Everyone agreed with what he said when he was summoned by the King. Now the palace fell into rage, and he answers back at the King.'[14] This inscription is unique, as are many aspects of the whole business. Never on any occasion in Egyptian history is the temper of the King mentioned, or even alluded to.

So what had caused the row? Could it be that the general had to leave the palace because of a major problem? Was this the reason for Horemheb's hatred of the royal family? For hate them he surely did. Upon his own accession to the throne, Horemheb immediately set about erasing all trace not only of Akhenaten's reign, but also of every other so-called Amarna king including, in ascending order, Smenkhare, the boy king Tutankhamun and Ay. He immediately outlawed the use of their names, whilst the years of Akhenaten's reign became simply the time of 'the rebel', 'the rebellion' and 'the enemy of Akhetaten'.[15] Everything and anything connected with the Amarna kings came under attack, including their now abhorrent worship of the Aten. Horemheb destroyed their temples, toppled their statues, defaced their reliefs and chiselled out their inscriptions. Worse still, tombs located in the cliffs on the edge of the city and built for Akhenaten's family and courtiers were systematically despoiled and looted, their enshrined mummies cast out and desecrated. Horemheb's final act was the destruction of Akhenaten's beloved city of Amarna, which by 1335 BC was deserted. Buildings were systematically torn down and the stones were carried away and used for construction elsewhere in Egypt. Horemheb's importance in the Amarna period cannot be belittled in any way. He hovered like a dark angel on the fringes of the royal family, ready to bring them down and crush them on his rise to the top.

Could it therefore be argued that, like the priesthood, the military, far from being a mute instrument of the crown, actually became so powerful that, in the end, it not only determined royal policies but eventually installed its own leader upon the thrones? Could Scota have sensed the threatening clouds drawing in around her father and his new religion? Did she then realize that their peaceful days at Amarna might be numbered?

We now return to the object of Akhenaten's particular loathing, the Theban priesthood at Karnak. What happened to them? We know that due to the activities of Akhenaten's predecessors, Tutmosis IV and his father Amenhotep III, the Amun priesthood had been stripped of their influence. Supernaturally charged and economically wealthy, they no longer possessed the political strength needed to protect their own interests, let alone topple the throne. In addition, the temple establishment at Karnak had neither the necessity nor the occasion to develop substantial military or police powers, coercive resources that were intimately linked to obtaining political power in ancient Egypt.[16] Did Akhenaten really succeed in killing off the priesthood for good? Was the temple of Amun at Karnak really sacked, as the surviving inscriptions indicate, or did it continue to function independently of the Pharaoh of Egypt?

Let us re-examine the facts. We have already seen how, in Year 5, Akhenaten disposed of his most reviled opponent, the High Priest of Amun, into the eastern desert. Following this he issued orders that the very name of Amun be struck from every monument in the land. How did he achieve this? Visions of the Egyptian army storming the gates of Karnak and shepherding the priests into a corner of the temple whilst the stone masons hacked their way through the temple of Amun all too readily spring to mind. Although supporting evidence is somewhat limited, perhaps it is not too far from the truth. In July 1905 the French Egyptologist Georges Legrain, whilst excavating the remains of Karnak Temple, stumbled across a large granite stela lying in the north-west corner of the temple of Amun. Erected during the reign of one of Akhenaten's successors, his son Tutankhamun, and now in the Cairo Museum, it hints at what may have happened to the great Karnak precinct.

Now when his majesty arose as king,
The temples of the gods and goddesses, beginning from
    Elephantine down to the marshes of the Delta,
Had fallen into neglect,
Their shrines had fallen into desolation and become terraces
    overgrown with weeds.
Their sanctuaries were as if they had never been,

Their halls were a trodden path
The land was in confusion, the gods forsook the land.
If an army was sent to widen the frontiers of Egypt, it met with
    no success at all.
If one prayed to a god to ask things of him, they did not come.
If one made supplication to a goddess in like manner, in no way
    did she come,
Their hearts were weak of themselves with anger, they
    destroyed what had been done.[17]

The ferocity of the statement is clear. The gods of Egypt
have been affronted and the temples were indeed closed as
Akhenaten had ordered. The message continues for some
time as Tutankhamun laments at the affront accorded to his
father Amun and the way his temples have fallen into ruin.
Although at first glance it does appear that Akhenaten
succeeded in his aims, can this inscription be believed? It is
difficult to envisage that the Theban priesthood would have
relinquished their grip upon the Egyptian state so easily.
There are a number of crucial arguments to consider.

To begin with, there is the matter of slave donations.
During Egypt's successful imperial expansion into both the
Near East and Nubia throughout the Eighteenth Dynasty, a
series of large endowments of slave labour was awarded to
the various temples of Amun around the country. Are we
really to believe that by closing down the temples, in
particular Karnak, Akhenaten would run the risk of
releasing thousands upon thousands of exceedingly
disgruntled slaves upon the streets of Thebes? Another
equally important point is the subject of the temple
economy. This was a vital cog in the Egyptian state wheel.
In simple terms, food offerings inside the temples, once
blessed by the gods, were subsequently distributed to the
surrounding community. It was by these very means that the

poorest sections of society survived. If Akhenaten had closed the temples, how would these people continue to exist?

From the surviving inscriptions upon the Boundary Stela surrounding the city of Akhetaten, we also know that Akhenaten swore that he would never enlarge the Aten's territory. If this is correct, then it implies that the limits of the city and its immediate environs were the sole frontier of the Aten. Taken literally, his words might even suggest that by Year 6 the king had decided to isolate himself in Akhetaten, and swore never to leave it.[18] In arguing this point some Egyptologists have noted Akhenaten's unwillingness to pass the northern and southern stelae. Does this mean that the dissensions between him and the Amun priesthood were at first amicably settled, he being content to live and worship in his own way in his own place?

On the available evidence, not a soul from the Theban set-up seems to have followed Akhenaten to Amarna. The names of the nobles of Amarna are not those known at Thebes. In fact, Akhenaten appears to have rejected all the ancient families that once held administrative posts for generations in favour of new men, many of whom were rank outsiders to the political system. At the death of Akhenaten, we already hear of tentative moves by Smenkhare, once co-regent and now king, to honour once again the imperial god Amun. The figure of Smenkhare first appears during the grey area at the end of Akhenaten's reign. Who this enigmatic individual is is open to much speculation.

In the Berlin Museum there exists a stela of unknown provenance. According to the inscription, it was a votive dedicated by a man named Pasi, who was a common soldier at Amarna. Two kings are clearly depicted seated side by side on a couch with lions' legs; thickly cushioned footstools support their feet. One king, who sits below the rays of the Aten, wears a pectoral and the Double Crown of Upper and Lower Egypt. He turns to a second king, who wears the Blue Crown, and touches him under the chin in a gesture of endearment. The king wearing the Blue Crown then reciprocates by placing his left arm around the other's shoulders. Two empty double cartouches flank the sun-disc to the right and, at a slightly lower level, to the left; they were certainly intended to be inscribed with the names of the Aten. The question is, whose names were to be inscribed in the three cartouches to the right of the table of offerings? Many Egyptologists believe that the two cartouches would have shown the names of Akhenaten and the third the name of Nefertiti-Nefernefruaten. According to this Nefertiti was the king in the Blue Crown and subsequently regarded as Smenkhare.[19] This argument is further enhanced by examining the royal titles of King Smenkhare. Surely it can be no coincidence that his throne name was also Nefernefruaten, the same throne name as Akhenaten's Chief Wife, Nefertiti?

There is also an alternative argument. Some Egyptologists refuse to entertain the idea that Nefertiti was in fact Smenkhare. Instead, without any concrete evidence to back up their arguments, they suggest that Smenkhare was either Akhenaten's brother, Tutankhamun's older brother or even Akhenaten's male lover!

Although the evidence is tentative, it would appear that Smenkhare ruled independently for three years after Akhenaten's death. An inscription bearing his name has been discovered in the temple of Amun at Karnak about three years before the Restoration Stela of Tutankhamun was even inscribed.[20] Not only does this confirm that Karnak had remained open throughout the reign of Akhenaten, and not 'fallen into neglect' as the stela suggests, but more importantly, that there had to be a priesthood of

Amun, in some shape or form, for Smenkhare to do business with in the first place. It is highly likely, therefore, that the Amun priesthood in effect maintained their status, enjoying their privileged position at Karnak.

Why and how did the cultic reforms collapse as they eventually did? Given the king's supremacy and overall control, it is difficult to see why this would have happened, especially as there was no immediate hostile reaction to Akhenaten's relatives and close associates – although this may have more to do with the conversion back to Amun and the fact that there were very few members of the royal bloodline remaining. But we have already witnessed the dissent from the general Horemheb and his hatred of everything connected with the reign of Akhenaten. There is also evidence in the city of Akhetaten itself that there were even whispers of opposition against Akhenaten stemming from the Egyptian people. At the foot of the cliffs beyond the north-east corner of the village, in which the men who worked on the official tombs lived, there are over twenty 'chapels' with benches built along the sides of the front halls. On the walls can be found a faint dedicatory text to the god Amun, confirmation that the workers of Amarna, in defiance of the theology of the king, continued to worship the much-loved state god.[21]

Why then were the Egyptian people turning against their divine king? Let us examine the facts of Egyptian religious life. The ancient pantheon of gods encompassed the many different aspects of a divine nature and provided the necessary order within Egyptian society. Accordingly, the Egyptian people had always found comfort in their own local gods, and from time immemorial they believed that Osiris, the god of the underworld, offered them the hope of a better life after death. Akhenaten swept away Osiris, the afterlife and all the other gods from the official state religion, and put nothing in their place. Moreover, the religion of the Aten contained no ethical teaching. The 'Hymn to the Aten' does not offer the necessary rules for a good life or any notion of a judgement at death. Atenism may have been logical and beneficial to the king, but it was too remote from the people and did not provide what his subjects wanted and expected. There can be no doubt that Akhenaten's policies created immense social problems, which were only resolved when the old gods were restored upon his death.[22] It is not surprising then that the worship of the Aten did not hold any appeal for the ordinary Egyptian.

There is, however, another possibility that is perhaps worth considering. There were an enormous number of deaths in Akhenaten's family during his seventeen-year rule, far more than would normally be expected. Cracks in the established order soon began to appear and by Year 12 they took a decisive turn for the worse. In this year, Amarna played host to an international pageant, in which the nations of the empire gathered to convey tribute to Egypt. It was a magnificent assembly. Inscriptions on the walls of Amarna give us an accurate indication of Egypt's immense authority in the Near East. In the first scene Akhenaten and Nefertiti are shown carried shoulder high in the royal palanquin made of electrum. Following immediately behind them are the six royal daughters, with Scota, now aged thirteen, at the head. As the hosts of nations bow before their eminent protector, shade-bearers hold their protective screens on long poles over the heads of the two monarchs while the fan-bearers near to them wave their flowing feathers to waft a current of air across the glorious couple. Once they arrive at the Hall of Tribute, they are seated upon two thrones under the canopy of a decorated pavilion. It was here that their courtiers and visiting ambassadors and envoys would approach.[23]

And what an assemblage it truly was. From the southern lands of Nubia, envoys brought ingots of gold, silver, and elephants' tusks. They also brought gifts of tame leopards, monkeys and enchanting gazelles. From the eastern provinces came musk and myrrh. In addition, sandalwood, spices, scents for cosmetics and incense to burn to the Aten were laid before the royal couple. The bearded Syrians, with their robes tied tightly around their bodies, brought their valuable chariots, horses and weaponry. An antelope was included in the tribute, with an oryx and a lion, perhaps tamed. Libyans, who wore side plaits from the crowns of their heads and a feather stuck in their hair, brought ostrich eggs and ostrich feathers for the queen's fans and plumed headress. All these scenes are full of action, in row upon row of foreign visitors carved on the walls. They are carrying their gifts, pulling chariots, leading animals and carrying weaponry and the pelts and skins over poles over their shoulders. It has to be said that everyone is noticeably enjoying themselves.[24] This glittering and joyous occasion is the last glimpse we see of a happy and united royal family seemingly at peace in an admiring world, worshipped by their subjects at home and abroad. Dark days were ahead.

Throughout the Eighteenth Dynasty the consistent feature of Egypt's involvement in Canaan and the Levant was her interest in the ports and the cities that bordered the inland trade routes from Megiddo to the lands of Hatti, Mitanni and Babylon. This interest reflects the traditional significance of Byblos and its importance in the trade that moved between Egypt and her major commercial partners, the kings of the Near East. Shortly after Akhenaten's Year 12 celebrations, war broke out between two of Egypt's most powerful neighbours, the Hittites in Anatolia and the land of Egypt's ally, Mitanni. The Egyptian vassal states in Syria soon began to be drawn into the conflict. The fortunes of the main contenders ebbed and flowed for quite some time, but eventually the Hittites prevailed and Egypt's ally was defeated. The king of Mitanni, Tushratta, was murdered and the Mitanni capital, Naharin, was wiped from the map of western Asia for ever.[25]

For a time Egypt had successfully kept out of the major struggles. But trouble soon erupted between power-hungry dynasts, such as the King of Ammiru, Abdi-Asurta, in Syria, eager to exploit the general unrest of the region for their own advantage. Before long one by one of Egypt's vassals, such as the Prince of Tyre in the Lebanon and the King of Sumer in western Asia, began to fall into the hands of rivals as Akhenaten idly stood by and watched. The Canadian Egyptologist Donald Redford once said, 'One of the most displeasing characteristics of the way of life Akhenaten held up as a model, was a refined sloth.'[26] Egypt was on the point of being dragged into a war it did not want to be a part of. After the prominent campaigning days of the early part of the Eighteenth Dynasty, when the likes of Tutmosis III dominated the lands right the way through the East, the demand for an equally strong pharaoh was now even more evident. Unfortunately, the king's practice of making triumphal promenades from time to time around his dominions and settling the quarrels of the local dynasts had now fallen into disuse. What is more, the armed forces had become an instrument of Akhenaten's central domestic policy rather that a professional fighting force. They were used to protecting the ways of the Aten rather than fighting in foreign theatres of war. An army demoralized by inaction and neglect of martial duties was in no position to take the field, even under a dynamic leader. From the diplomatic correspondence, often referred to as the Amarna Letters, it is not surprising that we read of defeats and withdrawals in both Syria and central Palestine. Akhenaten, and more importantly Egypt, would now pay a heavy price for this apathy towards its dominions.[27]

The Amarna Letters provide us with a fascinating account of the relationship between Egypt and its Near Eastern neighbours. Consisting of around 382 cuneiform tablets, they were found in 1887 by a local village woman digging for ancient mud-brick to use as fertilizer. This initial discovery led to further illicit diggings and a number of tablets soon began to appear on the open antiquities market. At first the academic community regarded them as fakes and their importance was not immediately recognized. It was not until a year later when Wallis Budge, assistant in the Department of Egyptian and Assyrian Antiquities at the British Museum, believing the tablets to be genuine, purchased them in large numbers, that scholars finally began to sit up and take notice. In 1888 he wrote:

> Rumour, which always magnifies and tinges with the marvellous all discoveries made there [Egypt] asserted that thousands of tablets had been found: but hard fact soon showed that only three hundred pieces of inscribed clay had been dug up by the natives. Of these a considerable number were small fragments and several of them only formed a complete tablet. Some of the larger tablets were found in pieces, but I am sorry to say many of them were broken by the natives, either that each man might have his share, or for the purpose of easy carriage on the persons of those who helped to dig them up.[28]

Because of his foresight, the significance of the find was soon realized. Today the British Museum, the Bodemuseum in Berlin, the Louvre and the Egyptian Museum in Cairo each holds its own remarkable collection of the letters.

The vast majority of the diplomatic communications

derived from the so-called Place of the Letters of Pharaoh, a building identified as the official 'records office' in the central part of the city of Akhetaten. The archive is composed of a huge number of letters between Egypt and the great powers, such as Babylonia and Assyria, and the vassal states of Syria and Palestine. Most are written in the dialect of Akkadian, which was the diplomatic language of the time. The letters provide a vivid record of high-level diplomatic exchanges that, by modern standards, seem rather less than ambassadorial. For instance, an Assyrian ruler complains that the Egyptian king's latest gift of gold was not even sufficient to pay the cost of the messengers who brought it![29] The King of Babylon refuses to give his daughter in marriage to the pharaoh without first having proof that the king's sister, already one of the pharaoh's many wives, is alive and well.[30] The King of Karaduniyash complains that the Egyptian court has detained his messenger for the past six years. [31]

We can tell from the letters that Egypt's dominant position in the Near East was under threat. The ensuing crisis, and the state of the Empire under Akhenaten, is poignantly documented in the increasingly desperate pleas for assistance from Syro-Palestinian states under siege. For example, one letter that arrived from an Egyptian vassal named Rib-Ada, writing from the besieged port of Byblos, repeatedly demands military assistance, or failing that an Egyptian ship to permit his own escape. He wrote no less than sixty-four letters, and there is no evidence to suggest that Akhenaten even replied. His letter says:

> I am unable to send my ships, since Aziru is at war with me, and all the majors are at peace with him. Their ships go about as they please and they get what they need. Moreover, why does the king give the majors, my

friends, every sort of provision, but to me not give anything? But now I write for troops, but a garrison is not sent and nothing at all is given to me. As for the king, my lord, having said 'Guard yourself and the city of the king where you are,' how am I to guard myself? I wrote to the king. My lord, they have taken all my cities; the son of Abdi-Ashirta is their master. Gubla is the only city I have. I indeed sent my messengers to the king, my lord, but troops are not sent and my messenger you do not allow to come out. So send him along with rescue forces. If the king hates this city, then let him abandon it; but if me, then let him dismiss me. Send a man of yours to guard it. Why is nothing given to me from the palace?[32]

When even this pitiful plea went unanswered, he wrote to the Egyptian general Amanappa:

> To Amanappa, my father, thus Rib-Ada, thy son;
> At the feet of my father I fall down . . .
> Why hast thou held back and not spoken
> To the king, thy lord, in order that thou mayest march
> Forth with archers . . .
> So speak this word to the king, thy lord . . .
> That he sends help to me as quickly as possible.[33]

Again Rib-Ada received no communication from Egypt.

While the situation was ominous in Asia, particularly in the face of Akhenaten's inaction, conditions in Egypt were no less dismal. After the Year 12 celebrations an enormous number of deaths began to afflict the royal family. In a short space of time Akhenaten appears to have lost four daughters, his mother, Queen Tiye, his favourite second wife, Kiya, and who knows how many courtiers and dignitaries. It is evident that a plague was now raging through the Near East.[34] It may have been introduced to the Egyptian royal family during the Year 12 celebrations.

We first hear of the plague in the diplomatic correspondence that originates from the Phoenician coast. The pestilence broke out in Sumer, the Egyptian headquarters for the region, and later in the port of Byblos, terrifying not only the inhabitants but the Egyptian officials stationed there as well. Fearful that the town might be quarantined and that he would receive no more aid from Egypt, the Governor of Byblos wrote frantically to Akhenaten: 'They are trying to commit a felony when they report in the presence of the king, "There is plague in the lands!" '[35] We also hear from the King of Alashia (Cyprus) that Nergal, the god of pestilence, was abroad and rife in the land, reducing the production of copper ingots for the pharaoh.[36] Furthermore, the annals of the Hittite Empire also show that around this time a devastating plague was indeed raging in the Levant. It appears to have decimated the entire Hittite royal family, including the reigning king, Suppilupilimas, and the population as a whole. It would appear that during border skirmishes with Egyptian troops, at the site of Amqa, the plague quickly took hold of the Hittite armed forces and swept through their empire. The epidemic also seems to have carried off Arnuwanda II, the king's son and successor.[37]

Is it conceivable that the same plague was responsible for the multiple deaths at the Egyptian court? There is evidence to suggest that it was. In the Department of Western Asiatics at the British Museum, there is a fragment of an Amarna Letter entitled the 'The Betrothal of a Princess'. Remarkably, the cuneiform inscription implies that Queen Tiye, the mother of Akhenaten, did indeed die from the plague. Addressed to Naphururea, the Akkadian name for Akhenaten, it says:

Say to Naphururea, the king of Egypt, my brother: Thus
Burnaburiyas, the king of Karaduniyas, your brother.
For me all goes well. For you, your wives, your house-
hold, your sons, for your horses, your chariots, may you
all go very well.

After the wife of your father had been mourned, I sent
Hua, my messenger, and an interpreter, to you saying,
'A daughter of the king was once taken to your father.
Let them take another to you.'

And you yourself sent Haamasis your messenger and
Mihuni, the interpreter, saying . . . 'The wife of my
father was mourned . . . that women . . . she died in a
plague' . . . and I wrote saying 'That women may be
taken.'[38]

Could it be then that the Aten cult was abandoned in the
wake of these disasters? Did the Egyptian people begin to
make a direct connection between the horrors of the plague
and the abandonment of Egypt's traditional pantheon and
modes of worship? Did they view the many royal deaths as
a divine punishment for neglect of the old gods?

Akhenaten now slips into what is one of the biggest
black holes in ancient Egyptian history. Whether he died or
fled Egypt, we do not know. His mummy has never been
found. He certainly disappeared as his dream rapidly
collapsed around him. With religious upheaval, political
inadequacies and now the plague, it must have looked like
heavenly retribution from the old gods of Egypt against
Amarna. Certainly the populace must have thought so, and
no doubt would have been pointing the finger of blame
directly at the royal family. If this is correct then it is feasible
that Scota must have felt disheartened and in fear for her
life. Not only had she witnessed several members of her own
family die from the plague, but in addition there was a good

possibility of a social uprising against her by the people as well. The only sensible thing left for her to do was to flee, in effect, to escape the misery of what was once grand and beautiful. How soon after the disappearance of Akhenaten she made the decision to leave Egypt is unknown.

With the mystery of why Scota had to leave Egypt perhaps solved, we turn to one piece of speculation. Who was her husband, Gaythelos, as recorded in the Bower manuscript? We know that near the end of Akhenaten's reign, Scota was promoted to Chief Wife and therefore Queen of Egypt. So at this time it would not have been possible for her to marry another. This would suggest that her union only occurred after the death of Akhenaten. Traditional Egyptologists believe that Scota was in fact married to Smenkhare. In Cairo Museum a coloured potsherd used for inscribing shows an Amarna male leaning on a staff, and a woman offering him a lotus.[39] In 1908, I believe, its discoverer misidentified the couple as Smenkhare and Scota and, regrettably, this label has stuck for the past hundred years, even though there was no accompanying inscription to say who the couple actually were and no other related finds to identify the couple positively. Many Egyptologists have accepted the classification ever since.

The historical annals are clear: Scota married a foreigner. So who could Gaythelos be? According to the Bower manuscript, he appears to have been of Greek origin, whilst other annals refer to him as coming from the East or possibly Scythia. One thing is certain: he was not of Egyptian blood. This presented me with a problem. From my knowledge of Egyptian history I knew that it was strictly forbidden for an Egyptian princess to marry any foreign dignitary. In Amarna Letter number EA4, when Kadasman-Enlil, the King of Karaduniyas, asked Amenhotep III for the hand of his daughter in marriage, Amenhotep replied: 'In according with the practice of old, from time immemorial no daughter of Egypt is given to anyone'.[40]

There is, however, another tantalizing possibility. In the diplomatic correspondence entitled 'Servant of Mayati', there is a remarkable letter from Abi-Milku, the Prince of Tyre. The letter is addressed to Akhenaten, but the evidence indicates that it was not answered. This was quite unusual, as one of the few people Akhenaten *did* reply to was the Prince of Tyre. Perhaps this is the final confirmation that the reign of Akhenaten was over. From the information available, it appears that not only was Abi-Milku regarded as the 'servant of Mayati' (Scota's nickname), but he also refers to her as 'my mistress'. He even calls Tyre, 'the city of Mayati'.[41] Why would a foreign ruler name his city after an Egyptian princess? Never before is this documented in Egyptian history. The fact that he refers to Scota in the form used for a partner or wife could be the answer to this. Was Gaythelos, in fact, the medieval name for Abi-Milku, the Prince of Tyre?

From the above evidence it would appear that Scota did indeed marry a foreigner and flee Egypt, at the age of about 18. In effect the Amarna dream had now turned rancid. The ordinary citizens abandoned the city and moved *en masse* back to Thebes, leaving what could be considered a ghost town. After the somewhat messy ending to Akhenaten's reign, Horemheb now waited in the shadows to see what would materialize. At this time, Egypt was spiritually weak and the next few pharaohs reflected this. Smenkhare's few years on the throne ended abruptly. Whether he also died or fled Egypt is not known. Tutankhamun, when he grew too old to be of any use, was murdered and the old vizier Ay, a man who did not want the job of pharaoh in the first place, was pretty ineffectual. Whether Horemheb had anything to do with these three kings' downfalls we can but guess.

However, with all four Amarna kings now dead, he at last saw his chance to become the strong pharaoh which Egypt badly needed. Maybe as he climbed on to the throne at Thebes, he had the blood of the entire Amarna dynasty on his hands.

CHAPTER EIGHT

 ❧

ESCAPE FROM PERSECUTION

A millennium of neglect and decades of Israeli hostilities are responsible for the sad modern city of Tyre, situated about 150 kilometres south of Beirut in modern Lebanon. My initial excitement had turned to immense disappointment as I forlornly picked my way through the shattered buildings that surrounded the quayside in March 1999. If Scota had been alive, she would have wept to see the pitiful condition of her once magnificent city. In its heyday Greek historians such as Herodotus and Homer paid tribute to the enormous wealth and taste of its inhabitants. Tyre's merchants were among the most successful in the world and its citizens the most flamboyant. In the sixth century BC the Old Testament prophet Ezekiel described it with a mixture of hatred and admiration: 'O thou that art situate at the entry of the sea, which art a merchant of the people from many isles. Thou hast said I am perfect beauty. Thy borders are in the midst of the seas, thy builders have perfected thy beauty.'[1]

According to tradition, the city was founded on two

floating islands by the ancient Phoenician god Melkart. With great strength he successfully anchored the rocks, and he taught the people of the mainland to build boats and to sail by the stars. It was the city whence Europa came, and the home of Jezebel, who gave her name to scarlet women everywhere. The Hebrews called Tyre Tsor, meaning 'rock', and the ancient Egyptians referred to it as Tar. Today, it is known by its Arabic name, Sour.[2] Of all the cities that sprang up along the Phoenician shore, Tyre was the most dynamic. But today, the town, which was once the commercial centre of the Mediterranean, is afflicted with what appears a terminal case of melancholy. Nobody goes to Tyre any more, except marauding armies and stray tourists. Abandoned and forgotten, the city has developed a self-protective shell of secrecy.

During the first millennium BC, Phoenicia was the name given by the Greeks to this coastal strip of modern Lebanon and northern Israel, although the indigenous people have always referred to themselves as Canaanites. Nowadays it is bordered by Israel in the south and is hemmed in by Syria on all other frontiers. No bigger than Wales, Phoenicia formed an important part of the so-called Fertile Crescent, the supposed origin of all Western civilization. A quarter moon shape of land, it stretched from the basin of the River Euphrates in the north to the delta of the River Nile in the south. Phoenicia was a kingdom with a much-celebrated Biblical tradition. It was here, on a beach just south of Beirut, that Jonah was said to have been washed up by the whale. Noah is reputed to be buried deep in the Bekaa Valley whilst Jacob's final resting-place is hidden high within the mountains.[3] Even those who know practically nothing of the ancient Near East have some vague impression of the Phoenicians. They were widely famed as navigators, voyaging far afield to explore the west coast of

Africa, mining for silver in Spain and constructing the great city of Carthage, just off the Tunisian coast. Inhabited since the earliest of times, it has been its location that has always given it such a key strategic importance.

If Tyre's history is no longer visible in its monuments, it can still be gauged by its layout. The city is built on a peninsula jutting out into the sea. The tip of the promontory is built over what were the original two islands, traditionally joined together by Melkart and inhabited by the ancient Phoenicians. From the higher ground, on the southernmost tip of the peninsula, the limits of the ancient city with its famous ports are just discernible. On the northern side is the Sidonian Harbour, still in use today by small fishing vessels, whereas to the south lies the much-silted up Egyptian Harbour. In about 25 BC in his much acclaimed *Geography*, the Roman geographer Strabo commented: 'Tyre is wholly an island built up in nearly the same way as Arados in Greece and it is connected to the mainland by a bridge constructed when Alexander the Great was besieging it. It has two harbours, one that can be closed and the other open; the latter is called the "Egyptian Port".'[4]

Facing south, with my back to the modern town, the quayside fell steeply seawards to the right and ended in a narrow shelf strewn with columns. Directly in front, down a gradual slope, lay the Egyptian Harbour with both its masonry and its rock-cut installations visible just above the water. Beyond was a huge bay, as far as the eye could see, about 4 kilometres long and 2 kilometres wide; the cordon of reefs which once enclosed it are now only visible from the air. To my immediate left was the El Mina excavation, under the direction of Dr Ali Hussein of the American University of Beirut. Only a small percentage of the site is now open to the public; a chain-link barrier fences off the remainder. For the past twenty years, the university's aim has been to expose the recognizable Egyptian Harbour works that had become buried under the surrounding sand dunes. It was easy to see how; nature had encroached where once the arm of the sea had separated the island from the coast.

In its glory days, the Egyptian Harbour must have been huge. No doubt it had to accommodate an endless procession of large ships belonging to the ancient empires, laden with luxury goods and commodities bound for cities unknown. Looking down on this ancient landscape, I tried to imagine what the port must have looked like at the time of Scota. It was easy to visualize it packed with the huge Egyptian vessels, their sails catching the slight breeze, the men working to secure ropes under the blazing sun. However, there are some that would have you believe that such a scene as this never took place.

A fierce debate rages within Egyptology, and has done for many years. In simple terms, were the ancient Egyptians seafarers or not? The argument seems to have started with the troublesome definition of the Egyptian term 'great green'.[5] There are those who believe it refers specifically to the Mediterranean Sea, whereas others vehemently disagree. We saw in Chapter 1 how some scholars deem that the ancient Egyptians did not even want to go to sea.[6] In the words of ancient historian Alexandria Nibbi, 'There is no evidence that the ancient Egyptians ever looked, much less went, any further west. Speculation about the Old Kingdom "explorers" and "colonists" diffusing Egyptian culture far and wide has no basis in fact and is implausible given that the Egyptians never even explored their own river to its upper reaches.'[7]

So, before we can undertake a full examination of precisely how Scota escaped from Egypt, and the ways in which the Egyptian party finally arrived in Britain, it is imperative to prove, beyond doubt, that the ancient Egyptians were indeed willing and able seafarers. If I cannot do that, then my entire investigation falls to pieces.

No civilization, ancient or modern, depended more on water for its existence and growth than Egypt. From the earliest period down to modern times, the Nile was the main highway through the country along which commerce and military expeditions moved. In comparison, travel by land, across the barren desert, was an arduous and time-consuming matter.[8] The Egyptians were perfectly placed to cross the eastern Mediterranean and trade with the Levantine coast. In addition they also had access to the Red Sea by travelling overland from the city of Coptos, just downstream from Thebes, to the Red Sea port of Quosier. From here it was possible to travel down the Red Sea over 2000 kilometres to modern day Somalia or Yemen.[9]

The River Nile is orientated almost exactly north–south, and by happy coincidence the prevailing wind blows from the north directly up the Nile. Thus boats can go upstream under sail and return with the current in a controlled drift or under oars. Accordingly, the Egyptian term for movement north or south was determined by signs that depicted a boat either with its sail raised or with its mast stowed away. The technical terms used to describe locations aboard a ship, such as starboard, were employed to denote either right or left once on land. What is more, a kneeling man holding a bow followed by a boat sign illustrates the Egyptian word for an expedition and a temple is also said to 'hold the prowrope of the Southland and the sternrope of the Northland'.[10]

It is therefore not surprising that boats were a dominant feature in the lives of the ancient Egyptians and, as a result, profoundly affected their mental processes and religious thinking. In common with many other ancient cultures, the

Egyptians believed that the dead had to cross a stretch of water called the 'Winding Waterway' before they could encounter resurrection in the afterlife. Travel by boat was so ingrained in the Egyptian psyche that it was considered natural to depict the sun god Ra travelling through the sky or the Netherworld in his barque.[11]

Our knowledge of Egyptian boats derives from a variety of sources, including both clay models and painted pottery dating from as far back as the fifth millennium BC, which depict vessels with upswept bows and sterns. A representation of a boat with full sail occurs on a predynastic vase discovered in Middle Egypt. Dating to around 3500 BC, it is now in the British Museum. Information can also be gleaned from reliefs and paintings on temple walls. Tomb scenes dating to the Old Kingdom have survived which show the making of papyrus boats. The boat-builders are clearly shown cutting the papyrus reeds and then tightening the ropes on the hull.[12] The earliest recorded Egyptian boats were known to be reed rafts, and because of their fundamental simplicity, they continued to be used on the Nile. However, probably our best source of information is the numerous model boats that have been found deposited in tombs. Made of wood, they were plastered and brightly coloured, propelled by oars and a sail. It was these boats that would enable the occupant to make his way safely to the underworld. For instance, the tomb of Tutankhamun contained a beautiful model of a fully rigged sailing ship.

In about 3500 BC the Egyptians took an epoch-making step by becoming the first people to exploit a source of energy other than human or animal muscle. By inventing the sail, they learnt how to harness the wind to propel their craft. The earliest sail was quite simple in design, square-shaped and hung on a pole mast set far up in the bows. Incredibly, one such sail from an ancient Egyptian boat still survives today. It was discovered in the most unlikely of places: swathed around a mummy dating from the first century BC. In the autumn of 1986, the authorities of the Guimet Museum, Lyons, took the decision to examine every Egyptian mummy that was housed in their collection. Unwrapping the protective material around one, they discovered that the binding cloth consisted of one huge sheet of trapezoidal linen some 5.5 metres high and between 4.5 and 5.5 metres wide. It was quickly recognised as a sail, especially as a piece of a wooden ring and fragments of rope were still attached to the edges where it was once tied to the yard.[13]

Boats made of wood soon replaced the popular papyrus raft. The only timber available around the Nile itself was acacia, which tends to be short and brittle, so, from the Old Kingdom onwards, *circa* 2686–2181 BC, cedar wood was imported from the Lebanon. With stronger boats and sails, the Egyptians now had the ability to make sea journeys. The earliest seaworthy ships were employed on the Byblos route and the Egyptians referred to these ships as *kbnt*, meaning 'Byblos boat'.[14] One such voyage is depicted on the mortuary temple of King Sahure. Dating to around 2491–2477 BC, Sahure records how he sent a fleet of ships out from the coast of Egypt, skirting across the lower corner of the Mediterranean Sea, to arrive at its final destination somewhere in the Levant. He was so proud of his achievements that he included a representation of the vessels arriving back home.[15] Other voyages attested to, at least from the Old Kingdom onwards, are the trips along the Red Sea to the land of Punt, traditionally thought to be at its southern end, to acquire incense, myrrh and other valuable products.[16]

With access to better timber, improvements in the design and production of Egyptian ships were encouraged and soon larger sea-going ships began to arrive on the scene. From an inscription on the Palermo Stone, dating to the Fifth Dynasty, we know that the size of some ships reached a staggering 100 cubits long – over 50 metres – and could easily support a crew of 100 men. The same source also speaks of ships 40 and 60 cubits long. Additionally, the records of the Middle Kingdom, *circa* 2040–1782 BC, document the construction of really large ships, some reaching 50 metres long, with a beam of around 20 metres. Clearly these huge ships were not built solely to travel up and down the Nile. They were not glorified cargo vessels and must have been intended for open sea journeys.[17]

But perhaps the best examples of sea-going ships, at the height of their development, date to the New Kingdom period, *circa* 1570–1070 BC, and are depicted on the mortuary temple of Queen Hatshepsut at Deir-el-Bahari, Thebes. Her ships were apparently 20 metres long and 5.5 metres wide.[18] They were built for her expedition to the fabulous land of Punt, and overseas voyages were by now becoming almost commonplace. Inscribed upon her temple walls, the accompanying text states that Hatshepsut was fulfilling the wishes of her godly father Amun, maintaining that she became 'the very first Egyptian ruler whose forces would tread upon the incense terraces'.[19]

Although badly ravaged by time, the reliefs show a remarkable procession of ships, some with sail furled and about to draw up at shore, and others with the oarsmen carefully guiding the vessel into the harbour. It is apparent that the huge rig of these well-built ships would not permit them to manoeuvre in confined quarters under sailpower. In a separate scene, another vessel appears to have moored already, as a light rowing craft has been loaded with trade-goods bound for the natives of Punt. This is followed by a further scene where the Egyptian ships are shown departing.[20] There are a couple of significant features that confirm that Hatshepsut's expedition was indeed a sea journey: first, there is the display of slung skin bottles used for storing water, a provision not normally required for a journey on the Nile; and secondly, various saltwater fish are depicted beneath the ship. It is generally accepted that the River Nile only contained freshwater fish such as carp and Nile perch.[21]

It is surprising that many scholars believe that the Egyptians did not set sail upon the high seas, as records even illustrate the existence of a fully functional navy. As we have seen, the New Kingdom period was a great time for imperial expansion during which pharaoh after pharaoh led their armies regularly through Palestine, Phoenicia, Syria and beyond. On the walls of Karnak Temple there survives a remarkable account of just such an expedition. Dating to around 1440 BC, the inscription states how Tutmosis III ferried his troops by ship around the Mediterranean coastline to the port of Byblos. When safely across, a convoy of prefabricated assault craft were rapidly constructed from the finest Lebanese timber. As soon as the craft had been completed, the entire Egyptian force crossed the mountains and travelled onwards deep into the Orontes Valley.[22]

During the reign of Amenhotep III, in around 1367 BC, a naval police force was ordered by royal decree, whilst during the reign of Rameses III, *circa* 1182–1151 BC, the first evidence of Egyptian warships can be seen. The written and graphically illustrated account of Rameses's fight against the so-called Sea Peoples is recorded on the walls of his great and remarkably well-preserved mortuary temple at Medinet Habu in Thebes. Documented on the outer wall of the Second Pylon, it is the longest hieroglyphic inscription known and shows many Egyptian warships cutting through the enemy lines.

From these few brief examples, it is clear that Egyptian wooden boats must have sailed on the open sea, trading with the countries around the eastern Mediterranean. The reasons why some scholars choose to think otherwise can only be guessed at. Perhaps it may have something to do with the lack of physical remains, and the debate will no doubt continue, as no wrecks of an ancient Egyptian vessel have so far been uncovered. But this does not necessarily mean that there are none. In the words of the eminent Egyptologist Professor Kenneth Kitchen: 'Absence of evidence is not necessarily evidence of absence.' The odd accident on the Nile, as well as losses at sea, can surely not be discounted. However good the sailor, the occasional disaster must have been inevitable.

It was a fellow Egyptologist, Bob Partridge, who first made me aware of the amazing exploits of the Norwegian explorer Thor Heyerdahl. Born in 1914 in Larvik and educated at Oslo University, Heyerdahl apparently left his homeland after completing his studies to settle in Polynesia, being adopted by the supreme Chief of Tahiti in 1937. It was there, whilst doing research on the origins of Polynesian animal life, that Heyerdahl began to examine the existing theories of how the people of the South Pacific had reached their islands. His opinion was that they had come from the South American coast via Easter Island on simple rafts made out of balsa wood.

After many years of research Heyerdahl presented his findings to the academic community. To his utter dismay he quickly discovered that, rather than being open to his ideas, the majority of academics rejected the possibility of trans-oceanic voyages between the South American continent and the islands of Polynesia outright. As a result, in order to prove his arguments, Heyerdahl took the bold step of constructing a replica of an aboriginal balsa raft, named the

Kon-Tiki, to test his hypothesis. In 1947, together with five companions, he left the coast of Peru and successfully crossed the 8000 kilometres of treacherous water to reach Polynesia in 101 days. Despite the scepticism of academic circles, Heyerdahl had proven that such transoceanic journeys were indeed possible. [23]

In 1969 Heyerdahl decided to test his theories on transoceanic voyages once more. This time he turned his attention to ancient Egypt, in particular reed boats made from papyrus. 'I wanted to find out if the ancient Egyptians themselves had originally been seafarers,' he said.[24] Historians already knew that reed boats were used on the Atlantic, as they survived tenaciously on both sides of the Straits of Gibraltar. They are still used today by fishermen living in the shadow of the impressive Nuraghi ruins on the west coast of Sardinia. Final confirmation, however, was provided in 1953 when members of a Spanish scientific expedition found that the ancient El Jolot, a tribe of the northern Sahara, was still building reed boats using Egyptian methods. Navigated by both sails and oars, the tribesmen explicitly pointed out that the vessels they used were identical to those that the ancient Egyptians had used.[25] So, could an Egyptian boat really sail across the open seas?

Heyerdahl's first obstacle was gaining the necessary permission. 'So, you want to rope off a bit of the desert behind the Cheops Pyramid to build a papyrus boat?' The thick-set Egyptian minister adjusted his horn-rimmed glasses and looked at Heyerdahl with a questioning smile. He glanced half dubiously at the Norwegian Ambassador, who smiled politely back as he stood erect and white-haired besides his compatriot as a sort of pledge that this stranger from the north was in his right mind. 'Papyrus sinks after two weeks. Not my words – they come from the President of the Egyptian Papyrus Institute,' said the minister. 'The head of the Cairo Museum also believes that the idea of a papyrus boat on the ocean waves is absurd and the archaeologists say that papyrus boats can never be sailed beyond the mouth of the Nile because papyrus dissolves in sea water and breaks up in the waves.'

'That is exactly what we want to test in practice,' Heyerdahl explained. The President of the Papyrus Institute had given his verdict in advance. He repeated it. But he admitted, laughingly, that since Heyerdahl was the only one of those present at the meeting who had actually seen a papyrus boat in real life he would gladly support the idea if Heyerdahl were absolutely determined to make the experiment.[26]

Having been given permission, Heyerdahl then began the daunting task of constructing an authentic Egyptian boat. Purchasing a staggering 12 tonnes of papyrus, he worked with an enthusiastic group of experts to construct the ancient-style vessel. After many months of preparation, the end result was a fully functional 15-metre long papyrus boat. Scientific experts said that it would disintegrate and sink if it ever left calm waters. Nevertheless, Heyerdahl was convinced the journey was possible. In a spirit of co-operation he embarked, under the United Nations flag, with a crew of seven men from seven different countries. They included Carlo Mauri, Santiago Genoves, Norman Baker, George Sourial, Yuri Senkvitich, Abdullah Djibrine and Heyerdahl himself. On 17 May 1969, the reed boat set out on the Mediterranean Sea and onwards into the Atlantic Ocean. The voyage was entitled the *Ra* Expedition, after the Egyptian sun god.[27]

After a total of fifty-six days afloat and after sailing an astonishing 5000 kilometres, the crew ran into difficulties when a tremendous storm descended upon them and battered the ship. Waterlogged and hemmed in by man-eating sharks, they had no other option but to abandon ship. Not to be defeated, ten months later Heyerdahl built himself a second, smaller papyrus boat, named *Ra II*, and attempted the remarkable journey once more. The success of *Ra II* in the 'quest for the sun god' is now part of ethnographic history. After fifty-seven days and 6100 kilometres across open waters, the papyrus boat reached Barbados in the West Indies. Once again, this voyage showed that modern science had underestimated long-forgotten technologies. Heyerdahl had proved beyond doubt that Egyptian boats were indeed capable of making open sea voyages.[28]

Having found the answer to whether the Egyptians were seafarers or not by logical consideration of the historical evidence, it is now time to examine how Scota escaped from the palace of Amarna and what direction her getaway from Egypt took. The Walter Bower manuscript provided me with very little assistance. Though it offered some hint as to the direction, it offered no clues whatsoever as to how Scota fled from Egypt. One thing is certain, it would not have been a straightforward mission. Not only was Scota the King's Daughter, but in Akhenaten's later years she was also given the title of king's Great Wife. She was effectively the most important woman in the Amarna set-up. As we saw in the last chapter, there was also the additional problem of the ambitious general, Horemheb. From his meteoric rise to the top of the ranks, there was just no telling the lengths he would resort to in order to achieve his aims. It would not be an easy task for Scota to slip away unnoticed.

A further hindrance was the way in which the Egyptian state was structured. From very early on in its history, every aspect of society was rigidly controlled, either by the state or by the temple precincts. This control was even more prevalent during the reign of Akhenaten who, as we have seen, maintained a tight grip on both. With the Egyptian people now increasingly alienated and hostile and, according to Akhenaten, the temple system abolished and defunct, to whom could Scota turn for help? She could not have approached the nobility as most of them had by now perished from the plague. The army was also out of the question as it now came under the control of the ambitious Horemheb. What she needed was a middleman, someone who was not beholden to Horemheb and the new order, a person who could obtain the use of a single vessel, or maybe more, without attracting any attention. But large-scale trade was a virtual royal monopoly, so did such men exist? Were there independent merchants operating outside the official channels?

On 6 February 2000 I received an e-mail from Robyn Gillam of York University, Toronto, who was investigating trade in ancient Egypt. An expert in her field of study, she kindly forwarded me details of her research to date. I was already aware that the status of a trader in ancient Egypt was a lowly one. No one who had made a success of his life used the term as a title. As the state and the temples controlled Egypt's commercial enterprises, trading was akin in status to making sandals. Some rich people enjoyed the benefits of trading but did not pursue it as an occupation, whilst the idea that the activity could bring wealth and position on its own terms was unthinkable.

The picture that is painted by a variety of texts is that the 'trader' – the commercial agent, the arranger of deals – was an ever-present figure in New Kingdom Egypt.[29] Consequently, I wondered if it was possible that a reference to the use of such private merchants had survived. I sat down and began to read Gillam's work. In next to no time I found the answers I had been looking for.

The Papyrus Lansing was originally discovered in Thebes in 1884, and purchased by an American missionary named Guilan Lansing. It is now in the custody of the Trustees of the British Museum. It dates to a later period than Scota's time but it explains how 'the merchants fare upstream and downstream and are as busy as copper. They carry wares from one town to another and supply him who has not, although the tax-people carry exact gold, the most precious of minerals'.[30] I was in luck. Here was a direct reference to the existence of private merchants. There is no indication whatsoever whether these were, in fact, merchants of the crown, or whether they were Egyptian traders at all. But if they were subject to the tax collector, as the Papyrus Lansing suggests, it is hardly possible that they were royal employees. People of the crown did not have to pay tax. If the papyrus was right, then Scota would have experienced no difficulty in obtaining a vessel through unofficial channels.

It is therefore feasible to suggest that Scota did indeed escape from Amarna. The question now remains: in what direction did she go? Unfortunately, no contemporary historical records have survived. One option that can immediately be discounted is setting a course due east and sailing towards the Levant and beyond. Not only have the Amarna Letters demonstrated that the entire area was engulfed in a long drawn out Syrian war but, in addition, a virulent plague was particularly widespread. Travelling east would have been far too perilous. What is more, this hypothesis appears to be confirmed by the Walter Bower manuscript: 'So Gaythelos gathered all together the followers and left Egypt with his wife Scota. He was afraid to return to the regions from which he had come to Egypt because of old feuds.'[31]

The only viable option would be for Scota and her followers to head directly north into the Mediterranean and then across the Aegean Sea or proceed west along the coast of North Africa. So, which route did they take? We shall return to the possible North African passage later. But first, it is time to examine Egypt's relationship with its Aegean neighbours.

We know of direct voyages from the Egyptian cities of Alexandria and Damietta, on the north coast, to the island of Crete during the seventeenth century AD,[32] whilst in the eighteenth century the Crete–Alexandria route was by far the most customary, both from the island and from Egypt.[33] In addition, the prevalent Aegean winds, blowing from the north-west, made for excellent sailing conditions throughout the Mediterranean Sea. Bearing in mind that climatic conditions do not appear to have altered to any great degree since the Bronze Age period, the prominent historian Peter Warren argues that there appears to be no inherent reason why direct voyages such as these could not have taken place during Pharaonic times.[34] After all, the island of Crete would have been the first port of call for any Egyptian vessel heading north into the Aegean.

Crete is situated approximately 300 kilometres north of Egypt and was the centre of an immense seafaring empire. It has been of paramount importance throughout history, for it is a stepping-stone between Europe, Asia Minor and Africa. It is part of a chain of islands leading eastwards throughout the Aegean. It appears to have been first inhabited during the Neolithic period, from about 6000 BC, but it was not until about 1700 BC that a highly sophisticated culture grew up around the palace centres. In 1899 the British archaeologist Sir Arthur Evans dug into an ancient mound at Knossos and discovered the remains of a palace. It was one of the most famous and significant digs in archaeology; on it still rests our whole view of the structure and the chronology of the Aegean Bronze Age. The main

Long view over the ancient site of Tara with earthen
ramparts in the immediate foreground.
(Author's own photograph)

Faience Bead necklace housed in Exeter Museum.
Identical to those beads uncovered in the
North Molton barrow.
(courtesy of John Allen, Exeter Museum)

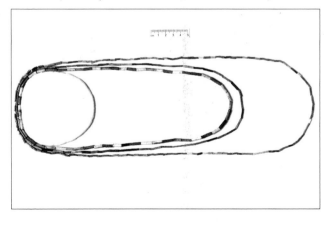

The remains of the Bronze Age boats unearthed by the
Wright brothers in 1937 at North Ferriby, Yorkshire.
(Courtesy of Hull Museum)

The Scotichronicon, dating to around 1435, depicting
Scota and Gaythelos fleeing Egypt for Ireland. (Courtesy
of Corpus Christi College, Cambridge University)

The entrance to Karnak Temple, the home of the Egyptian state god Amun, through an avenue of ram-lined sphinxes. (Author's own photograph)

Herihor depicted as King of Upper and Lower Egypt worshipping before the gods at Khonsu temple. The insignia upon his brow, the royal ureaus (cobra) denotes his claim to kingship. (Author's own photograph)

On the left, a limestone figure of Akhenaten, the father of Scota and on the right, the famous bust of Nefertiti, Scota's mother. Both were found during the excavation of Amarna in 1911. (Courtesy of Berlin Museum)

A typical domestic scene of Akhenaten, Nefertiti and their daughters. No other Egyptian pharaoh ever allowed himself to be depicted in such a manner. Scota is singled out by her father, as he embraces his beloved daughter. (Courtesy of Berlin Museum)

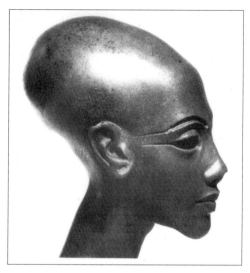

A brown quartzite bust of an Amarnan princess, thought to be that of Scota/Meritaten, unearthed in the Thutmose workshop at Amarna. (Courtesy of Berlin Museum)

A pot shard from the Cairo Museum supposedly depicting Smenkhare and Scota. (Courtesy of Cairo Museum)

The ruins of Amarna, Akhenaten's city.
(Author's own photograph)

The ancient port of Tyre on the Lebanon coast. The city
of Scota as reported in the Amarna Letters.
(Author's own photograph)

The Aegean-List inscribed upon a statue base belonging to
Scota's grandfather, Amenhotep III, from his
mortuary temple at Thebes.
(Author's own photograph)

Tin ingot dredged off St
Mawes harbour,
Cornwall, in 1812 by
local bargemen.
(Courtesy of
R.Penhallurick, Truro
Museum)

The Mold Pectoral discovered in 1833 at Mold in North Wales. Its shape and style is reminiscent of ancient Egyptian shoulder capes. (British Museum)

The site of Glenscota, County Kerry, Ireland. It was here, during the battle with the Tuatha de Danaan, that Scota died and was laid to rest. (Author's own photograph)

work took place over the first four seasons, when Evans uncovered many beautiful frescos, a throne and a massive granary containing enormous storage jars, indicating that the palace once belonged to the wealthy ruler of a highly developed civilization. Evans therefore named the civilization the Minoan, after the legendary King Minos.[35]

'On the wine-dark sea there is a rich and lovely island called Crete, washed by the waves on every side, densely populated with ninety cities . . . One of the ninety cities is a great town called Knossos, and there for nine years King Minos ruled and enjoyed the friendship of almighty Zeus'.[36] According to Greek legend, Minos was a king of Crete who kept a monster called the Minotaur, half human, half bull, in a labyrinth in his palace. This creature was the offspring of the king's wife, Pasipahe, and was the result of her coupling with a white bull sent to her by the god Poseidon as a form of revenge against the family. Minos spent the final years of his life living in this massive labyrinth.[37] The Greek historian Thucydides informs us that he was the first man to hold sway over the Aegean with his fleet, and that he captured and colonized the Cyclades, freeing the seas from piracy.[38] But what the Minoans thought, what stories they told, how they narrated their history, are all lost to us. Sadly, all we have left are their palaces.

Links between Crete and Egypt are well documented and continue right the way through Egyptian history, until the Minoan civilization came to an abrupt and mystifying end in around 1390 BC. There is compelling evidence that a gigantic volcanic eruption occurred in the eastern Mediterranean around the time of the reign of Amenhotep III. Its epicentre was on the Aegean Island of Thera (Santorini) and it was such an enormous explosion that it appears to have decimated the entire Minoan civilization.[39] Until this moment, however, trade flowed freely between the two empires. In 1984, Dr Olga Krzyszkowska, in an article to the British archaeological journal *Antiquity*, argued that raw materials went in small quantities from Egypt to Crete as early as the Old Kingdom.[40] In addition, stone vessels such as jugs also arrived from Egypt. Several are known from Knossos, ranging in date from the predynastic period up to the Sixth Dynasty.[41] The extent of these contacts, however, was not fully appreciated until a decade ago.

During the Second Intermediate Period, the Hyksos capital of Avaris was effectively an Asiatic colony within Egypt. Until recently Avaris was thought to have been the Egyptian city of Tanis, near the modern fishing village of San el-Hagar. Both are situated in the eastern Delta. But Egyptologists have now identified the site as being 30 kilometres to the south, at Tell el-Daba. It covers an area of some two square kilometres on a natural mound partly surrounded by a lake. In 1991, during excavations by Vienna University, the Austrian archaeologist Dr Manfred Bietak uncovered many fragments of Minoan wall paintings among the debris covering a series of ancient gardens adjoining the ruins of the Hyksos palace. The combined technique of fresco and relief on lime plaster is typical of Minoan painting and unknown in ancient Egypt. Several of the scenes depicted bull-leapers, similar to those Sir Arthur Evans had uncovered at the palace of Knossos on Crete. The leapers all wore Minoan kilts, belts and boots. Furthermore, their hair was displayed in the characteristic Minoan loose curls.[42] Some scholars have suggested that not only were such reliefs evidence of trading connections between the Minoans and the Hyksos, but that the population of Avaris may actually have included Aegean families. Dr Bietak even believes in the possibility of an interdynastic marriage between the Hyksos and a Minoan princess. He suggests that the large griffin mural in Avaris is often associated with queenship in Minoan Crete.[43]

Despite this close alliance, evidence has shown that during the Eighteenth Dynasty it was Greece, particularly Mycenae, and not Crete, which had now become the prime destination of the trade routes from Egypt. Even if Scota had fled Egypt before the destruction of the Minoan civilization, she would not necessarily have asked the Cretan royal family for asylum. The Theban kings of the New Kingdom may not have truly forgiven the Minoans for associating themselves with the loathed Hyksos. In any case, some scholars have argued that the Minoan Empire had been destroyed long before Scota's flight from Egypt. From the available evidence it now appears that the great palace of Mycenae, situated on the Argolid peninsula, became the seat of a new powerful seafaring empire that would swiftly spread right the way through the Greek mainland and throughout the Aegean Sea.

Although it had been deserted for well over 2000 years, Mycenae had never truly been forgotten. The Greek writer Thucydides had visited its ruins and was happy to agree with Homer's poetic account of its pre-eminence as the 'capital' of the Mycenean Empire.[44] In the ancient world everybody accepted that this was the place to which the legendary Greek general Agamemnon had returned to be murdered after the sack of Troy, and it was the general belief that he and the other great kings of the empire had been buried there. The ancient Greeks believed that the origins of Mycenae were inextricably linked with Egypt. According to tradition, its founder was Perseus, son of Zeus and Danae, who was ostensibly of Egyptian descent – being the great-great-grandson of brothers Danaus and Aegyptus, the Egyptian founders of the Greek nation.[45]

Although abandoned after its destruction by Argos in 486 BC, Mycenae still has impressive ruins to show.

Situated on a low wedge hill, in between the lofty peaks of
Mount Zara and Mount Ilias, the palace commanded the
greater part of the Argolid plain stretching all the way
southwards, across the Greek mainland and down to the
Mediterranean Sea. Its natural advantage thus enhanced its
strategic location and, as a result, Mycenae was in a useful
position to control all road transport through the hinter-
land.[46] This was where most of the choicest products from
the Aegean and the Near East were gathered; and it was
from the Argolid that most exports went to neighbouring
countries. As a result, Mycenae became the ancient capital
of Greece from around 1550–1100 BC and found its voice
in the poetry of Homer in a single defining event: the Trojan
War.

Connections between the pharaohs of Egypt and the
kings of Mycenae appear, at first glance, to be very close
indeed. Evidence for this is provided by the large quantities
of Mycenean pottery found at some thirty Egyptian sites
and, in return, by the Egyptian objects subsequently found
on the Greek mainland. From as early as the reign of
Amenhotep II, in about 1427 BC, contact between the two
states is evident. In 1896, whilst excavating on the Acropolis
at Mycenae, the Greek archaeologist Dr C. Tsountas
unearthed a small blue faience figurine of a monkey
inscribed with the cartouche of Amenhotep II and his son
and successor Tutmosis III. Fragmentary in condition, it was
minute, measuring only 3.5 centimetres in length and 2
centimetres in width.[47] Representations of monkeys are rare
in Mycenean contexts and in *Aegean Paintings in the Bronze
Age* in 1990, Dr S.A. Immerwahr suggested that monkeys
never appear in Mycenean wall paintings.[48] There is no
doubt that the figurine came from Egypt. In addition, two
other Egyptian faience figurines, also inscribed with the
cartouche of Amenhotep II, have since been uncovered at

Mycenae and the palace of Tiryns.[49]

It was during the Amarna period that contacts between the two powers became especially intimate. The city of Akhetaten has produced an extraordinary amount of Mycenean pottery, far more than would normally be expected. Whilst excavating Akhenaten's city during the 1930s, the British Egyptologist John Pendlebury uncovered between 1500–1600 shards of Mycenean pots and vases. Indeed, after the digging season had finished and all the surveying and recording was complete, the archaeologists named this particular Amarna avenue 'Greek Street'.[50]

All throughout the 1900s the Greek Archaeological Society continued excavations at the citadel of Mycenae, with some astonishing results. In a small dark room, just beyond the Lion Gate, named the 'Cult Room', they unearthed four faience plaques bearing the name of Akhenaten's father, Amenhotep III. Furthermore, a blue faience vase bearing the name 'Amenhotep – Ruler of Thebes' was also discovered, together with a small beetle-shaped scarab inscribed with the name of Akhenaten's mother, Queen Tiye.[51] In 1982, Dr Veronkey Hankey argued that these finds were the result of an official visit of Egyptians to Mycenae some time in the last few years of Amenhotep III's life. The Egyptian embassy brought the plaques to Mycenae as a gift and, in return, they took the Mycenean pottery back to Egypt.[52] The use to which these objects were put on their arrival at Mycenae can only be surmised. It was once thought that the faience plaques were originally set into the door of an 'Egyptian Room' and some have argued that there was even an Egyptian temple![53] Even with all this overwhelming evidence, however, many scholars still refuse to accept that such items were anything more than secondary trade, possibly arriving in trading ships from the ports of Byblos and Tyre in the Lebanon or

Cyprus in the Aegean Sea.

Perhaps the firmest indication of links between the royal palaces of Egypt and Mycenae stands these days in a bleak, deserted Theban field on the west bank of the Nile. Called the Colossi of Memnon, two gigantic seated statues of Amenhotep III, carved from quartzite sandstone, are all that remain now of his much-plundered mortuary temple. Each of the figures is flanked by a representation of Queen Tiye. In 27 BC, an earthquake damaged the northern statues, and perhaps created some flaw in the stone, causing it to produce a characteristic whistling sound every morning. Ancient Greek visitors knew this statue as the vocal Memnon, suggesting that the figure was, in fact, the Homeric character Memnon singing to his mother Eos, the goddess of the dawn. In the third century, the Roman emperor Septimus Severus decided to repair the damaged figures and, in doing so, seems to have rendered them dumb.[54]

In the north-west corner of the temple ruins there are five large limestone statue bases. Little known outside the realms of Egyptology, it is thought that they once supported statues of the king, though nowadays only the sculptured feet remain. Running along the front and sides of each base, a list of toponyms have been inscribed in a single horizontal row.[55] Each toponym consists of a cartouche, or name-ring, surmounted by the figure of a bound prisoner. This was the customary way in which Egyptian pharaohs would represent those foreign localities actually, or even only nominally, under Egypt's domination. Inscribed on one of the five bases is a catalogue of major Greek cities, nick-named the 'Aegean List' by archaeologists.[56] Once the hieroglyphs had been successfully translated, the cities, in consecutive order, were Crete, Rhodes, Amnissos, Phaistos, Kydonis, Mycenae, Messina, Nauplia, Kythera, Illios,

Knossos and Lyktos.[57]

In 1826 the British Egyptologist John Gardner Wilkinson together with James Burton, an elder brother of the more famous architect Decimus, travelled to the city of Akhetaten. Their objective was to record the scenes from the open tombs cut into the terrace above the northern edge of the site. These private tombs were the gift of Akhenaten to his loyal followers. In the tomb of the high steward, Huya, are remarkable scenes which appear nowhere else at Amarna – or in Thebes for that matter – showing the royal family attending the great ceremony held by Akhenaten during his twelfth year. Among the scenes, as we have seen, is a vast concourse of peoples including the nations who are in embassy with Egypt, bringing precious gifts to lay before the throne of the Amarna king. The delegates and their gifts are represented in some detail – Nubians, Libyans, and Aegeans (often referred to as 'Keifitu') etc. A lone accompanying inscription enigmatically reads 'the isles in the midst of the Sea'.[58]

What were these 'isles'? Could this be a direct reference to Mycenae or perhaps those cities recorded on the 'Aegean List' at Thebes? It could refer to either mainland Greece or the numerous landmasses within the Aegean. There are a number of textual references, which include similar terminology throughout the Eighteenth Dynasty:

1) 'The gods of Egypt and the isles of the Sea'
2) 'The Isles of the Great Circle'
3) 'Causing thee to smite the dwellers in the isles in the Midst of the Sea'
4) 'Filling the heart of the king in all foreign lands and the isles in the Midst of the Sea'
5) 'Coming in peace of the Great Ones of Keifitu and the Isles in the Midst of the Sea'.[59]

On the balance of evidence it does appear that each city recorded on the 'Aegean List' may have been some kind of Egyptian protectorate. At the very least it implies that Amenhotep III, and perhaps even Akhenaten, had some influence over them. This is confirmed by the use of a bound prisoner symbolizing Egypt's authority over each city. Accordingly, it could also substantiate those places included on the itinerary of an official Egyptian visit to the Aegean and Mycenae during Amenhotep's reign. Dr Hankey, as we have seen, has already suggested this. Evidence from Pylos on the Greek mainland, in the shape of two fragments of tablets, gives the name *a-ku-pi-ti-jo* which some scholars have argued illustrates that 'Aigyptos' was already the Greek name for Egypt.[60] If the term 'isles in the midst of the Sea' does refer to locations in the Aegean, then not only does it confirm that Egypt had very close associations throughout this region, but it probably also confirms the existence of an Egyptian sea-faring capability.

We return now to the question of Scota's escape route. If relations were close between Egypt and Greece during the reign of Amenhotep III, would this necessarily mean that they would be sustained throughout the reign of her father, Akhenaten? The diplomatic correspondence has shown us that when Akhenaten came to the throne, he not only ignored the plight of many established Egyptian vassal states, but also refused to honour any agreements or treaties that had been entered into by his predecessors. For instance, the Amarna Letters show that Akhenaten did not fulfil his father's promise to the king of the Mittanian Empire, Tushratta, when he requested some high-quality gold statuary. Akhenaten sent inferior wooden statues overlaid with gold leaf instead.[61] At first glance this may appear to be a trifling matter, but such transactions were a vital part of ancient diplomacy. So did Akhenaten have a special relationship with Mycenae?

The firmest indication that he did indeed maintain close links has only recently come to light. In 1992 the Department of Egyptian Antiquities at the British Museum made a remarkable new acquisition. Dating to around 1340 BC, it consisted of a series of fragments from a painted papyrus uncovered at Amarna. Not only was it the first of its kind ever to be found, but the fragments derived from a purely pictorial papyrus. This is exceptionally rare in Egypt. The scenes are of very artistic quality and apparently depict the scene of a battle. Even when you consider the military ethos of the Amarna period, a scene of a battle is extremely unusual, especially considering that, as far as we know, Akhenaten was never involved in any military activity outside of Egypt.

The papyrus fragments were initially unearthed in December 1936 by John Pendlebury, working on behalf of the Egypt Exploration Society. They were discovered in a building on the eastern edge of Akhetaten, which seems to have been a chapel of the king's statue as it contained the remains of a wooden shrine and various cultic items dedicated to Akhenaten himself. Pendlebury wrote from Amarna, shortly before the end of the digging season: 'Finds in the building included a complete Mycenean vase and a number of fragments of papyrus – still awaiting proper treatment.'[62] After the excavation had drawn to a close, the fragments were carefully packaged and rushed back to England. In 1954 they were placed into the care of Professor Walter Fairman. For the next twenty-five years, Fairman devoted all his time to the study of the papyrus. Sadly, even after his death in 1982 his tireless efforts still remained unpublished. It was not until 1992 that the papyrus came to the attention of those at the British Museum, when a set of the fragments came up for auction at Christies.[63] They were immediately purchased by the British Museum and have since been conserved by Bridget Leach of the British Museum's Conservation Department.

By chance, the School of Archaeology, Classics and Oriental Studies at the University of Liverpool discovered in its keeping a small, white, cardboard box, with the label: 'R 43.2 Papyrus Fragments 30.xi.36'. When opened, it was found to contain two painted fragments, plus a small leather fragment, similar to those that had been bought by the British Museum. After consultation with the Egypt Exploration Society, they were ceremoniously presented to the British Museum for further analysis. It would appear that all the fragments came to Britain in one cardboard box. Fairman had mounted the larger pieces between glass, but had left some of the smaller fragments in the box, where they had remained until 1992.[64]

The papyrus is now preserved in two main areas, one measuring 11×6.5 centimetres and the other 10.3×10.47 centimetres.[65] Still in the possession of the British Museum, a replica is on display to the public in the Mycenean gallery. There can be no doubt that the papyrus represents some kind of battle, but due to its fragmentary condition it is nigh on impossible to distinguish where and when it took place. One scene shows a fallen Egyptian soldier being attacked by a group of Libyan archers. We know that the opposing forces are Libyan because of the characteristic headgear they are wearing. The next scene, in the middle, shows a group of running troops and a solitary archer shooting an arrow to his right. However, in the remaining scenes there appear to be a group of fighting men that are not either Libyan or Egyptian. They are unquestionably a part of the Egyptians' army, as one of them is depicted attacking a Libyan archer. Who can these mysterious soldiers be?

One clue is that they appear to be wearing headgear

unlike that of their fellow Egyptian troops. In fact, the helmets worn by two of the figures bear a remarkable similarity to the boar's tusk helmets usually worn by Mycenean troops. Together with the characteristic Greek colouring, the vertical demarcations and the short oxide metal-edged tunics, the only parallels to be found are those in the Bronze Age Aegean.[66] It was not unusual for the Egyptian army to include soldiers from other nations; in fact, throughout history, it seems to be the standard military policy. In the past, conscripts from Nubia and Syria had often been used as the proverbial cannon fodder in many an Egyptian campaign. Nonetheless, this was the first time that armed forces from the Aegean had ever been depicted. Does this mean that Akhenaten was hiring mercenaries direct from the King of Mycenae to fight on his behalf?

The key series of events of this ancient drama are now beginning to fit into place. If the Egyptians had fled north across the Aegean, to the palace of Mycenae, would they have found sanctuary? The inscribed material found in abundance at Mycenae not only reflects Egypt's position as a world power but, more importantly, through Egypt's unquestionable support, Mycenae's emergence as the dominant nation among the various Greek kingdoms. Would it, therefore, have wanted to endanger its prominent status, not only with Egypt, but with the eastern Mediterranean in general? Akhenaten's employment of Mycenean troops is significant. It demonstrates a powerful union between the two great empires, and one from which Mycenae had benefited greatly. After forging a formidable bond with Akhenaten, would the King of Mycenae jeopardize his position by harbouring the Amarna refugees against the will of the new power that had now taken over Egypt? As we have seen, Horemheb had no particular love for Akhenaten or his followers, and thus would not have looked kindly upon the King of Mycenae interfering in the internal squabbles of Egypt's royal court. Being a military man, he would have no doubt been quite prepared to go to war over the merest of upsets.

Despite such obvious perils it appears that some of Scota's followers did indeed head for Greece even though there is no direct evidence to confirm that Scota chose this particular route. Remarkably, it appears to be confirmed in the Bower manuscript: 'It is however stated elsewhere that many Egyptians fled in terror far from Egypt and their native land not just in fear of men, but in fear of the gods. Seeing the fearful plagues and portents with which they had been inflicted, they did not dare stay any longer. It is said that some crossed over to Greece'.[67]

If some of Scota's followers did head towards the safety of Mycenae, as both the historical and archaeological evidence strongly suggests, their time in the immense citadel would almost certainly have been limited. Not wishing to offend Horemheb, the King of Mycenae, having given the refugees food and shelter for a few days, would most probably have sent them on their way. We now return to the question of just how these ancient Egyptian exiles arrived on the shores of Britain. After all, it is a very long road that leads from the gates of Mycenae to the British Isles. There is, however, one possibility, and that is the ancient amber routes that traversed Europe.

Amber is a fossil resin, called succinite by mineralogists, and was found mainly in the Baltic region, although today no major deposit of Baltic amber is known. It is only by inference that palaeontologists have located the original amber forest, where the resin was exuded by extinct trees, in eastern Sweden and southern Finland, an area sometimes called Fennoscandia. Amber was one of the principal commodities for barter in early Europe and the Mediterranean. Archaeologists have found it as far away as Russia, western Norway and Finland, which indicates the establishment of trade as early as about 3000 BC.[68] Some ornaments have been found in an Egyptian tomb dating to the Sixth Dynasty and have been identified as Baltic in origin.[69] That amber may have been used by the ancient Egyptians, especially at a late date, is not denied. However, it appears that not all the amber artefacts can be classified as such. Worked resin is also known and was often, mistakenly, thought to be amber. Dark red in colour and exceptionally brittle, the resin is easily soluble in many ordinary organic compounds, such as alcohol and acetone, in which true amber, or succinite, is not.

It is not known exactly when Baltic amber was first used. For many centuries, cultures acquainted with amber wondered what this beautiful gift of nature was and how it originated. True to the customs of the times, many myths and legends resulted from attempts to explain the origins of the mysterious substance. For example, in Greek myth, the so-called Tears of Heliades were attributed as the divine origin of amber. The legend recounts the adventures of Phaethon, who grew to young manhood without knowing that one of his parents was immortal. Prevailing upon his mother, Clymene, to inform him who his father was, Phaethon was astonished to discover that he was, in fact, the child of the sun god Helios. Doubting the word of his mother, he sought out the sun god to seek proof of his parentage. Upon his death it was said that his mother wept with tears of amber.[70]

Some historians believe that from as early as 2000 BC the Near East was acquainted with amber. During the early 1900s, at the palace of Ninevah, a broken obelisk in the form of a tapered four-sided shaft of stone was uncovered, inscribed with Assyrian cuneiform writing. Dr J. Oppert, a noted Assyriologist, translated the text in 1876. He believed the inscription indicated the early existence of commerce between northern Europe and Assyria. His translation is as follows:

> In the sea of changeable winds
> His merchants fished for pearls
> In the sea where the North Star culminates [the Black Sea]
> They fish for yellow amber.[71]

Research shows that the Baltic tribes traded amber mainly along the European rivers. During the middle Bronze Age (1800–1200 BC) a central route began in Jutland, Denmark, and passed along the Elbe River southwards to what is now Hamburg, Germany. An important hoard of amber artefacts was uncovered at Dieskau, where the route separates, with the main branch following the Saale River. From this river, finds indicate that the route continued south along the River Naab and then to the River Danube, thence to the Inn River at Passau on the present border between Germany and Austria. Crossing over the Alps through the Brenner Pass, the route then followed the Eisock River until it joined the Adige River flowing into Italy.[72]

A second branch of the route followed the Elbe River into the Czech Republic. Another turned off at Passau and followed the Danube to Linz and Upper Austria. A hoard of amber found at Halsatt, Austria, proved that another branch followed the Salzach River. Other amber finds indicate that a western route, heading toward Britain, diverged from the main central route on the Saale, passing westwards just north of the River Main to connect with the Rhine, then travelling along the Rhine into the Aare River watershed.[73]

It is known that amber was traded to central European

cultures, who then traded it to the Myceneans and early Greeks. Amber from the source area of Sambia was shipped to the mouth of the Vistula River, where it was combined with amber from Jutland and then transported southwards along the Bronze Age trading route. Amber beads, pendants, amulets and hairpins have all been found in the tombs of the Mycenean kings. Whilst excavating the citadel at Mycenae, Heinrich Schliemann found over 400 beads which proved to be of Baltic origin.[74] In 1885, Otto Helm, a German scientist, chemically tested Mycenean amber and identified it as succinite.[75] But it was not until 1963, with the advent of modern scientific methods, that Curt Beck utilized infrared photography on prehistoric amber. Infrared has proved the most appropriate method for distinguishing between amber from different sources. The organic compound in the amber absorbs different wavelengths of the infrared radiation. The results were astounding. Having compared the spectra of Mycenean amber with the spectra of Baltic amber he found that they were identical. Beck concluded that Mycenean amber was indeed Baltic in origin.[76]

The mound tombs of the British Isles, especially in the vicinity of Stonehenge, have also yielded amber ornaments. In fact, there are reports of Baltic amber the length and breadth of the British Isles; one of the earliest historical accounts is recorded in Boece's *Historia Scotorum* which dates to 1527. However, it was not until the early 1970s that Dr P. G. Embrey of the Department of Mineralogy at the British Museum, and Dr R. Baker of the Department of Palaeontology at the Natural History Museum, were able to apply the same infrared analysis, that Beck had successfully used on the Mycenean beads, to the amber found in Britain. The results of their analyses were, once again, astonishing. Apart from only three items, all prehistoric amber in

Britain, like that of Mycenae, was Baltic in origin.[77]

These startling revelations pointed to a direct connection between the high cultures of the eastern Mediterranean and Britain. It is certainly feasible, indeed almost certain, that both Mycenean and British amber came from the same source, which implies that the Myceneans may possibly have had some prior knowledge of Britain during prehistory. If the Egyptians did have to leave the palace of Mycenae, then by travelling through the trade routes of Europe they would, in all probability, eventually have reached the North Sea. From there, it was only a short step to the shores of North Ferriby.

There is, however, another alternative to consider. If Scota did not cross the Aegean Sea with several of her country folk, as the Bower manuscript appears to suggest, then the only other option to escape the tyranny in her homeland was via North Africa. But would she have taken the harsh route through the desert or the treacherous waters of the Mediterranean Sea? It was time to follow her possible route into the west.

CHAPTER NINE

BRIGANTIA

When Thor Heyerdahl embarked on his epic voyage across the coast of North Africa and beyond, he knew little that Walter Bower had chronicled such a journey centuries before. The evidence from the Aegean region has confirmed that an Egyptian splinter group probably fled to the northern reaches of the Greek mainland. As we have seen, from here it would have been a simple matter to follow the ancient amber routes deep into the heart of Europe. The focus of attention now returns to our fleeing princess, Scota, her husband, Gaythelos, and the remaining refugees fleeing the tyranny of Egypt. Did their escape route go via Africa and, if so, did they set out across land or did they choose the easier sea route?

West of Egypt lie the countries of North Africa. Today these countries are, from east to west, Libya, Tunisia, Algeria and Morocco, all with Mediterranean shorelines and all, with the exception of Tunisia, extending southwards into the great Sahara Desert. The long and varied history of North Africa, up into the early Islamic period, presents an extreme contrast to that of Egypt. However, in many ways it is just as interesting. In one respect there is a parallel with Egypt, for North Africa also had its 'Red and Black Lands', its arable areas and its deserts. One solitary strip of arable land, of varying width, stretches along the Mediterranean coast, gradually merging (unlike in Egypt) into the desert towards the south.

This was not always so. Some 12,000 years ago, at the end of the last Ice Age, North Africa, including the Sahara, enjoyed a moist, tropical climate, and elephants, giraffes and buffalo roamed the land. It is known that the peoples of the Sahara had pottery as early as those in the Near East, certainly by about 6000 BC, and cattle as early as the ancient Egyptians, around 4000 BC. However, about 2000 or 3000 years later, the climate of the Sahara became much as it is today. Environmental variations subsequently produced periods of relative humidity alternating with periods of drought. By around 3000–2500 BC, the climate began to alter dramatically and produced today's barren and inhospitable landscape. With water supplies rapidly drying up, virtually the only means of human sustenance left was cattle-herding, which depended on a special form of nomadic pastoralism. The cattle were therefore taken deep into the desert during the short grazing season and spent the rest of the year in better pastures either to the north or to the south. The populations that could be supported in this way were obviously small in number.[1]

Throughout Egyptian history, the Western Desert, beyond the country's frontier, was home to the Tjehenu, which is usually translated as 'Libyans'.[2] They had been the traditional enemy of Egypt since the time of its unification, around 3100 BC, and from this time onwards were constantly mentioned as the object of Egyptian raiding parties. They were regularly depicted in tomb paintings and temple reliefs as both bearded and light-skinned or fair-haired and blue-eyed. Today, they would be called Berbers. At times, it is difficult to differentiate the Libyans from the native Egyptians inhabiting the western Delta of Egypt itself. It has been suggested that on clear ethnic grounds the ancient Egyptian wall paintings made a distinction between themselves and the Tjehenu, whose lands, they believed, lay towards the Mediterranean, west of the Nile Delta.[3]

At first glance, the actions against the Libyans during the early part of the New Kingdom appear to have been little more than punitive raids. The orthodox view is that there are no explicit references to conflict with Libyans in the Eighteenth Dynasty. For example, an official of Amenhotep III is recorded as having Libyan cattle in his stockyard, but whether these were booty, imports, or simply a type bred in Egypt is unknown.[4] Libyans are also depicted as being present at Akhenaten's court. Here they appear as ambassadors bringing tribute or witnessing the king's public activities. Compelling evidence in the guise of the 'battle papyrus', found at Amarna in the 1930s, does, however, appear to contradict the official view. We saw in the last chapter that Akhenaten deployed his troops against the Libyans. Does this suggest that relations between the two nations were beginning to deteriorate? Or was Akhenaten opposed to just one faction? There is evidence from various tomb biographies of a Libyan group, possibly bandits, who were deemed to be quite a nuisance by the inhabitants of Akhetaten.[5] Certainly after the fall of Amarna, relations between Egypt and Libya were soon on a downward spiral.

During the Nineteenth and Twentieth Dynasties, Egypt was faced with a disturbing series of invasions from Libya. Based on the sketchy details available, famine may have forced tens of thousands of refugees to flee towards the north west of Egypt. A more sinister explanation is that the

Libyan settlements in the Western Desert threatened to overwhelm the Nile Delta and so undermine the Egyptian administration in that region.[6] Whatever the explanation, the reigning pharaohs drove back the immigrants by force of arms. Both Merenptah (*circa* 1220 BC) and Rameses III (*circa* 1180 BC) fought off substantial Libyan invasions. Merenptah was said to have killed over 9300 Libyans and their allies, but the figures of Rameses III, if taken at face value, indicate that over 28,000 were slain! Even if these figures are adjusted, they still number about 12,000, and this emphasizes the seriousness of the invasions.[7] Egyptian records rarely record the numbers of enemy slain, and captives are usually numbered in the hundreds or less, not in thousands. The Libyan invasions appear to have been the culmination of extensive, somewhat long-term Libyan infiltration and settlement of the western Delta, which continued even after the great defeats described above. In time, however, these Libyan rulers spawned a traditional line of Egyptian kings of their own during the Twenty-second Dynasty.[8] It is even said that Queen Cleopatra married her daughter to Juba VI, a Libyan/Berber king.[9]

Bearing in mind this fluctuating, sometimes hostile, relationship between Egypt and Libya, would Scota have risked an overland journey into unwelcoming territory, particularly as the evidence from Amarna suggests that Akhenaten took some form of military action against Libyan tribes? Perhaps the Egyptians avoided the desert through enemy terrain entirely by sailing around the Libyan coastline, and therefore avoided any unnecessary confrontation. There is only one way to find out. It is time to return to Walter Bower's *Scotichronicon*: 'And so Scota and Gaythelos wandered through many provinces, passing though many places, enduring many perils and vicissitudes according as they were driven about by the violence of opposing winds. They entered Africa along the river Ampsaga and settled peacefully for some time in the province of Numidia although the people who dwell in that country usually have no fixed abode'.[10]

At least Bower's manuscript confirms that the trail led into Africa. Even so, establishing the precise route they decided on was not so straightforward. I was unfamiliar with the names Ampsaga and Numidia, and was sure that they were not modern terms. My suspicions were confirmed upon examining an up-to-date atlas of the region. Did such localities, therefore, ever exist? With a little scepticism, I decided to surf the Internet once more for answers. I soon discovered that they were not simply a figment of Walter Bower's imagination. Numidia, it would seem, was the ancient name for Algeria, bordered to the east by the old Roman province of Africa Proconsularis and to the south by the Sahara desert. Dating from 201 to 46 BC, its collaboration with the Roman Empire culminated with it being placed under direct Roman rule.[11] And Ampsaga was the old name for the Roman town of Constantine. Situated approximately 300 kilometres south-east of Algiers, it was once a large city sprawling over the top of a huge limestone cliff slashed by an incredibly deep and narrow gorge. Nowadays, the ancient city has all but disappeared.[12]

It is almost certain therefore that the Egyptians did avoid the Libyan desert and entered North Africa via Algeria. This scenario fits perfectly with what we already know about Egyptian/Libyan relations. Besides, the Bower manuscript makes no mention of any journey into the Libyan desert.

With Scota's route now confirmed, the only remaining question was whether I would find any trace of her presence in the bleak terrain of the Sahara.

In 1879, the German geologist and explorer Oscar Lenz reported seeing 'strange drawings or decorations' engraved on the rocks whilst travelling through Morocco.[13] Despite his report, these sightings went virtually unnoticed by the academic world. It was not until 1912, when the Treaty of Fez turned Morocco from an independent kingdom into a French protectorate, that interest began to intensify. In the years that followed, hundreds of rock-art sites were being discovered, mainly due to the interest and energy of French administrators, army and civilian doctors and civil engineers. In 1926, when the Prehistoric Society of Morocco was founded, the academic community finally began to sit up and take notice of this much-maligned avenue of prehistoric archaeology.[14]

Rock art in North Africa is widespread and varied, but little known in English-speaking circles. It first appeared with the big game hunters, after the last Ice Age, then continued through various styles and phases for some 4000–5000 years. Naturalistic in appearance, it consists of animal forms, such as lions and gazelles, depictions of various weapons or pictures of foot soldiers or men fighting on horseback.[15] Nowadays the best locations lie deep in the southern Sahara and can only be reached by the most hardy of tourists. Despite their inaccessibility, over the past ten years archaeologists have uncovered many new sites and so far some 243 have been recorded. Regrettably, daily exposure to extremes of both heat and cold has severely damaged many of the carvings beyond recognition and repair. Human degradation has not helped their plight either. The modernization of African cities has resulted in large quantities of inscribed sandstone slabs been broken up and taken away in lorryloads for building purposes.[16] Their archaeological importance, sadly, has now been lost forever.

On 19 February 1935, a paper was submitted to the Sixteenth International Anthropological Congress in

Brussels, which first suggested that there may be a connection between North African rock art and ancient Egypt.
Entitled 'Engravings of Magarat Sanat', it was largely
ignored by those academics present as having no real
historical interest.[17] Situated in northern Morocco, and
dating to prehistoric times, the Magarat Sanat is, in fact, a
large cave where the local nomadic tribesmen often took
shelter from the Sahara climate. For the next fifty years its
importance to North African archaeology was ignored by
scholars. However, in 1975 a French archaeologist, Dr G.
Camp, rediscovered the Magarat Sanat, so to speak, and its
hidden secrets were finally revealed to the world.[18]

On first entering the Magarat Sanat, Camp did not
notice anything out of the ordinary. The cave was wide and
spacious and it was plain to see why it had been used as a
temporary refuge throughout the millennia. Then, as he
gazed up towards the ceiling, his mouth suddenly fell open
with astonishment. On the roof there was the most incredible collection of engravings he had ever witnessed. Through
the use of campfires by the nomads, some of the engravings
were now blackened with soot, but many still had all their
colouring intact. As he meticulously set about recording
each carving, Camp soon realized that some of the
engravings were very unusual and did not correspond with
the overall design. After closer inspection, he concluded that
they not only bore an extraordinary resemblance to artistry
originating in ancient Egypt but that one particular
depiction of a war chariot was identical to those used by the
Egyptian army during the New Kingdom period.[19] However, I was soon to find out that this was no isolated
painting in a nomad's cave.

Perhaps the most telling example of all of a possible
Egyptian connection was to be found on the Yagour Plateau
in the High Atlas. The Atlas Mountains stretch from the

south-west of Morocco to the north-east for over 700 kilometres and form a natural barrier between the Atlantic and the pre-Saharan regions. A dozen summits exceed 4000 metres in altitude, 100 exceed 3500 metres and more than 4000 others reach 3000 metres.[20] But the range has never been insurmountable: numerous passes have always allowed the passage of men and animals. It is here, among the desolate peaks, that the so-called Great Disc or Talat n' Lisk can be found. It is a huge rock, approximately 2 metres high, and inscribed upon the side is a representation of a sun-disc.[21] Although at first glance it is not dissimilar to those depicted upon the tomb paintings from Amarna, precisely what it is and when it was carved is difficult to say. But could it be some passing reference to the Aten? Did Scota instruct one of her followers to inscribe it in reverence to their god whilst passing through? Further enquiries, however, proved fruitless. Infuriatingly, it has been so badly damaged that we can no longer tell what it was meant to be or even if there were any accompanying inscriptions. It seems that it had once been considered a suitable target for stone throwers and for the odd rifle shot. To say that the picture of the Great Disc fascinated me is an under-statement. I could not stop staring at this compelling image which so perfectly captured the strange ambience of the location. For as I had discovered through my research, the waves of the Triton Sea once lapped around the area where the disc was located.

The North African region is cut by a countless succession of now-dry riverbeds. One such stretch of water that appears to have suffered from Saharan desiccation is the curiously named Triton Sea. This is a rather misleading title, as nowadays it is an obsolete stretch of water. In Greek mythology, Triton was the son of Poseidon and was usually depicted as a creature of the sea with the head and upper body of a man, the tail of a dolphin and two horse legs at the rear. He acted as his father's official trumpeter, blowing on a large trumpet shell in order to appease the rough seas. Traditionally, it was the god Triton who directed Jason and the Argonauts when they had gone astray. 'And Triton consented to draw the Argo along by her keel, until once more she entered the Mediterranean Sea.'[22]

The first historical reference to the Triton Sea appears to be by the Greek writer Herodotus, who says that 'the sea has all now but dried up'.[23] In 1982 the geologist and writer L. Taylor Hansen stated in *The Ancient Atlantic*, 'Lake Triton was part of a huge inland sea in the middle of the Sahara Desert, just east of the Atlas Mountains.' The Ahaggar mountain range, now in central Algeria, was once an island in the middle of the Triton, whereas today Lake Chad would represent the final remnants of this ancient waterway. According to Hansen, the Triton was held by the curve of the Atlas Mountains like the 'rim of a cup', and the water was thus held 'covered by the sand from the Gulf of Gabes where it entered the Mediterranean to the mountains south of Lake Chad'.[24]

Where the Triton once rose, deep among the Ahaggar Mountains, there lived a mysterious tribe known as the Tuareg. Related to the Berbers, it seems that their ancestors originated in the Nile Valley. Reminiscent of the ancient Egyptians, their society was also divided between those who tended the land and those who did not. For thousands of years their economy revolved around trans-Saharan trade, their camel caravans carrying goods throughout the desert and beyond. Many groups have subsequently moved southwards over the past 2000 years in response to pressure from the north. However, small pockets of ancient Tuareg can still be found surviving in the High Atlas today. A secretive people, according to Taylor Hansen, they are renowned for jealously guarding their Egyptian heritage and beliefs. She recalls a remarkable conversation she had with an unnamed Arab. After much persuasion he told her: 'Near In-Salah there are three high peaks of the Ahaggar where once the Triton Sea rose up. No Arab will go there if he can help it. These peaks touch the sky with claw-like fingers. Once a friend of mine got lost and saw the ruins of one of their cities on the Atlas. It was built of giant stones, each one the size of an Arabian tent'. The Arab qualified his statements by saying that he had travelled to the areas of the Tuareg people as a messenger. 'On one of these times I took a message from my sheikh to Tamen-Ra-Set – that is the Tuareg capital city. That is where Amun-Okhakl, their king lives.'[25]

It is certainly feasible, indeed almost certain, that these mysterious Tuareg people were a surviving element from ancient Egypt. The most obvious association lies in the names of their city and their king. Here, reverence to the Egyptian state god, Amun, is obvious. The only problem in trying to connect this to Scota is that she was an Amarna princess and, as such, a worshipper of the god Aten. Yet, there are some interesting points to consider. Taylor Hansen says that the Tuaregs particularly despised the sun and blamed it for all their misfortunes. This fits in perfectly with what we know about the priesthood of Amun. The rise of the sun-disc, the Aten, certainly brought about their downfall, even if it was only short-lived. And, considering the reasons for Scota's hasty departure from Egypt, it could also be argued that her particular reverence for the sun brought about her own downfall. Could the Tuaregs' loathing for the sun, in fact, be a hatred of the Aten? Could their city, Tamen-Ra-Set, have been built by a small contingent of Scota's followers? At this we can only guess.

Precisely when and where Scota left North Africa is

difficult to answer. From the archaeological evidence, we know that Egyptian artefacts were arriving in Britain somewhere between 1400 and 1300 BC, so her time in Africa was no doubt brief. We now return to the question of what direction the Egyptian trail took. Luckily, the Bower manuscript does give a clear indication: 'At last they left Africa, boarding the ships which they then had at their disposal, and sailed to the vicinity of the island of Cadiz in Spain.'[26]

Examining a map of the region, it is easy to see why Scota would have chosen to cross the open seas to Cadiz. Situated on the southern coast of Iberia, it was not only just a short hop away from the North African coast, but also an extremely fertile island, easily defensible and encircled by a protective lagoon. It was these particular features that attracted all the great empires throughout history. From the seafaring Phoenicians to the warmongering Romans, each exploited the port of Cadiz for their own commercial gains. During the Elizabethan era, it was raided by Sir Francis Drake in the struggle to gain absolute control over the trade from the New World. It even managed to withstand a siege from Napoleon's army.[22] Cadiz was unquestionably *the* major port on the Iberian Peninsula.

Iberia is the peninsula which holds the two modern states of Spain and Portugal. It is separated from France by the Pyrenees, and Africa is less than 25 kilometres away by sea, across the Straits of Gibraltar. Accordingly, the peninsula acted as a bridge between Europe and Africa, and between the Mediterranean and the Atlantic. It covers an area of 595,706 square kilometres and is probably Europe's most geographically diverse region, with a coastline on two sides and terrain ranging from the near deserts in Andalusia, in the south, to the deep coastal inlets of Galicia in the north-west, and from the sun-baked uplands of the Castilla

La Mancha in the centre to the rugged, snow-capped Pyrenees. No wonder it is often referred to as a miniature continent.[28]

According to the orthodox view, the indigenous race of Iberia was a backward people whose sudden rise, around 800 BC, was attributable to Greek colonization. Greece at this time was emerging from a so-called Dark Age, the impoverished period between the collapse of the old Mycenean order in about 1200 BC and the reappearance of new political forms based on independent city-states.[29] These colonizing surges were to take the Greeks from Gibraltar, in the south, to the Caucasus in the north by 650 BC.[30] For the Greeks, the lure of Iberia with its mineral wealth – the copper mines at Rio Minto, the gold of the Sierra Morena, the silver of Cartagena – was just too strong to ignore. From their base at Massalia (Marseilles) they began to wield their power throughout the western Mediterranean, and it was during this period that they also began to exert a major cultural influence on the Iberian Peninsula.[31]

Despite various claims in later classical sources, however, no archaeological evidence has yet been unearthed of any Greek towns in southern Spain. In fact, it now emerges that the Phoenicians, backed possibly by their Egyptian masters, may have played a far greater part in the opening up of Iberia than was originally believed. According to the Roman historian Strabo, it was the Phoenicians and not the Greeks who were the first peoples to voyage to southern Spain. He states that in 1200 BC, only a few decades after Scota had escaped from the turmoil in Egypt, an identical fleet of ships, sailing from the Phoenician port of Tyre, was recorded heading towards Cadiz.[32] Is there some relevance here?

We saw in the last chapter how the trading cities of

Byblos and Tyre, on the Levantine coast, were an integral part of the political economy of the Egyptian Empire. As a result, contact with Egypt and other Near Eastern empires governed the Phoenicians' activities. As a renowned maritime power, they were ideally placed to forge alliances with inland empires, act as intermediaries between the great nations of the eastern Mediterranean, and organize regional trading systems to their advantage. Phoenician colonization of the central and western Mediterranean began to take place, and before long a stream of Phoenician explorers and traders deposited themselves on Iberian shores. Remarkably, their very first foundation is understood to have been Gades, the ancient name for Cadiz.[33]

So what does all this mean? Clearly, it can be no coincidence that the island of Cadiz, the principal landing place of the Phoenician Empire was also the first documented site where Scota set foot upon European soil. What is more, the Phoenicians' departure point, the city of Tyre, as we know, also just happens to be the city of Scota. Could the classical chroniclers have got their facts slightly muddled? When documenting the 'fleets sailing from Tyre', were they in fact making reference to the escape of Scota and Gaythelos a few years previously? It is a possibility. However, there is another alternative. Could it be that after safely landing on Spanish soil, Gaythelos sent back a message to his people to come and join him? This may explain why the Phoenician fleet headed directly towards the port of Cadiz. One thing is certain: the ancient Egyptians did possess a working knowledge of the lands in the western half of the Mediterranean Sea. Writing in a later period the Greek historian Herodotus observes:

Africa, except where it borders Asia, is clearly surrounded by water. Necho, Pharaoh of Egypt, was the first we know of to demonstrate this. When he finished digging out the canal between the Nile and the Red Sea, he sent out a naval expedition, manned by the Phoenicians, instructing them to come home by the way of the Straits of Gibraltar, into the Mediterranean and in that fashion get back to Egypt. So, setting out from the Red Sea, the Phoenicians sailed into the Indian Ocean. Each autumn they put in at whatever part of Africa they happened to be sailing by, and sowing the soil, they stayed there until harvest time. Reaping the grain, they continued their journey; so that two years passed and it was not until the third that they rounded the Pillars of Hercules and made it back to Egypt.[34]

Alas, the endeavours of this Phoenician delegation continue to be a mystery to all those that study them, mainly because virtually all of their archives have disappeared. In 1978, in an article in the *Proceedings of the Prehistoric Society*, Dr C. Szynet, an expert in the field of Semitic studies, warned the academic fraternity that it was impossible to retrace this Phoenician internal history.[35] Nevertheless, with the city of Tyre now at the centre of things and leading the trading onslaught into the west, it cannot be denied that the world had opened up to the ancient Egyptians. It should be no surprise, therefore, that a few years after Scota had left the perils of her homeland, ancient Egyptian artefacts were beginning to appear on the Iberian Peninsula.

From an archaeological perspective, we are now faced with immense difficulties, not because of a *lack* of material finds, but because there is just *too much* evidence in Iberia of artefacts of an ancient Egyptian nature. In addition, it is impossible to establish from where they came and in what period they were originally deposited. Phoenician foundations were now beginning to appear all over the Iberian coastline and, to the casual observer, they demonstrate all the signs of a highly Egyptianized society. Unable to explain this, scholars have called the concept 'orientalizing'. Almost overnight the indigenous people of the Iberian Bronze Age were adopting the fashions, cultural values and technologies of Egypt and the eastern Mediterranean.[36]

From the cemeteries of Cadiz, blue-green scarabs have been unearthed inscribed with the names of the pyramid-builders of the Third Dynasty, the lower portion showing the cartouche preceded by the royal crook and flail.[37] Other tomb deposits have also included mummy-shaped statuettes, made from limestone and inscribed with a vast array of Egyptian motifs, such as the sacred eye of Horus. Furthermore, an assortment of scarabs and amulets has been uncovered bearing the names of numerous ancient Egyptian gods such as Osiris and Amun. Some even depicted the White Crown of Lower Egypt.[38] Evidence has shown that these later items, in particular, were highly prized in Iberian society. Even the Iberian city of Andalusia was found to have 'a very strong Egyptian aspect noted by the endless burial of Egyptian alabaster jars'.[39] In 1922, Icard and Guielly, the original excavators of the great Phoenician city of Carthage on the Tunisian north coast, remarked about the many Egyptian finds on the Iberian peninsula: 'The extreme antiquity of the findings belongs to such a distant era that could be attributed to an Egyptian colony'.[40] Could they, without knowing, be referring to Scota and her people?

On 4 August 1897, in Alicante, Spain, a young farm worker by the name of Manuel Campello Esclapez stumbled across a bust of a young woman whilst digging in a field. Made from polychrome stone, it measured approximately 1 metre high, though it appears to have been part of a much larger statue. Afterwards, it was purchased by a French archaeologist, Pierre Paris, for the sum of 4000 French francs, and carefully transported to the harbour of Alicante for the journey to France. Having survived the voyage intact, it was taken directly to the Louvre in Paris and placed on display. Here it was rebaptized the Reina Mora, meaning the 'Lady of Elche'. In 1939, at the outbreak of the Second World War, the sculpture was moved to Toulouse, in the south of France, for security reasons. In February 1941 it was returned to Spain, where it is on public display in the Museo del Prado in Madrid.[41]

The Lady of Elche is a quite remarkable find. She wears a very peculiar head-dress consisting of huge coils on either side of the face. The orthodox theory is that the bust probably dates to the fourth century BC, but the jewellery she is wearing is definitely not from the Greek or Roman period. From the iconography, some archaeologists believe that the statue comes from a much earlier date. Regrettably, as nothing else was found with it, and there were no traces of a burial, a temple or even a dwelling, it is impossible to give an accurate date. But writer David Childree in *Lost Cities of Atlantis* remarks, 'The Lady of Elche is depicted with a flowing gown and an Aten symbol on her chest. Here we see a correlation with the so-called Atenists of ancient Egypt.'[42]

Although at first glance there does seem to be some correlation between Scota, the Aten and the Lady of Elche, without accurate dating it is impossible to clarify the situation. Having studied photographs of the statue, I would say that the sun-disc she displays across her chest bears more than a passing resemblance to the sun-disc inscribed upon the Great Disc on the Yagour Plateau, Morocco. Whether the Lady of Elche is, in fact, some throwback to a bygone Egyptian era we can only speculate. Since the native Iberians adopted Egyptian dress and customs and the Phoenicians also displayed strong Egyptian tendencies, it is difficult, to say the least, to identify any remnants of Scota's trail into Iberia. The path is, quite frankly, littered with artefacts heading off in all different directions.

From the initial landing at Cadiz, where did the Egyptians go to next? The Bower manuscript states:

> Meanwhile they were in distress from the long weariness of the sea and were hurrying towards the land of Spain to acquire provisions and rest. The local inhabitants rushed together from all sides in resentment of their arrival. Their aim was to oppose them in armed warfare, but soon a fierce battle ensued and the inhabitants were defeated and turned to flight. With no time to celebrate their immediate victory, the Egyptians, with Gaythelos at the helm, pursued the indigenous people back into their own land and proceeded to plunder a sizeable portion of Iberian territory by the River Ebro. Here the Scots had their settlement for some length of time'.[43]

Obtaining a map of the region, I sat down to investigate further. It was clear that the River Ebro does indeed exist. Emanating from the Cantabrian Mountains, in the northeast of Spain, its course runs straight down to the Mediterranean Sea. From the contours of the map, it resembles a flattened arrowhead, snaking its way through the surrounding mountain passes and meandering through the deep valley gorges. Strategically placed, it provided not only unlimited access to the Mediterranean but, through its adjoining tributaries, it also crossed the northern Meseta to the foothills of the Pyrenees. Acting as a natural boundary between the great nations of Carthage and Rome, the Ebro flood plain was rich in alluvial soils and would have definitely attracted any ancient migrant.

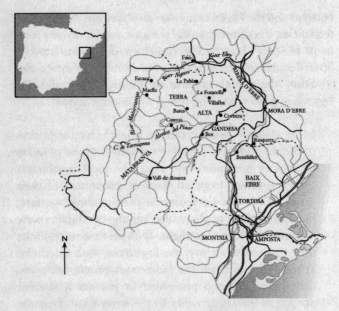

Map of Spain illustrating the River Ebro Valley

According to the Bower manuscript, after pitching their tents on higher ground, the ancient Egyptians swiftly built themselves a settlement on the River Ebro itself. The manuscript states, 'After the indigenous tribes had been subjugated for some time, Gaythelos built a very strong tower, encircled by deep ditches, in the middle of the settlement, and called it "Brigantia". Here their descendants multiplied greatly. It can still be seen to this day.'[44] Unfortunately, it does not record how long the Egyptians remained at Brigantia. So, was Walter Bower correct? Could this tower, reportedly constructed by the Egyptian refugees, still remain? It was a long shot, I knew, but if it could be proved that such monuments did exist in Spanish prehistory, at least it would give some credence to the suggestion that Egyptians actually colonized the Iberian Peninsula.

In 1995, Dr Maria Cruz Fernandez Castro in *Iberia in Prehistory* reported on the so-called 'towers in Spain'. She remarked upon the presence of conspicuous archaeological mounds that rise up from the flat landscape – conical in shape, and separated by only short distances. These towers were subsequently called *motillas*.[45] At first they were thought to be huge Arab fortresses, built by the Moors who had invaded the Iberian Peninsula in AD 711.[46] Then, when their prehistoric origin became apparent to historians and archaeologists alike, they were naturally thought of as megalithic monuments.[47] Over the past fifty years, excavations by various universities in Spain have tried to establish the nature of these strange structures.

In the summer of 1947 at La Penuela in northern Spain, Dr Joaquin Jimenez of the University of Madrid conducted the first full-scale excavation of a *motilla*. It revealed a complex structure and confirmed the notion of a well-fortified settlement with a tower in the middle of the enclosure – precisely how Walter Bower had described Brigantia. Three encircling defensive systems were uncovered, and the tower walls had to be reinforced on at least four occasions. At one stage even the gateway had to be blocked. The accumulation of occupied strata beside the wall, especially situated around the tower, pointed to the use of the fortification as a dwelling. Jimenez confirmed that the inhabitants paid great heed to their ancestors and their origins as they buried their dead within the confines of the fortification. Around the base of the tower he unearthed some graves that, according to him, contained highly advanced metal weapons: some bronze arrowheads and riveted daggers. Preliminary analysis confirmed that the weapons were of middle Bronze Age date, around 1340 BC.[48]

There can be no doubt that the *motillas* served a defensive purpose. It would appear that the perils of warfare were gradually becoming increasingly severe. This story would fit well with what was alleged in the Bower manuscript. With the Egyptian party being attacked by the locals, the construction of Brigantia would make perfect sense. Perhaps the firmest indication, however, is the date, around 1340 BC, which is roughly speaking the same time Scota would have entered the Iberian Peninsula. But this does not explain the lack of material finds. Be that as it may, with the study and excavation of *motillas* at present in its infancy, there is always the prospect of many more finds being unearthed in the next few years.

On 25 May 1999, at the Bloomsbury Summer School, London, the most compelling link between Egypt and Spain arose from a chance meeting I had with fellow Egyptologist Dr Joann Fletcher. It was here that I was first introduced to the mysterious Guanche culture of the Canary Islands. Dr Fletcher informed me that when Spanish adventurers first set foot on those islands in the mid-fourteenth century, they were surprised to discover a cave-dwelling, goat-herding people who mummified their dead. Could there be a connection between these lost people of the Canaries and the Amarna refugees?

The islands are approximately 150 kilometres from the north-west coast of Africa and are renowned for their warm climate and golden beaches. The name calls to mind the yellow songbirds that people like to keep in cages – but do not expect to find canaries fluttering around there. The native canary, a small brown finch with a poor singing voice, has nothing to do with the naming of the islands. There are many theories on the origins of the name, but songbirds do not feature in any of them. The Roman historian Pliny the Elder called the main island Canaria, a reference to the large wild dogs which he reported living on the island in his 7-volume *Natural History*:

> The island's name is Canaria, from its multitude of dogs of a huge size. Two of these were brought back for Juba, explorers said that in this island there are traces of buildings; that while they all have an abundant supply of fruit and bird of every kind, Canaria also abounds in palm groves bearing dates and in conifers. In addition to this there is a supply of honey and also papyrus grows in the rivers, and sheat-fish; and that these islands are plagued with the rotting carcasses of monstrous creatures that are constantly cast ashore by the sea.[49]

Gran Canaria is the most populous of the Canary Islands and tourists flock to its ocean-front hotels to bask in the sun. But few who visit the island are aware of its remarkable archaeological heritage. Hundreds of caves, occupied from ancient times to the present, hide in its cliffs and mountains. Burial mounds overlook the sea near the remains of the stone houses that once sheltered bustling fishing communities. Thousands of years before the first tourists came to the island – even before the Europeans set foot on its soil – a group of people from North Africa had made their home there.

According to Greek legend, the great hero Hercules first visited the islands as a result of the twelve labours that were charged upon him by Eurystheus, King of Tiryns. One of his tasks was to go to the end of the world and bring back the golden apples guarded by the Hesperides, the fabled daughters of the night. His route supposedly took him through the Straits of Gibraltar – hence their classical name, the Pillars of Hercules – until he reached the Garden of the Gods. Beyond was the paradoxical home of the night-time maidens. Successfully carrying out his assignment, Hercules returned home from what many historians thought could have only been the Canary Islands – about the only place to fit the ancient's description.[50] From then on the islands gained a reputation, passed down from one classical writer to the next, as a Garden of Eden. The Greek poet Homer identified the Canaries as Elysium, a place where the righteous spent their afterlife.[51] From the apparent contacts with adjacent lands, it is perhaps legitimate to presume that Mediterranean mariners had already visited the Canary Islands during the second millennium BC. After all, the legend of Hercules is said to date to the Mycenean Age (1500–1100 BC).

Nobody is really clear what the Canary Islands were like before the fourteenth century. There are no written records of the Guanches until the medieval invasion by the Spanish conquistadors. In 1402 Jean de Bethencourt, a Norman knight, was sent by Henry III of Castille to take the islands. He conquered Lanzarote and Fuerteventura, but he was defeated by the Guanches of Gran Canaria.[52] For a long time the Spaniards struggled to conquer the islands, pursuing the customary policy of divide and rule, making alliances with friendly kings and encouraging Guanche to fight Guanche, until resistance was finally quelled. Faced with the inevitability of defeat, the Guanches of Gran Canaria decided to end their lives rather than live in slavery. Their method of death was as drastic as it was spectacular; throwing themselves off the highest rock faces on the island.[53] Those who survived the invasion quickly adapted to the new state of affairs. Life on the post-conquest islands varied. Most Guanches were enslaved; collaborators were well treated and a minority inter-married. However, many were simply ignored by the colonists. A significant number did remain in hiding in the mountains, but many were coerced and intimidated by the Spanish Inquisition into 'abandoning their roots'. Within a few decades it is estimated that two-thirds of the indigenous people had disappeared in one way or another, and within a century or so this ancient society had all but vanished.[54]

In the centuries following the Spanish conquest, almost all of the Guanche mummies that had once filled the burial caves of the islands were destroyed. Only a handful remain today, and one of them is in the care of Cambridge University. When it was examined in the 1920s, and again in the 1960s, scientists concluded that it had been preserved by methods very similar to those of the ancient Egyptians.[55]

For most people, mummies are synonymous with ancient Egypt. They have gripped the popular imagination through highly publicized discoveries and macabre horror movies. For the ancient Egyptians, mummification was essential to secure eternal life. If the body had decayed or was unrecognizable, the afterlife would be jeopardized. It has often been said that the practice grew from observing that the hot, dry sand preserved bodies that were buried in it.

Unfortunately, there is no ancient Egyptian 'how to' book on mummification. Herodotus provides us with perhaps the most detailed account for the study of their techniques. He describes three grades of embalming. The most perfect process is as follows:

> As much as possible the brain is removed via the nostrils with an iron hook, and what cannot be reached with the hook is washed out with drugs; next, the flank is opened with a flint knife and the whole contents of the abdomen removed; the cavity is then thoroughly cleaned and washed out, firstly with palm wine and again with an infusion of ground spices. After that it is filled with pure

myrrh, cassia, and every other aromatic substance, except frankincense, and sewn up again. Afterwards, the body is washed and then wrapped from head to foot in linen cut into strips and smeared on the underside with gum, which is commonly used by the Egyptians instead of glue. In this condition the body is given back to the family, who have a wooden case made shaped like a human figure, into which it is put.[56]

When, for reasons of expense, the second grade is called for, the treatment is different. No incision is made and the intestines are not removed, but oil of cedar is injected into the body through the anus, which is afterwards stopped up to prevent the liquid from escaping. The body is then cured in natron for the prescribed number of days, on the last of which the oil is drained off. Natron or *neyjry*, meaning 'divine salt', is a mixture of sodium bicarbonate, sodium carbonate, sodium sulphate, and sodium chloride. It is found naturally in Egypt, most commonly in the Wadi Natron some 64 kilometres north-west of Cairo.[57] Its effect is so powerful that as it leaves the body it brings with it the viscera in a liquid state, the flesh is dissolved and nothing of the body is left but the skin and the bones. After this treatment it is returned to the family without further attention. The third method, used for embalming the bodies of the poor, is simply to wash out the intestines and keep the body for seventy days in natron.[58]

During the summer of 1998, Egyptologist Dr Joann Fletcher, together with Dr Joyce Filer of the Department of Egyptian Antiquities at the British Museum, examined the Cambridge Guanche mummy under strict laboratory conditions. An extensive skull X-ray showed that terrible damage had been done to the face. This damage could have been caused, said Dr Filer, by a heavy stick, not unlike those wielded by the Guanches and seen by the invading Spanish half a millennium ago. The brain was still in place, which certainly was not the practice in Egypt. Perhaps the injuries suffered by the Guanche man before his death would have made the type of extraction described by Herodotus impossible. However, a closer examination of the body showed incisions that virtually matched those found in Egyptian mummies. A computerised topography scan of the entire body revealed other clues. Along with the intact liver, there appeared to be a package of some kind in the abdominal cavity; except for this instance in the Canaries, the Egyptians are thought to have been the only people who 'packed' the bodies of their dead with their treated organs.[59]

During the Twenty-first Dynasty, Egypt witnessed the acme of the embalmer's art, and a new and unique method of mummification. Unlike their predecessors, the embalmers concentrated on making the body look as life-like as possible. This was done by making incisions in the skin and stuffing the desiccated corpse with sawdust, sand and mud in order to return it to the shape it had had in life. After the viscera were removed from the cut in the left-hand side of the torso, the body was stuffed. The evisceration cut was used to reach the neck which, after being packed, was stopped up with a linen plug. Then the torso was filled, followed by the lower back, buttocks and legs. Additional slits were made in the back, legs and buttocks to help pack them. Once the legs were filled, linen plugs were inserted at the tops of the thighs to keep the stuffing in place. Separate slits were used to stuff the arms, shoulders, feet and lower abdomen, and the mouth was used to fill out the face.[60]

Having confirmed that the mummification process used on the Guanche mummy was identical to that used by the ancient Egyptians, Dr Fletcher and Guanche archaeologist Mike Eddy decided to investigate further. They travelled to the Canary Islands, where they were amazed to discover that small step pyramids also existed on the islands, reminiscent of the oldest pyramids in Egypt.

Egyptologists trace the origins of the pyramids back to the modest pit graves of the predynastic period, where they were covered with simple mounds of sand and gravel. A little later, the graves of the rulers and the elite consisted of neat mud-brick boxes called *mastabas*, sunk into the desert sand. They were often massive rectangular structures with flat roofs and divided, like a house, into several chambers. The tombs of the pharaohs of the first two dynasties followed this pattern, but with greater complexity. Nowadays such tombs can be seen in the desert near the high cliffs at Abydos. Each tomb would have been marked by a pair of large stela and covered by a mound. These were the architectural antecedents of the pyramids.[61]

In purely architectural terms, Egyptian pyramids are divided into two broad types: step pyramids and true pyramids. The first step pyramids appear to have developed initially from the rectangular royal and private *mastaba* tombs of the early dynastic period (3100–2686 BC). The largest of these remaining belongs to King Djoser at Saqqara. Constructed during the Third Dynasty, not only is it the largest of its kind ever to have been built in Egypt, it is also the first known structure to have been built with stone masonry quarried and properly cut, rather than rough stones stacked together. It seems initially to have taken the form of one huge *mastaba*, but it was gradually extended and elaborated until it became a pyramidal superstructure consisting of six massive steps reaching a staggering height of 60 metres.[62]

Though clearly not as elaborate as the pyramid of King Djoser, according to Dr Fletcher the Canary Island pyramids do appear to have been constructed on similar lines. Some experts claim that the Spanish constructed the pyramids when they cleared the fields of stone before planting. However, the structures are quite substantial and would have taken a great deal of effort to build. One of them has been built on the edge of a cliff: if the object was to remove stones, why not just throw them over the cliff? The fact that the pyramids have an east–west alignment also indicates that they probably had a religious purpose, associated with the rising and the setting of the sun.[63]

It is now agreed that the original inhabitants of the Canary Islands were almost certainly Hamitic, a combination of ancient Egyptian and Berber, moving westwards from North Africa. It is possible that they used boats built of papyrus reeds; in the last chapter, we saw how the Norwegian explorer, Thor Heyerdahl, proved that such a journey was indeed possible.

Long before Christian times there were already seafarers, traders and colonists trafficking between the eastern Mediterranean and the old ports on the westernmost outpost of Africa's Atlantic coast. Here the Canary current swept everything it could get hold of to the other side of the Atlantic. All those who had passed through the Straits of Gibraltar, the ancient Pillars of Hercules, had found shelter here. Remarkably, on a handful of volcanic islands in the Atlantic, 150 kilometres from the north-west coast of Africa, there were once a people whose ancestors had possibly been Egyptian, from whom they had received the knowledge of the burial practices and perhaps even the religion of ancient Egypt. Were these forebears members of Scota's entourage who, for reasons unknown, decided to leave the main body of refugees and settle on the Canary Islands? It is possible that Scota's followers may have split into different factions. The building of step pyramids does indicate a particular reverence for the sun god Ra and not for the state deity of Amun. Unfortunately, the answers to these questions are most probably buried beneath the sands of the Canaries.

With the mystery of Scota's first footsteps upon European soil perhaps solved, I turned to a final piece of speculation. From the protection of Brigantia, could I demonstrate that she, and some of her followers, eventually landed upon British shores?

CHAPTER TEN

~~~

PROBLEMS OF PREHISTORY

Having successfully skirted the shores of the Atlantic seaboard, it was now the time to turn my attention to Britain once more. It soon became apparent, however, that there is a big difference between studying the trade routes and cargoes of the eastern Mediterranean world and studying the prehistoric exchanges across the English Channel. Much is known about the political, social and economic structures of the ancient empires from a wealth of old writings and archaeological material. But far fewer finds, and, as we have previously seen, no true written records, exist from the so-called barbarian societies of Europe before they entered Rome's imperial orbit. Apart from the three boats unearthed at North Ferriby, and the faience beads found at Tara, there was little archaeological information to go on so far. In that case, where would I find further evidence to substantiate the settlement of ancient Egyptians in the British Isles?

The study of both the British and the Irish Bronze Age has always been hampered by a lack of settlement evidence, a problem that persists today despite recent recognition that many supposedly Iron Age Celtic sites and their associated cultural material had Bronze Age beginnings.[1] It was also quite common in the past for people, deliberately or accidentally, to obliterate traces of their predecessors. Rulers, for instance, often destroyed the settlements and monuments belonging to a previous chief or monarch. We have already seen how the memory of Akhenaten was wiped out by his successors, in particular by Horemheb, and the city of Amarna was torn down and the material reused for other building programmes. For this reason alone, the likelihood of uncovering the boundaries of a characteristic 'Egyptian' settlement somewhere in Britain, or stumbling across the remains of an 'Egyptian' temple buried under some local farmer's field, was very unlikely.

An additional problem was the archaeological material at my disposal. With no written records to give an insight into the ideas and activities of these ancient communities, the material remains, such as pottery and metalworking, were the only surviving evidence. I would also find it extremely difficult to assess the total amount of information that could possibly have been retrieved. Unlike Egypt, where the hot, dry climate is ideal for preservation, the archaeological remains in Britain have either decayed because of the acidity of the soil or fallen to pieces owing to the moist environment.[2] My cause had also not been aided by the exploits of my fellow historians. The work of the 'antiquarian' is an important element in the advancement of our knowledge of prehistoric sites and settlements, but I was unaware of the colossal impact their activities would have on my investigation.

Among the wealth of ancient field monuments scattered across Britain, the most common and the best known are barrows, long or circular grass-grown heaps of earth or stones which mark the burial places of the prehistoric aristocracy. Though they had been in limited use from the later Neolithic period, around 2500 BC, it was not until the Bronze Age that the barrow truly came into its own. In fact, it was the predominant means of burial throughout this particular period. Barrows vary in size from around 10 metres in diameter to as much as 45 metres and from 1 to 6 metres in height. The simplest are known as bowl-barrows and consist of a straightforward mound formed by heaving soil inwards from a surrounding ditch. Although based on the same principles, in southern Britain a circular ditch was dug first and then the soil was raised into a bank outside. This was called a ring-ditch, and the burial took place in the flattened area inside.[3] Finally, there are long barrows, rectangular or wedge-shaped mounds of earth flanked by quarry ditches on either side. Each averaged 60–90 metres in length and approximately 3 metres high. In the highland parts of Britain, where mounds of stones were used instead of earth, these burials are referred to as cairns.[4]

Beneath the barrow a large pit would be excavated, where the first interment, or primary burial, would take place. The remains, either skeletal or cremated, would then be carefully laid out together with personal adornments and accompanying grave goods. It was not uncommon for other burials to be made at the same time and these are referred to as satellite burials. Barrows seemed to have retained their sanctity for hundreds of years after their initial construction, and further burials might be added to the mound at a much later date.[5] A classic example is the Tara Prince, referred to in Chapter 1, who was interred in a much earlier mound of Neolithic date.

For many centuries after they had been so painstakingly piled up, these minor monuments remained in peace at the heart of the landscape in which they stood. The only stirrings of interest in their contents in the early days occurred during Roman times, when certain mounds, predominantly in Derbyshire, Somerset and the Mendips, were cut into and explored. However, the earliest recorded barrow-digging, which was motivated by aims other than treasure-seeking, appears to date from Norman times. A now-vanished barrow group called the Hills of the Banners, near Redbourn, Hertfordshire, was excavated by a group of monks from the priory of St Albans. Having meticulously dug their way through the huge mound of earth, they disinterred and sanctified its occupant, a nameless Anglo-Saxon whom they took for St Amphibalus, converter of St Alban and the first British Christian martyr. Consequently, the bones were piously moved to the abbey church and a shrine was erected to receive them.[6]

By the beginning of the eighteenth century, barrows were recognized as the burial places of the ancient inhabitants of Britain. But few had been dug into for the purposes of gleaning information as to their origins, and the derivation and the period of the monuments remained vague and shadowy and their age but a guess.[7] Barrow-digging now became a recreational field sport for the rich and privileged and it culminated in barrow-opening on a large scale. The outcome was devastating. The desire for decorative relics led to the wholesale plunder of the graves. With a few notable exceptions, the methods used were quite appalling: the workmen recklessly destroyed any surviving burial remains, including pottery, and few, if any, made accurate records. As a consequence, much of the valuable archaeological information was lost to posterity for ever. What was most horrifying, however, was the speed at which they worked – one individual is reported to have dug over thirty barrows in a day, and nine in the space of two hours![8]

An intriguing account of one enterprise still exists. Over

150 years old, and remarkably well preserved considering its age, the genuine article can be viewed in the County Archives, Canterbury, in Kent. Having contacted the department responsible, Mrs Parkinson, Head of Archives, kindly forwarded me a copy. I sat down and began to examine the content. My worst fears were confirmed.

During the spring of 1844 the first archaeological conference on record was held in Britain. It was called the Canterbury Conference, and the document shows that a considerable number of different activities were on offer to amuse the paying guests, from do-it-yourself brain surgery to how to pickle human remains. There was even an unwrapping of an Egyptian mummy! However, the unquestionable highlight of the day was the official opening of a Bronze Age barrow mound on Breach Downs, Kent. Some 200 invited guests, including scholars and local gentry, flocked to the Downs in a procession of private carriages and hired vehicles to witness the uncovering. Upon their arrival, the labourers had already lowered the mound to within ½ metre of the presumed burials, and now, the archive states, 'his lordship dressed in an exploring costume superintended the uncovering of the skeletons'.[9]

It is clear from the report that no attempt had been made to protect the burial or its remains. No archaeological record was taken of the mound's contents or where they appeared and it would appear that 'the operation was constantly interrupted by drenching downpours, necessitating the frequent use of umbrellas'.[10] Unbelievably, a large number of the eager spectators had to take shelter from the rain in the burial pit itself! The document goes on to relate how 'the fair sex were well represented amongst the gathering', the local press noting that the ladies 'crowded around the tumuli and almost passionately expressed their gratification as beads, and the wire upon which they were strung, or amulets or armlets were handed to them for inspection'.[11]

It has been suggested more than once that barrow-diggers evinced a morbid delight in skeletons, graves and mortality that amounted to a gloating over the paraphernalia of the dead. In truth, they were just glorified treasure-seekers. The main concern was to adorn their display cases and mantelpieces with ancient pots, flints and trinkets. They had little feeling for the historical importance of the sites they so wantonly ransacked. Despite the advent of serious scholarship, it was a phenomenon that continued well into the nineteenth century. It is sad to think, therefore, that these minor field monuments, so vital to the study of Britain's prehistoric past, have suffered from such wholesale destruction. In the process, I believe that vital evidence in my search for Scota was destroyed. Ploughing and the increasing devastation of the landscape by modern farming methods, are not helping archaeology's cause either. It is a melancholy fact that of the great barrow cemeteries clustering around Stonehenge, only one remains relatively undamaged by agricultural operations.[12] I was now caught in somewhat of a dilemma. With what was left of the meagre prehistoric record, would it be at all possible to demonstrate that Scota had landed on the shores of Britain all those millennia ago?

From an archaeological perspective, I needed to examine, in great detail, every aspect of the material culture, including the burial remains and residence of race, language, trading links etc. There had to be ways of establishing whether there was a connection between the prehistoric peoples of Britain and their Egyptian counterparts. I knew from the beginning that I was going to experience immense difficulties. In the course of studying ancient Egypt, I was fortunate to have at my disposal a plethora of textual and historical information. In addition, there was an endless supply of real-life characters to examine, a numerous assortment of people whose achievements were either carved on temple walls or inscribed on papyrus parchment. In prehistoric Britain there were no such records. We have no knowledge of any prehistoric individuals. Before I could begin my investigation, there were two fundamental issues that needed answering. First, was there any exchange between Britain, its European counterparts and the countries of the eastern Mediterranean during prehistory? And secondly, was there any evidence of prehistoric invasions into British territory? Such questions were crucial in the pursuit of Scota. It was time for me to explore the hidden truth behind prehistoric Britain.

At the end of the last Ice Age, around 12,000 years ago, the climate of northern Europe gradually became warmer. Bare tundra was replaced by birch forests, which were subsequently replaced by pine woods. After dominating the natural world for centuries, the pines eventually gave way to a mixture of deciduous woodlands of oak, lime and hazel. Archaeologists have learnt about these past environments from the remains of pollen grains trapped in peat layers or in ancient buried soils. Before long, human communities began to move north, following the animals they hunted and gathering edible plants and fruits. The landmasses that we refer to as Britain and Ireland today were not islands then, but were linked to the rest of Europe by wide, low plains (now the Irish Sea, the Channel and the North Sea). As the glaciers melted and retreated, so the sea rose, covering these plains and isolating the communities on the islands. Ireland, in fact, remained connected to Britain by a land-bridge which did not truly disappear until 5000 BC.[13]

From as early as 10,000 BC, prehistoric people had started to reach Britain. For the most part they were

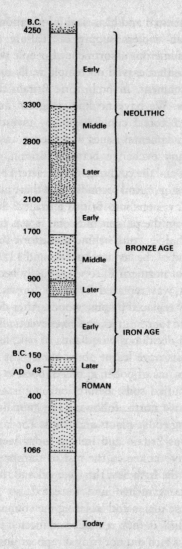

Timeline of British Prehistory

scattered bands of roving hunters living on game, fish and
wild plants. This period is referred to by archaeologists as
the Mesolithic, or Middle Stone Age. Six thousand years
ago woodland extended throughout the British Isles. There
were small patches of grassland on dry and infertile soils but
otherwise extensive forests covered these islands. All over
Britain small communities seem to have exploited two
principal ecological zones: the lightly wooded coasts and the
highland areas of open woodland where large mammals
browsed the forest edge. They grew no crops and had no
domesticated animals apart from dogs, a useful hunting aid
where smell rather than sight was the key sense in dense
forest. For tools and weapons they used flint, bone and
antler, and for shelter they either used caves, built huts or
windbreaks from brushwood or even constructed a form of
skin tent from animal hide. The landscape would have
looked very different from that of today, with broad tracts
of dense woodland and hardly any open grassland. Consequently, it would have been able to sustain only a small
population.[14]

Signs of a major change in the nature of these hunting
and gathering societies came around 4000 BC when groups
who practised an early form of farming inhabited Britain.
This period is called the Neolithic or New Stone Age. The
existence of these groups was not fully appreciated until the
spring of 1970, when Raymond Sweet, an employee of the
Eclipse Peat Works in Somerset, discovered a plank of wood
buried deep in the peat of the Somerset Levels. The plank
was subsequently sent to Dr John Coles of Cambridge
University who, after conducting rigorous scientific
analysis, concluded that it formed part of a prehistoric
trackway.[15] The precise dating of the trackway was
achieved by dendrochronology (tree-ring dating) and it has
since been established that the trees incorporated in the

trackway were felled in the winter of 3807–3806 BC.

To construct a trackway as complex as the one unearthed in the Somerset Levels required complex tools, and it is thought that farming equipment was most probably used. In fact, after further excavation, Coles discovered that the wood had been cut with a stone axe far more advanced than any other stone tool that had been previously unearthed in Britain. Returning to the site of the original timber find, he also uncovered a precious green jadeite axe by the side of the trackway, together with a pot filled with hazelnuts.[16] We know that the hunter-gatherers of Britain did not have the knowledge to make pottery, and the stone tools used to construct the trackway were not like those of the previous Mesolithic period. In archaeology, the appearance of pottery is usually associated with the appearance of farming, so who were the builders of the trackway, and where did they come from?

Farming seems to have had its origins in the Near East, where the wild ancestors of the early domesticated animals and cultivated plants are to be found. Once the knowledge of farming had spread to south-western Europe, it rapidly expanded northwards and westwards along the major river valleys that dissect the Continent. Farming in Britain, however, did not just happen overnight and its spread from Europe was slow. So far, two routes have been identified by which the techniques first arrived. One was by land along the Danube River valley in central and north-western Europe, and the other was by sea, across the Mediterranean to Spain and France and then to the Straits of Dover. With farming also came a series of assorted cultural traits, including pottery, polished stone axes, elaborate houses and enclosures.[17]

Unlike the hunter-gatherers, the Neolithic people cultivated primitive cereals and kept domesticated animals such as sheep, goats and cattle, which they had brought with them. The wild ox and the wild pig were the only indigenous species of animal in Britain when they arrived. They established their farms throughout both Britain and Ireland, although as their settlements are difficult to find, the remains of their burial mounds and ritual enclosures are all that have survived. They lived by herding their animals, growing grain and exchanging commodities, mainly raw materials.

Their farms were located in small, irregular plots that were probably sown with a crop year after year until the fertility of the soil was exhausted. Then they would set about clearing new plots from the wood and the scrub. When they arrived in Britain, they found an island which was thickly forested, and where good pasture and agricultural land needed to be created before it could be used. Clearing the land not only exposed fertile brown forest soils for cultivation but also created open grazing areas for the domestic livestock. From ancient plant remains preserved in the soil, we can see that the new settlers began work immediately, clearing away the forest with fire or flint axes.[18] Thus woodland clearance became a principal feature of Neolithic society, although it seems to have been much more extensive in certain areas, for example in the southern English river valleys, than in others, such as parts of East Anglia.[19] Open grassland and thickets of scrub soon replaced the thick forests of the Mesolithic.

Neolithic tools and hunting weapons were mainly of flint, which was obtained from the surface outcrops or river beds, or by digging shafts into the chalk. Axes were especially important in the clearing of woodland and the shaping of timber for houses. As a result, a booming axe trade soon began to flourish, with materials beginning to appear throughout Britain from Ireland, Cumbria, North

Wales and Cornwall.[20] Animal hide was now being used for clothing and there is even evidence to suggest that cloth may have been worn. Small implements were still made of bone and deer antler, and the baggy round-bottomed pots look like imitations in clay of the older leather vessels.

The early farmers probably increased in numbers fairly rapidly. Unlike the native hunters, who had to live from mouth to hand, the Neolithic farmers could build up a store of food, as surplus, in the form of grain and meat on the hoof. By the late Neolithic, from about 3000 BC, much of the original forest of Britain had disappeared through clearance, and the landscape began to appear more open. The population had grown to such an extent that labour could now be spared for communal works, and so the Neolithic period is often characterized less by houses and fields and more by temples and tombs. Although the term can lead to some confusion, at times this period is also referred to as the Megalithic era, deriving from two Greek words, *mega* and *lithos*, meaning 'large stone'.[21] The description is well deserved, for Neolithic structures are often made with large and heavy stones; for instance, the capstone of a tomb in Browneshill, County Carlow, Ireland, is reputed to weigh over 100 tonnes![22]

Down the years, these megaliths have been called by many names – druids' altars, dolmens, cromlechs, giants' graves etc.[23] Known generically as chambered tombs, they span the entire British Isles, including the far-off Orkney Islands, and come in a variety of shapes and sizes. Some scholars have argued that the monuments of the Neolithic dead were not just simple burial vaults but that they also had a significant ritual purpose.[24] From the orientation of their tombs, we can see that these farmers had a basic appreciation of the cycles of the sun and the moon. By the Middle Neolithic, they were building monuments to the dead that incorporated a growing concern with the movement of the celestial spheres. One of the best-known examples of Neolithic workmanship is the burial vault of Newgrange in Ireland, which, after intensive study, has been shown to align with certain calendrical dates. It was discovered that the chambered tomb had been deliberately orientated so that on midwinter's day, the rays of the rising sun would shine through a special aperture to illuminate the inner passage and chamber.[25]

The construction of great communal monuments must have brought together large groups of people. The most famous of these is Stonehenge in Wiltshire. There is a popular misconception that Stonehenge was built by the druids. In fact, their association with this great monument is a historical accident. In the eighteenth century, the British antiquarian, William Stukeley, became conscious that Stonehenge was built before the Roman period, but he did not appreciate just how long before. He wrongly assumed that since Stonehenge and the druids were pre-Roman, they must have been contemporary.

Neolithic constructions included elongated enclosures known as cursus monuments, then later stone circles and finally henges – rough circular earthworks with a bank surrounding an inner ditch and broken by one or more entrances. Henges varied regionally in age and size, but the effect was of a great wall so high that no outsider could see into the enclosure. It has been calculated that four workers, dividing their time between digging and carrying, could extract and shift approximately 4 tonnes of earth daily. Considering that the average henge required some 50 tonnes to be removed from each ditch segment, a gang could have completed its section in a fortnight. At Stonehenge it has been estimated that with fifty separate working parties, the monument could have been completed in a month.[26]

For one reason or another, from about 2000 BC onwards the great communal monuments of the Neolithic began to be abandoned or altered. Some were even commandeered to build burial mounds for single individuals. This was the dawning of a new age, the Bronze Age, and the old religious hierarchies of the Neolithic were eased out of power by a new secular aristocracy which paid greater attention to individual status than to the worship of their ancestors.[27] A marked transformation in the landscape followed, with settlements that could now be deemed as permanent. A system of territorial division was implemented, and the countryside was controlled to a much greater degree. Linear boundaries became a major feature throughout Britain.[28] The period also witnessed the first appearance of bronze metal, initially for decorative items but increasingly for tools and weapons.[29]

For the first time since the cessation of the Ice Age, there was now a marked change in the British climate. An examination of pollen remains has shown that the climate appears to have been a lot warmer and drier during the Bronze Age than it is today. Long, hot summers, lasting for anything up to six months at a time, were not uncommon.[30] The environmental conditions are also reflected in the drying up of bogs and the spread of settlements into what would now be regarded as inhospitable upland areas such as Dartmoor in Devon, and the Welsh mountains.[31] Similarly, evidence from the Somerset Levels indicates an absence of flooding or peat growth throughout the Bronze Age. There was no need for man to construct trackways to cross the bog surface to higher ground.[32]

With such excellent climatic conditions, a new pastoral economy rapidly developed together with a governing culture. A new and influential group of immigrants suddenly appeared and, before long, began to make their presence felt. From the information available, it would appear that there were three separate invasions stretching from around 2000 BC to the final onslaught in approximately 1300 BC.[33] They are often referred to as the Beaker culture, after the characteristic pottery drinking vessels found in their burial sites. Whatever skills or knowledge they brought with them, both they and the new type of pottery which they introduced quickly gained acceptance amongst the native communities. Where the Beaker folk originated from is a complex issue and archaeologists are still no nearer to establishing who these people actually were. Whole books have been written about the Beaker phenomenon, yet still little has been resolved. The distribution of their artefacts has, so far, been identified as spreading from the shores of North Africa to Norway in the north, Britain to the west and to the Danube in the east.[34] Whether Scota and her party were amongst these invaders is a matter of conjecture. However, evidence uncovered in Wessex suggests a possible Egyptian presence.

Although knowledge of metallurgy had reached the British Isles relatively late compared to other parts of Europe, around 2500 BC, once established, the new metal smiths pursued their craft with vigour.[35] The availability of copper deposits, principally in south-west Ireland, but also in western Scotland, North Wales, Devon and Cornwall, was a tremendous advantage and made the new industries that sprang up virtually self-sufficient. A knowledge of bronze, made by alloying copper from the west of Ireland and tin from Cornwall, was swiftly gained and, through its control, led to the rise of a fairly large population dominated by a few ruling families centred on Wessex, southern England.[36]

The ancient land of Wessex consists of the three modern counties of Wiltshire, Hampshire and Berkshire. The emergence here of a so-called Wessex elite demonstrated that the resident population was now being systematically organized to create and build gigantic monuments. The impetus for this drive is unknown but, from the archaeological remains, it certainly involved distinctions in social class. Whether this elite represented either an aristocracy, a military dictatorship or a priesthood, or perhaps all three, we cannot tell. Nor do we know if their power was born of slavery or whipped up by religious fervour or national pride. What we do know is that in Wessex and a few other localities in southern England, a small number of burials are found with very rich, exceptionally fine objects, and archaeologists attribute them to this elite band.[37]

The most famous Wessex burial was discovered in 1808 by the British archaeologist William Cunnington. Thought to have been the resting-place of a high-ranking leader, the remains were discovered in a small bowl-barrow named Bush Barrow, 1 kilometre south of Stonehenge. After days of careful excavation, Cunnington eventually uncovered the complete skeleton of a well-built man lying in the customary burial position. By his side were found three exquisite daggers, one with a finely decorated hilt held together by hundreds of minute gold nails, a flat axe, a polished stone mace-head, its handle decorated with cylindrical bone mounts, and three sheet-gold plates which once decorated the clothes of the deceased.[38]

The quality of the burial goods cannot be underestimated, and they confirm the importance of the deceased. People have suggested that he might have been the architect of Stonehenge when the large sarsen uprights and lintels were erected. This is really fanciful, however; it just happens that the grave goods uncovered by Cunnington were the most elaborate among the Salisbury Plain burials at the time. In 1818, at Upton Lovell, in Somerset, another fine barrow was discovered, this time containing the remains of a young woman. The grave goods were also of exceptional quality and consisted of the partial remnants of a complex amber necklace with spacer-plates, cylindrical gold beads, a bronze awl or brooch pin, various gold ornaments and an accessory vessel in the shape of a grape cup.[39]

Such finds have led some archaeologists to talk of an age of gold in Wessex. However, the amounts are small; the gold-work that has so far been unearthed could quite easily fit into a shoebox! On the other hand, a large number of Wessex burials do contain what could be called luxury items and in fact show a very close association with their prehistoric neighbours in Europe. Moreover, most of the rich material found in the Wessex graves does not occur naturally in that area.[40] Although there were limited deposits in East Anglia, the amber used in the Upton Lovell necklace most probably came from the Baltic, possibly from Scandinavia.[41] The gold probably came from the mines of Ireland, whilst stone for the battle-axes and mace-heads originated in highland Britain.[42]

Archaeologists had long suspected that there was a relationship between the Mediterranean and Britain during the Bronze Age. Nonetheless, it was not until the discovery of the Wessex graves that such contact could finally be confirmed. Bone mounts similar to those on the shaft of the Bush Barrow mace, and amber space-beads like those from the Upton Lovell burial, are commonly found in both the Aegean and the eastern Mediterranean. Amber discs bound in gold, and dagger pommels decorated with minute gold nails, are also characteristic of continental goods, and have been viewed as links with the rest of Europe.[43] How then did such luxurious items end their days as notable grave goods in British burials? They might have been part of an extensive commercial network, exchanged by traders for northern animal furs. They could also have reached Britain as gifts from seamen. They might have even been carried to Britain by Bronze Age invaders.[44]

The precise dating of the Wessex graves is open to question. Whilst some historians place them at the beginning of the Bronze Age, around 1800 BC, other scholars disagree and argue that there was a flourish of the Wessex culture much later on. After careful examination, the British prehistorian Dr Hugh McKerrell places the deposit of these luxury grave goods as between 1300 and 1100 BC, matching exactly the closest parallels for the faience beads mentioned in Chapter 1. Could this later element then be evidence of an ancient Egyptian presence? Faience beads have also been found in some of the Wessex burials, but unfortunately, with no carbon-14 dates available for the earlier phases of the Wessex culture, it is impossible to compare the initial Bronze Age findings with those from the much later period.[45] Whatever the answer, these men had considerable cross-channel connections. Presumably, they were powerful and influential local leaders, both male and female, who were able to exchange other forms of wealth for imports and so impress their own communities.

Metal now made an important contribution to almost every aspect of life. Consequently, the Bronze Age was a time of considerable experimentation and innovation. New metal types began to be introduced, such as palstaves (axes), rapiers and socket spearheads. Both Britain and Ireland soon became regarded as prolific centres of metallurgy and external relations with continental Europe developed rapidly. Burial hoards in Brittany, northern Germany and the Netherlands have all unearthed large quantities of British rapiers and palstaves. Bronze Age Europe was also now beginning to have an increasing effect on the material culture of Britain. For instance, short swords, called dirks, have been uncovered in British barrows and are clearly based on types found in Europe. British warriors also began to display a comprehensive array of long spears with finely pointed heads and decorated swords, both copying central European styles.[46]

If relations between Britain and the Continent were growing and, as the material evidence illustrates, commodities from Europe were now appearing in British graves and vice versa, how did these goods arrive here in the first place? Contact had to involve some kind of sea-crossing. With the demand for British metals escalating, Bronze Age man in Britain would not only have to gain the technical ability to produce seagoing craft; he needed to make them. The same problem would have faced the Bronze Age people of the Continent. But there is an apparent lack of prehistoric shipwrecks around the British coastline. The oldest remains so far are those unearthed at North Ferriby, Yorkshire. With an apparent flurry of activity around British waters, one would expect to find at least some additional evidence of cross-channel exchange, especially in the waters surrounding the southern shores, since commercial networks appear to have been strongest throughout these regions. Why is there no evidence of any of these prehistoric mariners coming to grief?

A study of the waters on which these prehistoric vessels sailed does provide some answers. Even though the English Channel at its most narrow end is only 40–50 kilometres wide, crossing it was fraught with difficulties. It is no calm stretch of water, by any means, and is often scoured by strong tidal streams. In addition, ships have to contend with varying weather systems, each blowing its own series of gales, depending on the direction in which the boat is sailing. The land itself was also a hazard. For those ships sailing from France or Spain, once in the English Channel the west-facing coasts of the Lizard, Start Point and the Isle of Wight were all key obstacles.[47] This implies that prehistoric man must have learned to build fairly sturdy craft before he could even attempt to make a crossing. But it does not explain the lack of physical evidence. I decided to contact Gillian Hutchinson at the National Maritime Museum in Greenwich. Perhaps she could solve the riddle for me.

As far as she was concerned, the apparent lack of wreck sites can be explained principally by considering the sea floor in the areas concerned. It would appear that most of the Channel bed is surfaced with a varying amount of loose sand and silts. This is especially true of the Narrow Seas, the warmest point of the Channel, where most of the voyaging almost certainly happened. A sunken boat and its cargo might be well preserved in these sediments, she went on to explain, but it would leave no visible clue to its presence. Moreover, suspended particles cloud the water, reducing visibility to a few metres. Not many divers swim in such areas for pleasure and those who do see only a small part of the seabed.[48] Even with the advent of advanced scientific techniques, few prehistoric sites have therefore been found in the English Channel to date.

Nonetheless, she did inform me of two Bronze Age wrecks found off the southern coast of England during the 1970s. Both date to about 1200 BC, and the first was discovered just below the famous white cliffs, at Langdon Bay, just east of Dover harbour. In August 1974, members of Dover Sub-Aqua Club began to report the finding of various bronze objects. Spotted in routine dives by members Mike Hadlow and Simon Stevens, the bronzes were resting in the chalk gullies at a depth of around 8–12 metres. By the end of 1975, following many more dives, a total of ninety-five bronzes had been uncovered, of varying shapes and sizes. Uncertain what they had uncovered, the dive team consulted the curator of Dover Museum, and the finds were subsequently identified as an assortment of tools, rapier blades, spearheads, pins, a knife blade and fragments of bracelets, seemingly derived from Bronze Age France. Over the next three years members of Dover SAC recovered another ninety bronzes. Nothing comparable was known from land sites, and after careful examination, in 1979 the British Museum, the National Maritime Museum and the British Sub-Aqua Club sponsored a full season of excavation work. Work at the site has continued since then and the total number of recoverable items amounts to a staggering 363.[49]

The centre of the site lies about 500 metres from the base of Langdon Cliff, and most of the finds discovered so far lie within a radius of 50 metres. This close concentration is one of the principal arguments for believing that the finds have always lain in this area, and have not been swept there from either a cliff-fall or another undersea location. The bronzes were exceptionally worn as a result of exposure on the seabed for some time, and a closer examination reveals their European origin. For instance, the spearheads had holes for fixing the shafts by means of pegs, whereas British spears were fastened to their shafts by means of loops. Due to the large amount of metal uncovered, archaeologists surmise that it had been assembled from a wide area on the Continent and was being brought to Britain for melting down.[50]

Of the ship itself, nothing has been found so far; the chances of finding such remains, even within the deeper stable clays of the site, must be remote, although the possibility cannot be dismissed. We can only guess what goods they would have been exchanged for. One thing is certain: in the amount discovered, it far exceeds even the largest European hoard that has ever been found.

In July 1977, the remains from yet another Bronze Age wreck turned up, once more in the English Channel but this time on a gentle shelving beach called Moor Sand near Salcombe in South Devon. The hoard's finder was a local diving instructor, by the name of Philip Baker, who at the time was escorting a class of the Youth Hostel Association on what turned out to be an unforgettable dive. Whilst guiding the inexperienced divers through the calm waters of the bay, in shallow water between two large rocks Baker suddenly glimpsed what looked to be a fine bronze sword blade buried in the seabed. After scanning the area in greater detail, one of the novice divers found another heavily eroded sword lying on the seabed 5–6 metres below the initial find. Being an avid collector of naval swords, Baker immediately recognized that the bronze weapons were unusual and probably quite old. On his return home after the summer season, he approached the local museum to make further enquiries. He learned that it was of French origin and dated to the middle Bronze Age.[51]

The possibility that these Bronze Age weapons had come from a shipwreck more than 3000 years old was something of national interest. Baker reported the find immediately to the proper authorities, and the site was officially designated under the Protection of Wrecks Act. Approved by Parliament in 1973, this Act allows the designation of a restricted area not only around the seabed site of a vessel, but also of the wreck's contents or former contents. It applies only in UK waters, excluding the Isle of Man and the Channel Islands, and states: 'It is a criminal offence for unauthorized personnel to tamper with, damage or remove any part of a wreck or its contents. It is also an offence to carry out diving or salvage operations; and to deposit anything which would obliterate or obstruct access to the site.' Archaeological activity can only be taken under licence.[52]

During the summer of 1979 the British Museum, the British Academy and the National Maritime Museum sponsored a further investigation of the Moor Sand site. This included a systematic search and survey of the entire area. Over a four-week period, a team of thirteen divers, equipped with the latest metal-detecting equipment, failed to find any evidence of a shipwreck. However, by the end of the season a total of seven bronzes, including two palstaves and four eroded blades, had been uncovered. The question was how the bronzes came to be in the sea.[53]

It is difficult to accept that the remarkably well-preserved sword first found by Philip Baker had lain for so long where he initially saw it, exposed on a bed of shingle at a depth of only 6 metres. The same can be said for the palstave found during the 1978 season, which was buried in loose shingle. On the other hand, the second palstave and the eroded blades did have the appearance of having been exposed to marine abrasion and corrosion for some time. Indeed, one of the blades was found pinned under a boulder and cemented to the surrounding gravel.[54] The biggest argument for a shipwreck was that the swords appeared not to have been of British manufacture. The first find, the sword discovered by Philip Baker, was made from a low tin alloy and had shallow grooves on the shoulder. These are found on the Continent, predominantly in southern Germany to the west of the River Seine. Most probably the finds were part of a cargo that was being brought to Britain via the Dover Straits.

At the very least these two underwater sites clearly illustrate that cross-Channel exchanges did take place and that objects drawn from different areas of the Continent were assembled for such ventures. But how does this relate to my search for Scota? We know that prehistoric 'invasions' of the British Isles were not uncommon. With the advent of farming, there can be no doubt that domesticated animals and plants had been carried by boat from the continent of Europe. From the Bronze Age onwards, the burial evidence also indicates, in the shape of Beaker pottery, that another group of people colonized Britain. There are a number of options. Groups of pioneers could have set off from the Continent in one-off, small-scale migrations or people might have arrived after a long-term mixture of contacts. But however they happened, there can be no doubt that prehistoric incursions into Britain by overseas travellers were, in fact, quite commonplace.

Moreover, throughout the Bronze Age period, the archaeological material shows that contacts between Britain and the Continent were widespread, with luxury goods from Europe being unearthed in British barrow graves and vice versa. Wessex graves demonstrate possible contact with the Aegean, in particular with the Mycenean Empire, and an amber bead with gold decoration in the unique Wessex style has been found in Switzerland. Adding together the evidence from both Langdon Bay and Moor Sands, there can be no denying that prehistoric seafaring around the British coastline was not in the least unusual. Bronze Age Europe was a complex web of networks and not a continent of isolated communities. With the evidence accumulated so far, I had no doubts that Scota and her party would not have encountered any problems in making the sea voyage from the northern tip of the Spanish coast to the British mainland. To the ancient British people, their arrival would have been something completely out of the ordinary. Even though there were many different incursions into Britain during prehistory, Scota and her followers must have looked so out of place that as soon as written records came into use, an account would have been kept of her landing.

CHAPTER ELEVEN

—◆◆◆—

THE DNA ENIGMA

Human beings have buried their dead for the last 50,000 years or more. Their associated monuments and grave goods have been the study of archaeologists for several centuries. However, recent advances in medicine and science now allow the human remains themselves to be investigated, revealing details about the people and communities to which they once belonged. Until now, the focus of my study had been solely on the material remains, such as metallurgy, pottery and so on, together with any significant historical data. The combination of the two had clearly shown that migrations did take place during the British Bronze Age. Regrettably, what it could not definitely confirm was whether some of these people were ancient Egyptians or not. For the time being, therefore, archaeology had served its purpose. I decided to turn my attention to another, related discipline, anthropology. Was there any anthropological evidence that would corroborate the fact that ancient Egyptians had settled in Britain?

Unlike archaeology, which is devoted to the analysis of

artefacts, anthropology is defined as the study of humanity. It is the study of past and present cultures, their language, evolution and biological variation. It attempts to scrutinize the entire human condition over time. Anthropologists undertake scientific comparative studies. For instance, they apply related disciplines such as anatomy and pathology to determine how peoples of the world are similar and how they are different. They pose such questions as: who were the first inhabitants of the world and how did they live? It is a very complicated and broad field – so broad, in fact, that it can be broken down into two related disciplines: physical anthropology, which is the study of human biological or physical characteristics and how they evolved, and cultural anthropology, the analysis of human culture and society.

Modern methods of forensic anthropology can reveal the age of a skeleton as well as the sex. People's skeletons can also give a fascinating insight into their social life. Unfortunately, with the study of human remains in Britain there is an inherent and obvious difficulty. We have already seen how, more often than not, the fleshy parts of our British prehistoric ancestors do not survive. The hair, eyes and skin, on which so much ethnic classification is based, and by which we so easily describe ethnic types, have decayed over time.[1] Besides, high acid levels in the soil, a common feature in Britain, rapidly destroy any surviving human remnants. It is not uncommon for whole skeletons to be ruined in such a manner. Moreover, after cremation became popular in Britain, during the later stages of the Bronze Age, nothing was left at all to assist in the identification of cultural and physical stereotypes.[2]

Despite these difficulties, the odd bone or tooth retrieved by the archaeologist can offer some clues to the identity of the individual. It can also illustrate evidence of injury and infection, and sometimes signs of a violent end. The explicit identification of race, however, is slightly more complex. During the formative years of anthropology, the establishment of ethnic identity was determined primarily by examining the features of the skull and face. There are two related disciplines. The first is called anthropometry and is defined as the study of human body measurements for use in classification and comparison.[3] During the nineteenth and twentieth centuries, anthropometry was regarded as a kind of pseudoscience used mainly to classify potential criminals by their facial characteristics. In 1895 the French scientist Cesare Lombroso, in his book *Criminal Anthropology*, claimed that murderers have prominent jaws and pickpockets have long hands and scanty beards![4]

But perhaps the most infamous use of anthropometry was by the Nazis, during the Second World War. Their Bureau for Enlightenment on Population Policy and Racial Welfare recommended the classification of Aryans and non-Aryans on the basis of the measurement of skulls. German scientists discovered that the head shape has a strong heritability factor in the measurements of breadth, facial and nose heights, jaw breadth and head circumference.[5] Accordingly, they concluded that all these components had to be genetically based. This related discipline is usually referred to as craniometry, or sometimes craniology, and centres on pinpointing variation, for example, in the orbit shape of the skull, the configuration of the nasal root or the nasal passage size.[6] In the early nineteenth century, the British used craniometry to justify their policies towards the Irish and black Africans, whom the British considered to be inferior races.[7]

Let us return to Scota for one moment. Attempting to prove a link between skeletal remains uncovered here in Britain and their ancient Egyptian counterparts would not be an easy task. When it comes to the examination of

Egyptian mummies, the authorities permit such investigation only under exceptional circumstances. However, by
applying the principles of craniology, it would surely be
possible to establish a connection between two independent
skeletons. The process is non-invasive and would do no
permanent harm to the remains. The only problem is
whether one could then link these two bodies to the same
genetic family. Curiously enough, an account of just such an
analysis exists. Resembling the plot of an Indiana Jones
adventure, the application of craniology was put into
operation on two members of the Amarna royal family to
establish a hereditary link.

In 1907, a wealthy American lawyer and amateur
Egyptologist, Theodore Davies, was leading an expedition
into Egypt's Valley of the Kings, just across the Nile from
the ancient capital of Thebes. The members of his working
party included his cousin, Emma Andrews, who acted as
Davies's personal assistant, painter Joseph Lindon Smith,
who was there to document any new discoveries, and
professional Egyptologist Edward Ayrton. On 11 January,
at the northern end of the valley, Ayrton busied himself with
organizing a team of local workers. Their aim was to clear
away a mass a rubble around the entrance to the tomb of
Rameses IX when, some 9 metres to the south, the workers
unexpectedly discovered a deep-filled trench that had been
cut into the hillside. Ayrton initially thought he had
uncovered part of Rameses's tomb, but when they began to
unearth pieces of broken pottery predating him it quickly
became apparent that the trench must have been part of a
much older excavation – an undiscovered tomb.

Working through the night, after hours of continuous
digging, the gang finally revealed a flight of ancient carved
steps and exposed the stone lintel of the outer entrance to a
buried tomb. It took a whole week to remove the rubble that

had accumulated in the accompanying passageway. At last, after some twenty-one steps were uncovered, leading deep into the cliff, the workmen came to a solid barrier, an intact limestone wall sealing an entrance some 2½ metres high. Ayrton immediately realized the implications of what he had found – an undiscovered tomb. However, there was something quite odd. Usually the entrances to such tombs were embossed with the royal seal of the occupant, but here there was no such seal, just a plain, bare wall concealing the entrance.

An account of the discovery of Tomb 55, as it was later designated, survives in Emma Andrews's diary, now in the Metropolitan Museum in New York, and today it continues to be one of the most controversial discoveries ever made in Egypt. Breaking through the sealed entrance, Davies and Ayrton eventually discovered a single-chambered tomb containing an assortment of objects.[8] They included a coffined mummy with the name-ring or cartouche intentionally damaged, a gilded wooden shrine which apparently belonged to the mother of Akhenaten, Queen Tiye, four canopic jars (for the embalmed organs) and a set of so-called 'magic bricks' which appeared to belong to Akhenaten himself.[9] These were four mud-bricks which were often placed on the four sides of the tomb during the New Kingdom in order to protect the deceased from evil. With the name of the tomb owner excised from the coffin, it was almost impossible for Davies or Ayrton positively to identify him or her. One thing was certain, though: this was not just any old royal burial – this was an Amarna burial.

After nearly 100 years, no consensus has yet been reached on the identity of the occupant. The mummified remains were found to be in a pitiful state. In 1907 Davies concluded that the mysterious mummy was clearly of a woman and published his findings in *The Tomb of Queen*

Tiyi.[10] Whilst unwrapping the ancient bandages, the first thing to be observed was the position of the arms. The mummy had been embalmed in the pose normally associated with a queen, with one arm folded across the chest and the other by the side, instead of both arms folded across the chest like a king. However, in July 1907, the initial hypothesis was proved to be incorrect when the mummy was sent for analysis to Sir Grafton Elliot Smith, Professor of Anatomy at the Cairo School of Medicine. He found, to everybody else's surprise, that what actually lay before him were the remains of a young man who, it would seem, had died in his early twenties.[11] Davies was outraged and immediately assumed foul play. To him the remains had to have been switched *en route* to Cairo.

So who was the mysterious mummy in Tomb 55? A shadowy figure does emerge just prior to the reign of Tutankhamun. As we have seen, his or her name was Smenkhare, meaning 'whom the spirit of the god Ra had anointed',[12] and the name figures prominently on a number of scarab stones and furniture from Amarna. From a scene in the tomb of Meryre, the Overseer of Akhenaten's harem at Amarna, Smenkhare is quite clearly shown as a reigning pharaoh of Egypt, although the reign does not appear to have lasted very long, perhaps three years at the very most. A wine jar docket discovered at Amarna, and dated to the first years of Tutankhamun's reign, is inscribed with the prophetic words, 'wine from the estate of Smenkhare, deceased'.[13]

The advent of modern forensic techniques has enabled scholars to establish an unlikely relationship between the Tomb 55 mummy and that of Tutankhamun, the last of the Amarna royal bloodline. In 1963, a leading anatomist, R.G. Harrison of the University of Liverpool, believed that applying these disciplines of craniometry and palaeopathology to the study of the remains of Egyptian mummies would shed new light on old questions. German physician Dr R.W. Schufeldt first used the term 'palaeopathology' in 1892.[14] The name is derived from two Greek words meaning 'ancient' and 'suffering', and though it was initially centred on the study of diseases or pathological conditions, today the focus of the discipline has changed dramatically, to include X-ray analysis, DNA cloning and so on.

With the assistance of a grant from the Wenner-Gren Foundation for Anthropological Research, Harrison travelled to Cairo in December 1963 to reassess the mummy in Tomb 55. The remains were found to consist of little more than a skeleton, but as a result of extensive anatomical and anthropometric investigation, which included taking precise measurements of the skull, plus a series of X-rays, it was found that the remains bore a very close resemblance to those of Tutankhamun. In fact, the measurements of the skull of the remains of Tomb 55 and the head of Tutankhamun were identical. It was thought advisable to re-examine the remains of Tutankhamun in order to assess the degree of conformity. Consequently, Harrison ended his report by saying, 'A reappraisal of the anatomical and radiological features of Tutankhamun is urgently necessary, and it is to be hoped that such an investigation may be made possible in the not-too-distant future.'[15]

In 1969 he got his chance, but the re-examination of Tutankhamun proved to be a much more difficult task, as he is the only pharaoh of Egypt whose remains still lie *in situ*, within his tomb, in the Valley of the Kings at Thebes. Any re-examination would therefore involve reopening the sarcophagus, a very complicated affair. Another problem was that the excellent radiological unit at Cairo, some 600 kilometres away, was the only one in the whole of Egypt which had the necessary equipment for the job. It would therefore be necessary to have the use of portable radio-graphic equipment to X-ray the remains within the tomb, since permission to remove them would be unlikely.

Through the immense efforts of Professor Ali Absalla of the Department of Anatomy at the University of Cairo, in March 1968 written permission was received from the Director-General of the Antiquities Service in Cairo. With portable X-ray apparatus, the expedition eventually took place at the end of December 1968. It was not an easy task. After all, the crowding of people and equipment into the confines of Tutankhamun's small tomb would present difficulties in opening the sarcophagus and examining its contents. Nevertheless, after much manoeuvring, the coffin lid was eventually opened to reveal the mummified body of the boy-king.[16]

When the modern bandages wrapped around the remains of Tutankhamun were removed, it was immediately obvious that the mummy was not in a very good condition and certainly not in one piece. The head and neck had been separated from the remainder of the body, and the limbs, in addition to being detached from the body, were broken in many places. For example, the right arm had been broken at the elbow, the upper arm being separated from the forearm and the hand, which lay across the torso so that the hand lay on the lower part of the abdomen. The left arm was also broken, at the elbow and at the wrist, the lower ends of the radius and the ulna (the bones of the forearm) being broken off. The left leg was broken at the knee and so on. After an initial assessment, Harrison proceeded with the analysis and X-raying of the skeletal remains.[17]

After many weeks of painstaking work, the initial find-ings were released to the public. Remarkably, Harrison's first impressions were confirmed. There was indeed close conformity of the shape of the skull of Tutankhamun with that of the mummy in Tomb 55. The diameters of the skulls were identical: in fact, on placing an X-ray of one skull on that of the other, it was virtually impossible to distinguish between the two. The cephalic index also demonstrated that the type of skull, in this particular instance brachycephalic (short-headed), was the same in each case. What is more, after blood and tissue analysis, it was proved beyond doubt that both mummies possessed identical blood groups, A2 MN. Taken in conjunction with other features, such as the resemblance in facial features, this strongly suggested a close kinship between the two bodies.[18] Even so, Egyptology today is still divided upon the gender of the mummy found in Tomb 55.

This use of skull measurements and blood group testing to investigate the affinity between two members of a human population living over 3000 years ago is perhaps unique. It is also a remarkable coincidence that the two specimens chosen for such groundbreaking work just happened to be two members of the Amarna set-up. And it provides us with a tantalizing possibility. From our knowledge of the Amarna royal family, we know that Scota was a direct blood relation of Tutankhamun, both having the same father, Akhenaten. From this we can deduce that Scota would also be directly related to the mummy discovered in Tomb 55. Bearing this in mind, could it be possible to conduct the same rigorous tests on the skeletal remains unearthed by Dr O'Riordain at Tara? This would confirm whether he was, in fact, descended from ancient Egyptian stock.

I decided to contact Dr Ian Robson of the Institute of Archaeology of University College, London, for advice. In his opinion, the use of skull analysis is difficult when dealing with earlier prehistoric material and especially if there is just an isolated skull, as is the case with the so-called Tara

Prince. Even if it is possible, the individual may be assigned only to the broadest category of ethnic stock – for instance, whether he was of Mediterranean origin or African etc. It would be more advisable, he went on to say, when dealing with excavated skeletal material, to think in terms of the area and the archaeological period concerned as a preliminary to more detailed anthropological analysis.[19]

Taking his recommendations into account, therefore, let us examine the facts. With regard to the area, the archaeological evidence unearthed at Tara and North Ferriby does indicate that the Egyptians could possibly have settled in Britain. In addition, the dated material falls into the timeframe of around 1400–1300 BC, the time at which Scota escaped from Egypt and may have arrived in Britain. Furthermore, confirmation is provided by the Walter Bower manuscript and other historical sources. If forensic tests could be applied to the Tara Prince, and perhaps any other related Bronze Age remains, it would put the question of whether the ancient Egyptians did inhabit the British Isles or not beyond doubt. Regrettably, I knew such tests would never be permitted, especially considering the controversial nature of the subject matter. From my investigations so far, I knew that presenting any claim of an Egyptian presence in prehistoric Britain to my fellow colleagues would invite ridicule. There had to be some other way of linking the skeletal remains. I now had to go in search of further evidence.

In 1956 an article in the *Proceedings of the Prehistoric Society* by Dr Graham Clarke remarked on the variation in skull shape between Neolithic and Bronze Age man during British prehistory. In the Neolithic era he found that there appeared to be a general correspondence to 'long-headed' skulls, whilst during the Bronze Age the skeletal remains show a marked difference. Instead, the shape of the skull became far more robust and 'round-headed'. He concluded that British Bronze Age skulls were almost always brachycephalic.[20] Clarke's work has profound significance for our understanding of possible Egyptian incursion into prehistoric Britain. For as we have seen, only eight years later Harrison illustrated that both members of the Amarna family he examined, Tutankhamun and the Tomb 55 mummy, also had brachycephalic skull shapes.

The evidence accumulated so far did look exceptionally promising. Cranial studies do provide us with some answers. Nevertheless, the study of racial affinities in prehistoric populations, though of tremendous interest and scholarly value, has been neglected over the years. It needs far more study before any definite conclusions can be made. Unfortunately, I could take the matter no further, so I decided to look into other related areas to find methods of achieving similar results.

In 1953 Britain celebrated the coronation of a new queen and the first ascent of Mount Everest by Sir Edmund Hillary. Far less publicity attended another momentous event, the publication in the prestigious scientific journal *Nature* of a short article proposing 'A Structure for Deoxyribose Nucleic Acid'. Building on an earlier but not widely appreciated work that had identified DNA as *the* genetic material, the two young authors, James Watson and Francis Crick, initially proposed the now-famous double helix models of DNA. James Watson was a bright, ambitious American scientist on a visiting fellowship to Cambridge University, whilst Crick was a somewhat dilettante ex-wartime engineer and physicist.[21] They had spent the past few years attempting to identify, with limited success, the three-dimensional structure of DNA by using the immensely difficult process of crystallography (the use of crystal refraction). However, illumination came, so to speak, when they secretly obtained photographs taken by London-based scientist Rosalind Franklin, illustrating the concept of X-ray diffraction. Unbeknown to Franklin, her photographs were provided to the Cambridge pair, who then proceeded to use her own discovery to further their own revelations.[22] Although their methods may have been deemed slightly underhand, their model of DNA opened the way to unanticipated biological discoveries. In the report they concluded: 'It has not escaped our notice that the specific pairing we have immediately postulated immediately suggests a possible copying mechanism for the genetic material.'[23]

Genes, the organizers of inheritance, are composed of DNA, which carries the hereditary instructions needed to build a body and make it work. DNA is found in almost all living cells. Each cell consists of two long chains of the alternating chemicals phosphate and deoxyribose. Each chain is then twisted to form a double helix, joined together by hydrogen bonds. Between each bond are the complementary bases of the chemical units adenine and thymine, cytosine or guanine, each of which projects towards the axis of the helix. Each bonded sequence is unique and as such determines an individual's hereditary characteristics. There are only two places in the cell where DNA is found: nuclear DNA is found in the nucleus of a cell and mitochondria DNA in the mitochondria, which are in the body of the cell. The latter is inherited only from the maternal side and is very useful when the nucleus of the cells may be missing or degraded.[24] New work in genetics means that it is now entirely possible to work out family relationships through the analysis of DNA.

Scientists can now extract tiny amounts of DNA from the bones and the teeth. As a result, recent advances in genetic engineering open up fascinating possibilities for

future work in human evolution and past human relationships. In the summer of 1984, the first attempt to clone
ancient DNA was carried out by a group of scientists based
at the University of California, Berkeley. From the skin of a
quagga, a relative of the zebra which has been extinct for
more than a century, the team of scientists located and then
reproduced the animal's DNA.[25] Cloning ancient DNA had
been impossible before Polymerase Chain Reaction (PCR)
techniques were developed in 1983. The two steps for this
process are as follows. First a DNA sample is extracted from
the subject and the two strands of the double helix are
subsequently split into single strands. Afterwards, the single
strands are immersed in nucleic acid, whose enzymes,
proteins, then produce the missing strand of the double
helix; the amount of DNA is thus doubled. This process can
be repeated indefinitely until enough DNA is produced for
scientific analysis.[26]

Perhaps the most startling discovery in recent genetic
analysis, however, has in fact involved the study of Egyptian
mummies. Incredibly, it is now possible to isolate and clone
DNA taken from 4000-year-old bodies. News of such
revelatory work first appeared in 1985, again in the
scientific journal *Nature*. It reported on the work of a
Swedish scientist named Svate Paabo, who for ten years had
based his research on previous efforts to clone extinct
animals. After examining tissue samples taken from twenty-
three Egyptian mummies, he discovered remote traces of
DNA in the tissues of one infant and two adults.
Unfortunately, the DNA sample in both the adult female
and the adult male mummy had deteriorated too much to be
used in the cloning process. Nonetheless, the cells taken
from skin on the left leg of the infant mummy contained
surprisingly well preserved DNA. After many long hours in
the laboratory, Paabo succeeded in producing a total of

3000 DNA subunits. The only difficulty he encountered was that the DNA molecules were rapidly broken up by the chemical actions involved in the cloning process. Accordingly, there was no question of reconstituting a functioning gene, far less a living body.[27]

Is it feasible that such genetic analysis could be applied to my own investigation? Surprisingly, it would only take thirty days to compare DNA from ancient Egyptian remains with that from prehistoric Britain. But I knew the powers that be would never allow such tests to be done. In 1998 I asked to examine and possibly test some of the mummies that had been uncovered at Tanis, in the Delta region of Egypt, to establish family links. Not only were my endless communications ignored, but a colleague informed me that my requests would be fruitless.[28] During the late 1970s and early 1980s the Manchester Mummy Project at Manchester Museum was granted permission, by the Supreme Council of Antiquities in Egypt, to carry out DNA testing on all Eighteenth-Dynasty mummies to ascertain the complex family relationships. The project, headed by Dr Rosalie David, is at the forefront of ancient Egyptian pathology. It has established the world's first Egyptian mummy tissue bank, supported by a Leverhulme Trust research grant to collect samples of tissue from the collections of Egyptians mummies worldwide except Egypt. Despite this impeccable reputation, at the final moment the Manchester DNA tests were postponed for reasons unknown, and today all mummies in Egypt may only be tested in Egypt.[29]

The application of DNA analysis to prove or disprove the racial heritage of specific skeletal remains is an exceptionally contentious issue. Surely, if the answers to puzzling archaeological questions of the last hundred years could be resolved, DNA testing would be the perfect way to come out of the dark and into the light. Nowhere has this been more of an issue in recent years than in the United States of America. One of the most important archaeological discoveries ever to have been unearthed in North America swiftly turned into a three-year nightmare for all those who were involved.

In July 1996 something very extraordinary began to unfold in the town of Kennewick, Washington. Two young bystanders at a local boat race were wading through the Columbia River when they stumbled upon what looked like a human skull in the muddy bed of the river. They reported the find immediately to the local police. Sergeant Craig Littrell investigated the site and to his surprise he found an almost complete skeleton. Thinking that they had a murder on their hands, the remains were sent to the State Crime Laboratory for forensic examination. The state coroner instantly recognized that the individual had been dead for a very long time indeed. Further examination mystified everybody, so local anthropologist Jim Chatters was called in to help solve the puzzle.[30]

Kennewick Man, as the remains have been called, was about 178 centimetres (5 feet, 10 inches) tall and was estimated to have been between forty and fifty-five years of age. The skull was long and narrow with a projecting nose, receding cheekbones, a high chin and a square mandible. When the back was examined, it was surprisingly not shown to be flattened by the use of cradleboards, a common feature of old American Indian skulls. Cradleboards were long pieces of wood that were attached to the skulls of newly born infants to elongate their skull. Chatters's immediate impression was that the features were, in fact, European in nature. But to his astonishment, after radiocarbon 14 dating, the remains were found to be 9300 years old. It was the oldest known skeleton ever to have been discovered in the United States. Shocked by what he had uncovered, Chatters immediately consulted Professor Catherine Macmillan of Washington University who, after meticulous analysis, agreed that the skeleton was indeed Caucasian.[31]

There was sufficient surviving DNA to test against various populations around the world and to confirm, once and for all, whether the skeleton was indeed of European origin and not Native American as believed. But before any investigation could take place, the remains were seized by the Army Corps of Engineers on the basis that the remains were pre-Colombian and, by law, under the Native American Protection and Repatriation Act, had to be returned to the tribe of its origin. So, without being tested, the remains would simply return to the tribe which, at that time, just happened to live in the area where they were initially discovered. There was an immediate outcry, and the country's top anthropologists and archaeologists joined forces to file a lawsuit against the United States Government preventing them from handing back the skeleton to the Native Americans for burial. As a result, the body has lain in FBI headquarters ever since and the government continues its three-year effort to block DNA testing on it.[32]

DNA tests on Kennewick Man could confirm whether he was indeed European in just ninety days. However, if the government get their way, then he will be handed back to the Indian tribes for secret burial with no crucial scientific testing having been done. Why is this 9000-year-old skeleton causing so much uproar? It is quite simple. If Kennewick Man was indeed proved to be European in origin then this would suggest that the Native Americans' claim to be the 'first peoples of America' would be untrue. Not only would they lose their rights to the title, but they would also lose all the benefits that such a claim has brought them; for example, extensive land rights. Unfortunately, in this instance, the politics of political correctness has so far triumphed over the needs of genuine scientific enquiry.

When the existence of a particular ethnic group is difficult to determine through the archaeological record, the application of DNA testing can help solve the problems of identity. In today's political climate, however, the subject is often too racially sensitive to even contemplate. As I write, news has come through that the United States Government has finally lost its case and DNA tests will be conducted on Kennewick Man. The associated Native American groups are now lodging an appeal against the court ruling. Whether the genuine results from studying Kennewick Man will ever be made public is another matter.

Deep down, I knew that DNA tests would also never be conducted on remains dating to the British Bronze Age. The possible outcome of such tests would be just too controversial. But there are other ways to prove genetic relationships.

In 1628, the first description of the human circulatory system appeared in William Harvey's *De Motu Cordis*. Amongst other things, the publication analysed the possibility of transfusing blood between different individuals. Early experiments had concentrated on the transfusion of such chemicals as beer, water and even dilute acid solutions into animals. A blood transfusion was reported between two dogs in 1665. Over the next few years the transfusion of blood from animals to man was attempted, but following legal problems concerning the death of a transfusion individual in Paris, the practice was banned in both France and Britain and fell into disuse for more than 100 years.[33]

In 1900 Austrian scientist Karl Landsteiner made one of the most important discoveries in the study of human blood. He found that mixing the serum – the liquid part of the blood – taken from a random group of people resulted in the clumping together of the red blood cells. However, repeating the tests on another group of people, he found that the clumping of the cells did not always take place. Why did it happen in some cases but not in others? After meticulous investigation Landsteiner discovered that the red blood cells from some people had a specific chemical on the surface, whilst those of other people did not possess such a chemical. Based on these observations, Landsteiner reported three blood groups, which he named A, B and O, and indicated their potential importance in relation to blood transfusion.[34] Soon afterwards his fellow workers, B. Sturli and N. De Castello, reported the existence of a fourth blood group and named it AB.[35] A new avenue of genetics was about to open and nowadays we classify all human blood groups as either type A, B, AB or O.

In 1901 in *Libyan Notes*, English historians D. Randall-Maciver and A. Wilkin remarked, even before the discovery of blood groups, 'Many of those people now living in the regions of North Africa, especially the Berbers, were remarkably European in appearance and could, if suitably attired, pass for Scotsman or Irishman.'[36] If their assumptions were correct, they confirmed a North African/British connection, one which, on the evidence already presented, I had come to suspect. Maybe what Randall-Maciver and Wilkins should have concluded is that many of the Scots and Irish people bore a remarkable similarity to those people occupying the lands of North Africa!

In 1986 an article appeared in *Genetic and Population Studies in Wales* which first suggested there might be a genetic connection between the population of Wales and North Africa. Written by Irwin Morgan-Watkins, the aim of his investigation was to examine the ABO blood groups of the indigenous Welsh population in an attempt to trace any ancient genetic marker. To achieve his objective it was necessary to go beyond the information normally supplied by blood-donor records and examine the historical links between old Welsh surnames. Morgan-Watkins aimed his analysis, therefore, at all single males and females with Welsh surnames together with those married women who were found to have Welsh maiden names. In addition, the National Blood Transfusion Service grouped every blood sample on both cell identity and serum. The groupings were checked and then rechecked each time a person donated blood. In doing so, the gene frequencies, the expected percentage of groups A, B and O, were subsequently calculated. Having successfully worked out the gene frequency percentage, Morgan-Watkins then devoted his time to studying the history of the tested regions for further clues.[37]

During the last 800 years, in the southern part of Pembrokeshire there has existed a large community of non-Welsh-speaking people. Historians agree that in order to consolidate the Norman conquest of Britain, King Henry I transferred a considerable population of Flemings to south Pembrokeshire in 1108, in the belief that they would form a useful bastion against any Welsh uprising opposed to his rule. Most of them came from the banks of the River Tweed, where they had served a similar purpose against the Scottish. It is possible that this contingent was further reinforced following the implementations of a clause in the Magna Carta that said all Flemings must be expelled from England.[38]

It has also been argued that throughout its early history, this same region was continually subject to Viking incursions. That the Vikings were therefore responsible for the names of islands such as Gateholm and Grassholm Caldey, and of a village called Hasguard, is very probable.[39] The Royal Commission on Ancient and Historical Monuments has also concluded that the old place names of Castle Martin, Rhos and Narberth appeared to be Norse in origin and, as such, they deduced that they were branches of a Norse settlement.[40] Tradition has it that Viking settlements were not prevalent in Wales. The most important narrative source concerning the Vikings in Britain is the *Anglo-Saxon Chronicle*, and it also makes no mention of Wales. The first version was compiled in Wessex in the late ninth century, and in the following three centuries it was continued in various places by several authors. Far from being just lists of kings and battles, it contains detailed entries for some years, poems, summaries and personal comment by the analysts.[41]

Morgan-Watkins's research was about to alter the history books radically, as historians did not believe that the Vikings had actually colonized Wales. By applying the gene frequencies A, B and O, he discovered that in southern Pembrokeshire there was a very high A frequency coupled with a corresponding low O one. He decided to compare his results with those in England. To his amazement, he found that, even though the A frequency did fall as he proceeded north towards the Scottish border, in the southern half of England, particularly in the south-west, where one would expect to find a high A frequency due to its close tribal links with Wales, the opposite appeared to hold true. The A blood frequency, in fact, actually decreased the further south he went. What is more, by examining the blood serum of those people settled in traditional Viking areas, for instance in the city of Chester and its environs, he discovered that each person he tested also had a very high A frequency – identical to the results in Wales. The link between the Viking race and the A blood gene was also confirmed by the very high A results he subsequently found in the former Norse kingdoms of Man and the Western Isles. If the Vikings had married Welshwomen to any appreciable degree, their issue would have been much lower in A.[42] As a result, he confirmed that a number of people he had tested in this part of Wales were genetically descended from Viking stock. If his conclusions are correct, then the same methods could be applied for locating other nationalities, including the remnants of Scota and her followers.

The blood group B is the rarest of the ABO genes to be found in Western Europe. It gradually decreases in intensity as one passes westward from the borders of the ancient Near East through central Europe to the edge of the North Sea. Nonetheless, when Morgan-Watkins divided Wales into western and eastern halves, he was astonished to find that the B gene was significantly more frequent in the west than in the east – the reverse of the general European pattern. What is more, on the moorlands and the moorland fringes, where it has been claimed that some of the earliest Bronze Age peoples arrived and settled, the incidence of the B gene rises. This leads one to conclude that in Wales the B gene is a very ancient phenomenon. Recent studies by other scientists have confirmed Morgan-Watkins's initial findings in relation to the B gene frequency.[43] Dr E. Brown of Edinburgh University has shown that in Scotland there is an interesting similarity between the distribution of the B gene and megalithic monuments.[44] The presence of the B gene falls off markedly where no tombs are found. In addition, a raised B frequency has also been detected in central and south-western counties of Ireland, and according to the British geneticist Robert Damson it 'may reflect a pre-historic settlement'.[45]

We are now left with one final enigma. Very high frequencies of O blood, similar to those found in much of Wales, Scotland and Ireland, are rarely encountered. Apart from a few islands in the Aegean Sea and pockets in the western Caucasus, Morgan-Watkins discovered that the only other region of the world which produced similar gene frequency results to those of Britain was North Africa, particularly the so-called Hamitic tribes, which, as we have seen, are the accepted descendants of the ancient Egyptians. Along the Atlantic seaboard the only other correlation with Britain was to be found upon the peculiarly named 'island of Ra', just off the North African coast.[46]

This was in itself truly remarkable. From only a small sample of Welsh people, Morgan-Watkins had established, categorically, that some of their ancestors had not only migrated from the East, but that many had possibly derived from North Africa itself. Little did Randall-Maciver and Wilkin realize that their profound comments would be scientifically confirmed in the years to come. Feeling satisfied with these conclusions, I decided to look for further physical confirmation of Scota and her followers. This search led me on an investigation into the varied landscape of ancient Britain.

CHAPTER TWELVE

SYMBOLS OF POWER

On 15 March 1999, a letter arrived from Steve Ottery, Curator of the Isles of Scilly Museum. It read, 'Did you know that at the excavation of Knackyboy Carn on St Martins, in the early 1950s, five blue faience beads, similar to those found in the tomb of Tutankhamun, were discovered?'[1] Ever since I had found out about the faience beads uncovered at Tara in 1956, I had been recording and evaluating every faience find that had been made in the British Isles. However, this discovery on the Isles of Scilly was indeed quite a shock, especially as my reasons for contacting the Museum in the first instance had been about another matter.

The Isles of Scilly lie in the Atlantic Ocean 45 kilometres south-west of Land's End in Cornwall and consist of around 100 islands, of which only the largest five are inhabited. Populated since prehistoric times when, according to geologists, the islands were still joined to the British mainland, nowadays the only way to reach the Scillies is by either boat or helicopter. The earliest historical account

dates from Roman times, written in around AD 240 by the
Roman historian Solinus. Called 'Siluram Insulam' –
translated as the Scilly Isle – it indicates that even during the
Roman era the Scillies may have been only one large island.[2]
In fact, it is argued that the islands may only have taken
their present form as late as the sixteenth century.
According to tradition, the celebrated Arthurian land of
Lyonesse was thought to lie somewhere between Land's End
and the Isles of Scilly. Evidence of drowned houses, field
walls and graves can be traced at very low tide where, it was
said, in a single night 140 towns were inundated by the sea.
Supposedly, the church bells can still be heard ringing
beneath the waves.[3]

Situated on the uninhabited island of St Martins,
Knackyboy Carn was a grass-covered round barrow crossed
by the remains of a field wall. It was just to the north-west
of the prehistoric settlement of Nornour. All that remains of
what had evidently been an important burial site is a flat-
topped hill. The mound is circular, around 15 metres in
diameter and under 1 metre high, and is composed largely
of stones. According to local lore, in 1912 the cairn was
illicitly broken into by two of the islanders in search of good
stone for the field wall they were constructing. One of these
islanders, Mr Alexander Gibson, tells of finding tiers of pots
with blue, glassy beads, together with two large pottery
urns.[4] The official excavation in 1948 by Bernard St John
O'Neil revealed that much of the material of the mound had
been dug over in the past, although under a portion of the
original barrow an unpolished flint axe was discovered.[5]

Once in the cairn, O'Neil found a narrow stonework
passageway leading to the inside chamber. It measured over
3.5 metres long and nearly 1 metre wide, and a total of
twenty-two burial urns were eventually recovered. Sadly, all
showed evidence of having been tampered with. The first set

of burials were carefully placed into grooved-out hollows upon the cairn floor whereby a layer of cremated ashes, probably from a funeral pyre, was heaped over them. At a later date, a straight-sided urn was placed on top of the ashes, filling the entire cavity of the chamber right up to the roof. Amongst the ashes, O'Neil unearthed some star-shaped faience beads.[6]

The concentration of faience beads in the British Isles appears to be exceptionally high in comparison with other European regions. So far, a total of 286 have been positively identified. Problems still surround their origins, however, and many archaeologists refuse point blank even to entertain the idea of an Egyptian provenance. In 1970, Dr R. Newton, Director of Research of the British Glass Industry, and Dr Colin Renfrew of the University of Sheffield, suggested that the faience beads unearthed in Britain were, in fact, of local manufacture.[7] So determining whether the beads were Egyptian or not would need specialist help. I decided to enlist the assistance of the British Museum and contacted Gillian Varndell, Curator of Prehistoric and Romano-British Antiquities. She did not think we were yet able to draw a line under this problem. Though forensic examination of the British beads has indeed shown correlations with their Egyptian counterparts, much speculation and discussion still surrounds their source.[8] Could I therefore find corroboration elsewhere to verify whether the beads were indeed Egyptian or not?

Thankfully, further scientific investigation has continued since the initial assessment by Stone and Thomas in 1956 that the Tara beads were of Egyptian origin (see Chapter 1). In an article in *Proceedings of the Prehistoric Society* in September 1972, Dr Hugh McKerrell of the National Antiquities Museum of Scotland in Edinburgh confirmed their initial findings. By analysing the lead content in faience beads found in Scotland and Wessex, he discovered that identical lead composition also occurred in Egyptian faience beads dating from the Eighteenth Dynasty onwards. Furthermore, the closest resemblance he found to the Wessex beads were those unearthed in graves at Abydos, in Middle Egypt.[9] The faience beads found at Lakenheath and Ringwold, both in Scotland, were also identical to Amarna beads dating from around 1350 BC. Perhaps the firmest indication, however, was a pear-shaped white glass bead discovered at Gilchorn, in Arbroath. It was first mentioned in an article in 1921 in the journal *British School of Athens*, where the author, Dr A.F. Harding, remarks not only on the close parallels with similar glass beads from Eighteenth Dynasty Egypt, but that an identical bead had actually been recorded from the palace of Mycenae.[10]

After continuing with his investigation, McKerrell stumbled across something quite unexpected. Not only did he find comparable tin contents between Egyptian and British faience beads but, more importantly, he discovered that a glaze might have been applied to many of the British beads. To confirm his initial suspicions, further laboratory tests were carried out and it was noted that the glaze colour achieved, in each case, was much darker than the normal faience blue, which was predominantly turquoise in colour. The significance of this was appreciated only after he closely examined the two faience star beads from Fyvie, in Aberdeenshire. Both showed a similar dark blue glaze. The similarities to lapis lazuli were striking and McKerrell concluded that the glaze could well have been applied to make the beads look like lapis lazuli.[11]

The ancient Egyptians called lapis lazuli *khesbed*. It is a form of limestone, rich in the blue mineral lazurite, which is dark blue and often flecked by impurities of calcite, iron pyrites or gold. The Egyptians believed that its appearance imitated the heavens, so they considered it to be superior to all other materials except gold and silver. Lapis lazuli was used extensively in jewellery, from predynastic times onwards, but unlike most other stones, it did not occur naturally in the deserts of Egypt. Consequently, it had to be imported directly from Badakhstan, in north-eastern Afghanistan, or indirectly, as trade goods from the Near East.[12]

The deliberate preparation of a glaze formula to achieve this dark, matt blue must be given serious consideration. It has a significant bearing upon the eastern origin of the faience beads. No lapis lazuli has been found in Britain and it would hardly be likely that such careful imitation, if this were the explanation for the composition on the Scottish beads, would have been carried out here. On the other hand, the possibility of an Egyptian origin is strengthened by this thesis, as the colour and formulation of the glaze found on the Scottish beads fits far better into an Egyptian context than a British one. The ancient Egyptians spent much effort in an attempt, often incredibly successful, at imitating lapis lazuli. We have seen how lapis lazuli was greatly prized in Egypt. During the opening of the tomb of Tutankhamun in 1922, its finder, Howard Carter, discovered, amongst many splendid things, a golden box containing powdered casserite (tin oxide).[13] The relationship between the deposition here in the tomb of a pharaoh and the use and value of the powdered material seems fairly clear. Tin oxide was of immense significance to the Egyptians. McKerrell concluded that it was this tin-containing material that was most likely to have been used in the glaze on the British beads.[14]

Apart from gold and silver, tin was one of the most highly prized materials in the ancient world. Its principal use was in the making of bronze, though its early history is little known and no real evidence can be found to show when it was first discovered. It does not occur naturally in the metallic state. The manner in which it is usually found in nature is in stratified layers of rocks. The only tin mineral of importance is the oxide, or casserite, which is heavy and usually dark brown or black in colour. It occurs in two forms: in granite or granite rocks, and occasionally associated with copper ore; and in pebbles, gravel or sand, derived from the break-up of rocks, which have then subsequently been carried and deposited by water. It is often found in the same alluvial gravel as gold, and since both are obtained by the same method, namely by washing away the accompanying lighter material with running water, it is quite possible that during the search for gold, the heavy tin oxide would have been noticed.[15]

Egypt was fortunate in possessing large deposits of many different types of stone and metal, which were extensively exploited. The main mining areas were in the Eastern Desert, Sinai and Nubia. Certain minerals, including gold, copper, malachite and alabaster, were particularly highly prized, as were limestone, granite and other rocks used in the construction of temples and other monumental architecture. As we have seen, some minerals had religious and symbolic significance in addition to their practical value. For instance, the Egyptians regarded gold as a divine substance. The flesh of the gods was thought to be made of gold, and their bones of silver, an even rarer material not available locally.[16] But what Egypt did not have easy access to was a steady supply of tin. Very small quantities have been uncovered near Gebel Mueliah in the Eastern Desert region and in the neighbourhood of Quesir on the Red Sea coast, but there is no evidence to suggest the Egyptians knew about these deposits or worked them in ancient times.[17] It made me think: where was Egypt obtaining its huge supplies of tin?

In the Valley of the Kings, located on the upper side of the south-eastern slope, there stands one of the most outstanding tombs of the entire Theban necropolis. Built during the time of Tutmosis III, about 1450 BC, it belonged to the Vizier Rekhmire, meaning 'wise of god'. Among its many splendid wall paintings, there is a scene that shows a series of porters carrying metal ingots. One man carries on his shoulder an ingot of copper, and the following two each have a basket full of oblong ingots. The accompanying inscription reads: 'Bringing Asiatic copper which his majesty carried off from his [Syrian] victory in the land of Retenu in order to cast two doors of the temple of Amun.'[18]

In 1943 Egyptologist Norman de Garies Davies in *The Tomb of Rekhmire at Thebes* remarked that the great temple doors were made of copper in the mixture of six parts to one, the 'one' presumably being tin. His hypothesis was based on the actual colouring of the tomb wall paintings. The so-called 'Asiatic copper' appears to be lighter in colour than genuine copper and perhaps, he argued, it may have been some kind of special copper alloy.[19] It is certainly feasible, as a light colouring would indicate high levels of tin. Surprisingly, finds of tin in the ancient Near East are exceptionally rare. It is strange that a metal which constitutes a major technological change in society and which presents no problems in extraction should scarcely be evident in its own right. Only a few items of tin have survived, for instance a cast tin bottle and a tin ring from Egypt that probably date to the later years of the Eighteenth Dynasty, and a twisted tin wire bangle found at Thermi in Lesbos. Infuriatingly, apart from these few minor objects, no articles of pure tin or even tin ingots have been recovered which date to before 1500 BC.[20]

Despite the lack of material finds, one would think it would be easy for scholars to pinpoint the tin-producing areas of the Near East. Regrettably, it is not so straight-forward. Over the past few centuries, archaeologists have showered maps of the Near East with an endless array of tin sources which, after closer scrutiny, appear as figments of the imagination or, at best, minor occurrences unlikely to have been known in ancient Egyptian times.[21] Alas, Egypt therefore had no alternative but to import its tin. So where did it come from?

In 1934 Egyptologist Dr E.A. Wainwright believed he had found the answers. In an article in the *Journal of Egyptian Archaeology* he announced that his informants had, at last, discovered the origins of Egypt's tin. It was, in fact, the Levantine port of Byblos. Unhappily for Wainwright, it was subsequently revealed that the Australian engineers he had relied upon for his information, Sams and Robinson, had actually found large quantities of silver and copper. Having been misinformed that copper and tin are always found together, they mistakenly told Wainwright that what they had found was tin. The Byblos tin was purely fiction.[21]

There is no doubt that tin ingots were indeed traded throughout the Levant during the second millennium BC. The museums of the eastern Mediterranean are full of them. For instance, in the autumn of 1976 two tin ingots were found in the sea near the Phoenician port of Dor, just south of Haifa. Over a period of ten years local fishermen successfully raised around seven tonnes of tin and copper ingots, which were subsequently sold to scrap dealers in Haifa for remelting. Only two ingots survive and are now in the Museum of Ancient Art at Haifa.[23] Precisely where they came from and what period they date to is difficult to answer.

Turkey has also been claimed as a likely source of Egypt's tin. Regrettably, scientific analysis of Anatolian metal from the second millennium BC has revealed that it consisted of scarce amounts of tin bronze. So Turkish mines were unlikely to have been exploited during ancient times. Links between Egypt and Mesopotamia were strong throughout antiquity, especially under the Akkadian Empire founded by Sargon in about 2370 BC. Apparently, Assyrian traders were a common sight in the Anatolian markets and in exchange for gold and silver the merchants gave cloth and tin 'transported by black donkeys bred in Assyria'. The quantities of tin traded could have been considerable. A cargo of approximately 12 tonnes is mentioned in one communication. Nonetheless, in about 1757 BC Hammurabi, King of Babylon, destroyed this lucrative trade, defeating the Assyrians and sacking their capital, Mari, situated 90 kilometres up the River Euphrates. A period of wars followed and central Anatolia, once rich, was left in ruins. Moreover, there is no evidence that Egypt ever traded with the Assyrians for tin.[24] In summing up, if the Egyptians were not obtaining their tin from the east, as the information provided suggests there was only one other option open to them, and that was to look to the west.

'Tarshish was thy merchant by reason of the multitude of all kind of riches; with silver, iron, tin and lead, they traded in thy fairs.'[25] With these words the Old Testament prophet Ezekiel described the riches of the port of Tyre. He also paid tribute to the mysterious land of Tarshish. Where and what was Tarshish remains a mystery to historians and archaeologists alike. Part historical, part legend, according to many scholars, it appears to have been a kingdom that the ancient Greeks once referred to as Tartessos. For them it was a friendly monarchy located somewhere in south west Spain on the 'shores of the ocean where silver abounded'.[26] The first biblical narrative recounts the arrival of the Greeks from Ionia in their fifty-oared ships, who reached Tartessos and were befriended by the local king, Arganthonios, whose name in Greek literally means 'he of the silver land'.[27] Apparently, this monarch ruled for eighty years and lived until he was over 120 years old!

Another traditional story, perhaps, is slightly more credible. Here a ship from the Greek island of Samos was blown off course in a ferocious storm. It finally passed out through the Straits of Gibraltar, and shortly reached the shores of Tartessos. Here its goods were traded for a vast profit and the Greeks eventually returned home. Upon their safe arrival, they gave six talents of silver to make a huge bronze cauldron in honour of the goddess Hera, wife of Zeus.[28] It is said that the Greek historian Herodotus actually saw the cauldron for himself, since he described it in great detail: 'jutting griffins' heads on the rim and the three huge statues of a kneeling man, which support the vessel'.[29]

Could Spain therefore have been the provider of Egypt's tin? If so, it is possible, bearing in mind the lack of other available sources, that Scota in her powerful position as Chief Wife was aware of these lands. This would provide us with some kind of explanation as to why the Egyptians eventually decided to settle upon the Iberian Peninsula, even if only temporarily. Examining a map of the metal regions of Spain, it becomes apparent that the whole of north-west Iberia is rich in abandoned mines. In 1873 in an article in the *Proceedings of the Society of Antiquaries*, British archaeologist Edward Howorth described the enormous excavations he had witnessed in Galicia, where nearly half the country's tin was produced.[30] The Romans also found Spain full of mines. The coastal strip between Italy and Spain was vital to Rome's trading links and was subsequently annexed by them in 123 BC.

Nevertheless, in spite of the odd Biblical quote and the exploits of the Greeks and the Phoenicians, there is no evidence to suggest that the east had any knowledge of Iberia's mineral wealth during the middle Bronze Age. Almost no prehistoric artefacts can be ascribed to any ancient workings. I could take the matter of Iberian tin no further.

We are on firmer ground, however, in locating tin in Britain. Imagine my surprise when I found out that a tin ingot, similar to those found in the eastern Mediterranean, had been uncovered in Britain. During the summer of 1812 at St Mawes, Cornwall, some local bargemen were going about their daily business, scouring the sea bottom for sand. Sand was extensively used in the early nineteenth century to improve soil quality, and is still worked commercially today. After a short while, they discovered, in the dredge, something that looked like an ancient block of tin. Resembling the letter H in shape, it was said to be of the 'purest metal'. It was exceptionally corroded and since it had no official stamp, which denoted the duty paid to the Duke of Cornwall, they agreed that it must have been deposited in the water some time before. There were even suggestions that it must have been manufactured in the days when the Phoenicians supposedly visited the Cornish market for precisely this metal at some point during the Bronze Age. If this conjecture was correct, they concluded that this particular block of tin was from a hoard that had accidentally slipped in the water whilst being put on board a Phoenician ship for exportation.[31]

This Cornish ingot is perhaps one of the most enigmatic finds ever to have been unearthed in Britain. Measuring 91.3 centimetres in length and weighing roughly 72 kilograms, it was large enough to make over a tonne of 10 per cent tin bronze. But after its initial discovery it attracted little attention from the academic community and did not receive the international fame it deserved until after an account of it had been published in 1863 by Sir Henry James, Director of the Ordnance Survey. The ingot may have been exported from a port on the Falmouth estuary, as tin has been to the present day. The ingot has generally been credited with great antiquity because it was said to contain crystals of casserite (tin oxide).[32] However, this need not necessarily imply a great age. It is not possible to date metals such as tin, so no more is known about the St Mawes ingot today than when it was initially dredged from the harbour.

The ingot is on display in Truro Museum. I decided to enlist the help of Roger Penhallurick, the Curator of Truro Museum and one of the country's leading specialists on ancient tin production. In his opinion, it is impossible to say whether or not Cornish tin supplies could have reached Egypt during the Bronze Age – although that is not to say that they could not. He did say, however, that tin exports from Britain to Egypt occurred as early as AD 600, as a letter from the Patriach of Alexandria, in Egypt, has proved. He kindly forwarded me details of tin production in prehistoric Britain.[33] By examining the history of early British tin mining, could I find any evidence to suggest earlier links with Egypt?

The south-west of England, in particular Cornwall, was one of the richest mining regions in the world in ancient times. It combined extremely rich copper and tin resources with one of the best preserved prehistoric landscapes in the British Isles. However, very little attention has been paid to the possibility of prehistoric mining and metal production in the area. Although evidence for modern-day mining is quite literally everywhere, searching for evidence of mining during the prehistoric era is not quite so rewarding.[34]

British tin is likely to have been obtained by the method called streaming. This is perhaps, a misleading word which really refers to the washing of the casserite once it has been dug up. In actual fact, in a traditional sense, streaming is really opencast mining, because the casserite lay in what the miners called the 'tin ground' at the bottom of moorland basins and valleys near to the sea. They were, in fact, still being worked up until this century, so it makes dating a very real problem indeed.[35] The Bronze Age copper mines, such as those in Ireland, have all been hard rock mines where the diagnostic evidence has been the surviving workface, bearing all the characteristic marks of working. By contrast, the exposed gravel faces of the stream workings have been rapidly weathered away. After more or less 4000 years of continual mining and, it has to be said, pretty extensive exploitation in the last few centuries, it is remarkable that any prehistoric evidence has survived at all.[36]

In my conversations with Roger Penhallurick, he informed me that whilst collecting data for his book, *Tin in Antiquity*, he found references to over forty prehistoric artefacts having been discovered in tin streamworks. These included spearheads, rapiers, rings and brooches. However, he confirmed that the chance of finding any more is remote.[37] Apparently, what must be remembered is that every object was recovered by chance and we can count ourselves fortunate that someone with sufficient interest was around at the time to record what was dug up. The last recorded discovery from a tin streamworks was in 1930, only a few miles away from the St Erith valley, where a stone axe was discovered. Regrettably, it was taken off to London and has not been seen since.[38]

Nonetheless, a scattering of tin ingots found beside a reef in a small river mouth has provided unique evidence for the West Country's trade in metal from a very early period in history. In 1992 divers from the South-West Maritime Archaeological Group discovered forty-four ingots scattered in the Erme estuary, Devon. Lying among the loose rocks, at a depth of around 7–10 metres, the divers would not have spotted them without the use of metal detectors and most probably would not have given them a second look. The group was working close by on a designated wreck site and recognized the importance of the objects immediately. Ranging in size from a fist to a rugby ball, the tin had blistered, producing nodules and scars. Accretions of shells and worm casts covered them and the sea had done its worst to abrade and corrode them. The ingots as recovered weighed 84.6 kilograms, equivalent to a man. The forms included round and oval buns and possibly little H-shaped ones similar in appearance to the St Mawes ingot.[39]

Although I was slightly disheartened at the lack of evidence so far, the absence of any real Bronze Age workings does not necessarily mean that Cornwall was not a main provider of tin throughout the prehistoric era. The distinctive shape of the St Mawes ingot is unique, and it is also possible that another ingot of this type was found near Camborne in Cornwall, although any record of its discovery is now lost. What is striking, however, is the similarity between the St Mawes ingot and those found in the eastern Mediterranean. In fact, having examined the block of tin myself, I would say it bears more than just a passing resemblance to the ingot depicted in the tomb of Rekhmire in Egypt. Could that alone indicate a connection between the Bronze Age Mediterranean and Cornish tin?

Tradition has it that the Phoenicians were the very first peoples from the East to discover the vast supplies of tin in Cornwall. Whether this was during the Bronze Age or the Iron Age is unknown. The Roman chronicler Pliny the Elder recorded the exploits of one such Phoenician explorer. What survives of his account is now recorded in the verse entitled 'Ora Maritima' meaning 'seacoast'. Written in the fourth century AD, by the Latin poet Rufus Festus Avenius, it describes the journey from Massalia, modern day Marseilles, beyond the Pillars of Hercules to the lands of tin beyond. The traditional interpretation of this Atlantic voyage is up the coast of Iberia, across the bay of Biscay to the oestrymnides (identified as the southern islands of Brittany), arriving two days later at a holy island called Hierni, which is taken to be Ireland (Hibernia). It was here that dwelt the Albiones – presumably people of Albion, the ancient name for Britain.[40]

In the early seventeenth century, John Twnye proposed a Phoenician connection in his work *De Rebus Albionicus Britannicis*. He suggested that the stereotypical Welsh and Irish skin boats, called coracles, were also Phoenician in origin. What is more, he even said that the dress of the Welsh women throughout the sixteenth century was a survival of an old Phoenician form of dress.[41] The writer/historian Samuel Bochart developed the same line of thought throughout his *Geographic Sacra*, which was first published in 1646. In his opinion, the name of Britannia was first applied by the Phoenicians, in whose language Bartanac signified 'the land of the tin'.[42]

In its time, Cornwall has also been cited as the location of the Casserides, the legendary 'islands of tin'. Herodotus, writing in the fifth century BC, was the first to make mention of these tin islands, though, unfortunately, he did not reveal their exact location. But they were for him 'the place where we get our tin'.[43] That the ancient Greeks should have sailed so far west is no surprise. The first Greek known to have circumnavigated the British Isles was a man called Pytheas. A native of Massalia (Marseilles), he was a mathematician, geographer and astronomer who believed that the earth was round. According to him there had to be regions of continuous daylight, given the angle of the earth's axis. In the fourth century BC, he left Massalia, sailed past the Straits of Gibraltar and reached the British Isles. There he mapped, with great accuracy, what is today England and Scotland. He continued his voyage to discover Iceland, then headed into the Baltic Sea, where he observed icebergs and nightless day before returning home. Although the reports of his travels and sightings were viewed by his contemporaries with great scepticism, today Pytheas is acknowledged as a great man of science.[44] So ancient Greek vessels were not unknown in British waters, something which has been confirmed in recent years. In 1974 an anchor-stock was dredged up off Port Felon at the tip of the Llyn Peninsula in North Wales. Such anchors are common in the eastern Mediterranean, where they 'litter the roadsteads and ports as well as off perilous headlands and reefs'. The British find is unique, however; the only other examples found in the Atlantic were ten dredged up from the Bay of Setubal, just south of Lisbon.[45]

In the first century BC, the Greek writer Diodorus Sicculus gave another important account of Cornish tin, which is generally thought to derive from the lost work of Pytheas. A contemporary of Julius Caesar and native of Agyrium, his version is by far the single most important description by any classical author of the mining and trade of Cornish tin.

> The inhabitants of Britain who dwell about the promontory known as Belerion are especially hospitable to strangers and have adopted a civilized manner of life because of their intercourse with merchants of other peoples. The men, who work the tin, treat the bed, which bears it, in an ingenious manner. This bed, being the rock, contains earthy seams and in them the workers quarry the ore, which they then melt down and cleanse

of its impurities. They then work the tin into pieces the size of knucklebones, and convey it to an island which lies off Britain and is called Ictis. On the island of Ictis the merchants purchase the tin of the natives and carry it from there across the Straits of Galatia, or Gaul. Finally making their way on foot through Gaul for some thirty days, they bring their wares on horseback to the mouth of the river Rhone.[46]

The precise location of Ictis has caused considerable controversy. Some historians suggest the Isle of Wight, which was known in Roman times as Vectis, with ancient Hurst Castle as the main fortification for the important port site.[47] But in my discussions with Roger Penhallurick, we both came to the same conclusion that the most likely spot was St Michael's Mount. Overlooking Mount's Bay on the Land's End peninsula, it does, geographically, seem to fit the criteria. The religious history of the mount began in the fifth century when St Michael was said to have appeared to some fishermen, who saw him standing on a ledge on the rocks high above the sea, although its earlier fame as a tin trading post cannot be ignored: The coastline around this area of Cornwall is much the same as it was during the days of Pytheas, and there are no geographical or historical reasons why St Michael's Mount should not be accepted as the legendary Ictis. Cormac's glossary, compiled around AD 900, also favours this site, for the name 'Ictis' survived in Irish as Muir-n-Icht, 'the sea of Icht', the Irish name for the English Channel.[48]

This was all well and good, but links with the Phoenicians, the Greeks, and even the Romans did not prove that Cornwall was exporting tin to the eastern Mediterranean during the Bronze Age. More recently, however, a Mycenean tin connection with western Europe has been proposed. This view has been strengthened by a whole host of Mycenean swords uncovered at specific European sites that produced tin-decorated pottery. Like the ancient Egyptians, obtaining a regular supply of tin in sufficient quantities must have been a problem for Mycenean metal-smiths. But, as with Egypt, is it feasible to suggest that Mycenae was trading tin with Cornwall? As we have seen, the Mycenean Empire's heyday was contemporary with Akhenaten's reign in Egypt; only a few years after Scota fled Egypt, the palace culture of Mycenae collapsed. So could Scota have heard about the tin land of Britain indirectly through the Egyptian royal contacts with Mycenae?

There are a number of archaeological finds which point to possible Mycenean/British connections. One particular object recognized by archaeologists as a possible Mycenean export is the Pelant Dagger, thought to have been uncovered in a Cornish Bronze Age barrow whose exact whereabouts are shrouded in mystery. The earliest reference appeared in an album of watercolour drawings, dating to 1871, compiled by Borlase. Now displayed in the Truro Museum, the question of dating is, as always, problematic. According to Dr P. McNamara of the University of Durham, it shows striking parallels with daggers or short swords made around 1350–1230 BC.[49] In addition, Dr Keith Branigan of Bristol University has recently published a report on a probable Cypriot 'hook-tang weapon' ploughed up in the 1950s near Torrington in Devon. It appears that five were already known from Sidmouth, Devon, and one from Egton Moor, Yorkshire.[50] Whether they can all be deemed to be archaeological finds or are just simply relics from a lost traveller is open to discussion, as none were found in a stratified layer or in an undisturbed barrow. Nevertheless, they reinforce the arguments in favour of contact between

Britain and the Mediterranean civilizations, including Egypt, in the middle of the second millennium BC.

We have already observed how solid the bond was between Egypt and Mycenae during the later part of the Bronze Age. If the Myceneans were obtaining tin from Cornwall, and the evidence so far suggests it is a possibility, then one would naturally expect that, through their close ties, Egypt would eventually be made aware of tin supplies in the west. Perhaps the Egyptian term 'isles across the sea', mentioned in Chapter 8, may have a deeper meaning than was originally envisaged. Maybe scholars of the past have made some passing reference to such a connection. I was keen to discover any evidence that Egypt either traded or was even acquainted with the vast tin supplies in Cornwall during Scota's era.

In January 1832, in St Just, Cornwall, a local worker named John Lawry uncovered the foundations of what initially appeared to be an ancient burial site whilst demolishing a stone wall for the local vicarage. From the remaining ashes it would seem that the ground had been burnt. After picking his way through the rubble, he stumbled upon a small figure of a bull made of bronze. Unsure of what it was, or where it had come from, it was shown to 'some of the most learned antiquaries in London' who, after much consultation, agreed that it was Phoenician. Subsequently, the little bronze figure was sent to the British Museum for further investigation. On 21 September 1929 Truro Museum received a letter from the Department of Egyptian Antiquities which stated quite categorically that the bull was, in fact, an Apis bull, of Egyptian origin.[51]

The cult of the Apis bull possibly dates back to the very beginning of Egyptian history. His principal sanctuary was located near the temple of Ptah at Memphis, the ancient capital of Egypt. The bull was closely linked with the pharaoh, both being the divine manifestations of a god. Unlike many other sacred animals, the Apis bull was always a single individual, selected, more often than not, for his particular markings. According to the Greek historian Herodotus, the Apis bull was conceived from a bolt of lightning, and was black with a white diamond on his forehead, the image of a vulture on his back, double hairs on his tail and a scarab-shaped mark under his tongue.[52]

At the death of each Apis bull, there was national mourning, and the embalmed corpse was taken along the sacred way from Memphis to the necropolis of Saqqara, south of Cairo. Here it was buried in its own granite sarcophagus, often highly decorated, in the underground catacombs known as the Serapeum. Because of the divine nature of his birth, the mothers of the Apis bulls were venerated as manifestations of the Egyptian goddess Isis; they were accorded similar burials to their offspring, in the Iseum, a set of galleries to the north of the Serapeum.[53] Even the calves of the Apis were buried with much ceremony, but their catacombs remain undiscovered.

Mystery continues to surround the St Just bull. According to letters now housed in Truro Museum, as recently as 1981 Carol Andrews, Curator of the Department of Egyptian Antiquities at the British Museum, argued against an Egyptian origin for it. She said that not only were Apis bulls not much worshipped outside of Egypt, let alone Britain, but the St Just bull did not resemble an Egyptian Apis bull in the slightest. In her conclusion she commented that the St Just bull was probably of local manufacture.[54] I was not to be defeated. In a German book called *Agyptische Bronzefiguren,* published in 1956, I found a depiction of a bull that bears a remarkable similarity to the St Just figurine. Both stand with their feet together and both possess a curiously thick and upright neck.[55] However, as the St Just bull is without provenance, and until scientists invent a method of positively dating the age of bronze, it is at present not possible to confirm whether the St Just bull is Egyptian or not. Nevertheless, I believe it is one of the strongest pieces of evidence that we have found so far. Imagine my surprise when, some months later, I stumbled across another find that even eclipsed the St Just model.

In an article in the *Proceedings of the Prehistoric Society* in 1953, Dr T. Powell of the University of Liverpool reported on one of the most puzzling archaeological finds of the past 200 years. Called the Mold Pectoral by archaeologists, it was unearthed at Mold, in North Wales, during the early nineteenth century.[56] It is one of the largest pieces of prehistoric goldwork so far discovered in Europe, and it has been one of the principal treasures in the collection of prehistoric antiquities in the British Museum for more than a century. Consisting of a shoulder cape made from a single sheet of relatively thick gold, its surface is covered with a rich repoussé of ribs and bosses, perhaps intended to look like beads. Strangely, the best parallels for such shoulder capes come from ancient Egypt.[57]

In the summer of 1833 a large mound, recognized by the local inhabitants as a tumulus, was demolished to fill up a small gravel pit, and to level the surrounding field. At some stage in the operation the team noticed that the mound consisted of larger material than the initial grave subsoil, and a number of large stones were uncovered. Underneath, approximately 1 metre from the top of the mound, they found the remains of a burial. Lying in the centre of the mound, it appears the burial was initially enclosed in some kind of rough cist, formed from huge boulders, which had subsequently collapsed. Accordingly, it was impossible to tell how many chambers there were. From the many remains and stone artefacts, the site was clearly of late Stone Age date. At least one cremation urn was found in the body of the barrow. Nothing of it survives, but it would suggest that the barrow was most probably of Bronze Age date. One skull was recorded, although it was too fragmentary to save, owing to the collapse of the roof. Incredibly, just to the left of the cremation urn, the locals found a corslet made from the purest of gold. In addition, several pieces of tarnished bronze were revealed that had been riveted to the gold with small nails. The gold sheet was apparently folded so as to enclose a quantity of unburnt human bones. On top they found a quantity of amber beads – in one account some 200 or 300 – disposed in rows and lying in some relation to the remains. Regrettably, only one amber bead survives.[58]

The surviving fragment of sheet-gold consists of one large piece around 57 centimetres in length and 21 centimetres wide, together with two medium-sized pieces approximately 34 centimetres × 19 centimetres and 26 centimetres × 14 centimetres. Remarkably, based on the accompanying finds, the Mold object was dated to around 1350–1250 BC.[59] It has been suggested that the gold ornament was possibly a ceremonial cape, worn as a status symbol or for display. It is possible that similar capes, made out of cloth, were also in use during the Bronze Age, with gold ornaments sewn into the cloth. In an article in the *Journal of the Cork Historical and Archaeological Society* in 1945, Dr L. Binchy reported on the discovery of a similar burial in 1805 near Castle Martyr, County Cork. Here the skeletal remains were said to have been covered with a series of similar gold plates.[60] Furthermore, amber beads were also reported from the same burial, although once again nothing survives except one small gold plate now in the National Museum of Antiquities, Dublin.[61]

It has been suggested that the goldsmith responsible for

the Mold object might have had no ethnic connections with Europe. In fact, based on the uniqueness of the design and shape, some scholars have argued that it probably derived from the eastern Mediterranean, or that the goldsmith involved had some knowledge of the techniques of Mycenean metallurgy. In 1947 the British antiquarian Gordon Childe suggested that these objects might have had ultimate Egyptian prototypes. He argued that the Mold Pectoral reflected in general form and attributes the broad collar of ancient Egypt.[62]

In ancient Egypt the ornaments for the neck are developments of a single charm strung upon a cord. At one extreme they became pectorals, at the other collars. The traditional collar in Egypt is so universal that it is virtually an item of everyday dress. The most popular version is the broad collar, composed of cylindrical beads or tubes, strung vertically in rows in a semicircular or circular shape and terminating in two end-pieces. Such collars are found painted on statues and reliefs from the early Old Kingdom, but have rarely been uncovered intact, though a notable gold and faience example dating to the Sixth Dynasty is at Boston Fine Arts Museum. In the Middle Kingdom they were depicted on painted wooden coffins. They were made from various materials including metals and stone. More elaborate versions substitute beads fashioned as hieroglyphs for the simple tubes of the main body of the collar. The majority of collars were designed to be worn with a *menkhet*, a counterpoise, which hung down the back of the neck and balanced some of the weight of the collar in front.[63]

Thankfully, pictures of the Mold Pectoral survived at the British Museum. I contacted the Curator of the Department of Prehistoric and Romano-British Antiquities, Gillian Varndell, who kindly forwarded me copies. These I compared with detailed pictures of collars in the collection of the Cairo Museum. I was immediately struck by the similarity in design. In fact, the embossed gold work on the Mold Pectoral appeared to be an attempt to imitate the beadwork on ancient Egyptian collars.

It has been shown that early Bronze Age metal types are very rare in the north-east of Wales, nor are there any important graves of this period. The late Bronze Age is also poorly represented in metal types. Together with the associated finds, by a simple process of deduction this confirms that the Mold Pectoral had to derive from the middle Bronze Age period – the time when Scota and her followers would be setting foot upon British soil for the first time. Remarkably, another important burial at Llangwm, 30 kilometres south-west of Mold, was found to include, amongst the grave goods, two-segmented faience beads.[64] In addition, a large gold torc (neck-ring), also of middle Bronze Age date, had also been unearthed in this region. Found in 1899 at Ysgeifiog, a village some 13 kilometres north-west of Mold, it was made from a solid rod of gold. Intriguingly, the only other example of such astounding workmanship derives from the Irish site of Tara.[65]

I therefore felt that it was time to pack my bags and cross the same stretch of water that Scota had done all those millennia before. I would now literally be walking in Scota's footsteps, to trace the final part of her journey and that of her followers.

CHAPTER THIRTEEN

THE LOST COLONY

Little did I realize when I began my search for Scota that events would take me full circle. When I first found out about the boy prince buried at Tara, I could never have dreamt that I would end up returning to this site, this time on the trail of an Egyptian princess. It was hard to imagine, as I wandered through the breathtaking countryside, that this could be the last resting-place of this ancient refugee. It must have seemed so strange to Scota when she arrived. After all, this place was so different from the barren red deserts of her homeland.

From the information available, we know that the earliest surviving Irish manuscript to contain a reference to Scota was the *Lebor Gabala*, or *Book of the Taking of Ireland*. It is only a passing reference, and amounts to just a couple of lines, but it does refer to Scota, daughter of an Egyptian pharaoh, landing with her fleet on the shores of Ireland. In Irish tradition the Hill of Tara was the seat of the High Kings of Ireland and, according to the Bower manuscript, Scota's descendants *were* those high kings.

Map of Ireland illustrating the principal locations cited in the text

What had happened to Scota in the intervening period? Perhaps I could find some answers in the historical annals?

In 1921 the pioneering Irish historian Eoin MacNeill studied the documents of the Irish 'synthetic historians', a phrase coined by him to describe those who compiled and wrote the annals, genealogies and legends of early Ireland. He concluded: 'Thus the central doctrine of the historical fabric was the remotely ancient rule of the race of Mil in Tara, and the supremacy of Tara over all Ireland. Around this doctrine were grouped and dated all the traditions, mythological and heroic, of the nation.'[1]

Who was this ancient race of Mil? As we saw in Chapter 2, the *Lebor Gabala* is devoted to recording the early history of Ireland, the memoirs of those peoples from overseas who were ultimately the ancestors of the great lineage of the country. According to the text there appear to have been five separate invasions. I decided to browse through the first volume, to see if I could discover which race the ancient chroniclers had ascribed to the Egyptians.

On the map of Europe, Ireland can be seen to be a neat geographical entity tucked away in the north western corner. But despite its remote location, it was not isolated from the Continent, for it had the advantage of being connected to its nearest neighbour by an easily navigable stretch of water. Its out-of-the-way position, rather than acting as a deterrent, in fact attracted both friend and foe to come and settle. As a result, Irish tradition, prior to the arrival of the people of Mil, documents the arrival of such legendary tribes as the Formorians, the Nemedians, the Partholonians, the Fir Bolgs and finally the Tuatha de Danaan.

According to the Walter Bower manuscript, the tribe called the Formorians were considered to be on the scene long before any other races came to Ireland. Living mainly in the oceans or on offshore islands, the Formorians were often portrayed as one-legged, one-armed giants.[2] Or in the words of the *Lebor Gabala*, they were regarded as 'men with single noble legs and with single full hands'.[3] The first people to invade Ireland were the Partholonians, although where they originated from is unknown. In fact, very little is known about them at all, and after fighting with the indigenous Formorians for around 300 years, they were apparently wiped out in an epidemic. Next came the race of Nemed, or the Nemedians. They suffered the same fate as their predecessors, dying from an epidemic, although a few did survive, only to be pursued by the Formorians.[4] After that came the Fir Bolgs who, according to the annals, came from either Greece or Scythia. In reality, they consisted of three tribes, the men of Domnu, the men of Gallion and the men of Bolg. They eventually intermarried with the Formorians and held the country of Ireland until the arrival of the Tuatha de Danaan.[5]

No sooner had the Tuatha de Danaan arrived than they forced the reigning Fir Bolg tribe into partial serfdom. It was they who originally established the site of Tara, in the Boyne River valley, as the ritual inauguration and burial place of the ancient kings of Ireland. They were generally regarded as the gods and the goddesses of the Celtic tribes, but it is believed that their true origins date far back into prehistory. They were said to be the 'children of the mother goddess Danu'. The so-called Children of Don in Welsh mythology parallel this Irish pantheon of deities. In the beginning it was said that Danu flooded the earth to form the river named after her, Danuvius. These waters fell and nurtured a sacred oak tree named Bile. Afterwards, Danu and Bile gave birth to the being that became the 'father of the gods'. In Irish myth this was referred to as the Dagda, or the Good God.

His children, the descendants of Danu and Bile, became the gods and the goddesses of Irish legend and are subsequently identified as the Tuatha de Danaan.[6]

Although the *Lebor Gabala* is a primary source for the study of early Ireland, Eoin MacNeill, seems to have obtained his information about the sons of Mil from another Irish source. A few times in his work he mentions the *Annals of the Four Masters*. This, in fact, became my best lead. Dating to the seventeenth century, and now preserved in Dublin University Library, it was compiled in the Franciscan monastery of Donegal by four monks named Michael, Conary, Cucogry O'Clery and Ferfasa O'Mulconry. They began work in 1632 and completed it in 1636, and it was published in seven large volumes.[7] It is regarded as among the most prominent of the pseudo-historical accounts of ancient Hibernia (Ireland). I therefore contacted the Irish Texts Society in Dublin who kindly forwarded me a copy of the first volume. I was in luck. The opening section of the manuscript deals with the origins of the Irish race. Seemingly compiled from an amalgamation of recorded history and oral tradition, it made a number of specific references to the sons of Mil:

The Milesians attempt to invade Ireland and are beaten back by the combined spiritual forces of the Tuatha de danaan. After circling the island three times, just as the full moons of the seventeenth day, the Milesians are able to approach the shore. After landing the Milesians now have to fight with the Tuatha de danaan on land. Eremon loses his horse in battle, and it gives its name to the River Liffey, Gabor Life. The Milesians then go onwards to consolidate their invasion by arriving at Tara, seat of the High Kings. Under setting the guise of a truce for three days, the high kings demand that the

Milesians retire to their ships. They have every intention of making it impossible for the invaders to return'.[8]

The *Annals* then goes on to relate how forty-eight married couples, four servants and Scota, daughter of a pharaoh, accompanied the Sons of Mil across the sea from Spain when they went to seek land from Ireland. They proposed to take Ireland at Inbatr Slaine because of the prophecy that said a famous company would take Ireland at that place. Of the Milesians who invaded the Tuatha de Danaan lands, Eber and Eremon divided the land between them – Eremon getting the northern half of the island, and Eber the southern half. In this battle died Scota, daughter of a pharaoh, wife of Eremon.[9]

The account of Scota's death at the battle of Slieve Mish is also confirmed in the *Lebor Gabala*, where it states that the sons of Mil originated from northern Spain. The fleet subsequently left Spain and sailed to Ireland to take it from the Tuatha de Danaan. On the third day, after landing, they fought a bloody battle at Slieve Mish. In this battle fell Scota the daughter of a pharaoh, after which the sons of Mil fought a battle at Tailtinn, against the three kings of the Tuatha de Danaan, named Mac Cuill, Mac Ceacht and Mac Greine. The battle lasted for a long time, and the sons of Mil were eventually victorious and took the seat of Tara.[10]

It is obvious from both accounts that the battle of Slieve Mish was probably long and bloody. We also know from the text that Scota died. Whether she led her people into battle like the warrior queens of old is unclear. Unfortunately, there is also no record of how many of her followers perished in the ensuing confrontation. Perhaps the Tara Prince was a victim. We do know that Scota was present during the onslaught, and that the beleaguered Egyptian forces finally overcame the Tuatha de Danaan. It does seem strange, however, that Scota was not afforded the proper burial, according to the rites of her ancestors, and that her comrades in arms apparently decided to bury her in a traditional British grave.

It now became my priority to find Scota's final resting-place. She had not been lain to rest at the site of Tara, of that I was certain. It would appear that she had died in battle before the final onslaught upon the site of Ireland's sacred high-kingship. I could take the matter no further by examining the archaeological evidence. I knew from my own research that the solitary finds so far uncovered at Tara, such as the faience beads and the remains of the young boy, were all that Tara had to offer in the way of material support. We have already discussed these in some detail and, as we have seen, they both have an undeniable Egyptian 'feel'. To discover exactly where Scota was buried I needed to examine the ancient annals once more. It was time to return to the Walter Bower manuscript.

After only a few hours of meticulous scrutiny, I eventually discovered the truth about Scota's grave. As I had guessed, she had not been buried at Tara. According to the Bower manuscript, she had been buried 'between Sliab Mis and the sea'.[11] This location would fit in well with what I had uncovered with regard to the battle against the Tuatha de Dannan. The account continues, identifying her grave, named Fert Scota, as being situated in a glen called Glenscota, meaning Scotina's or Scota's Glen.[12] Astounded at how relatively easy it had been to uncover the truth behind her final resting-place, I excitedly contacted Dr Andrew Halpin, Assistant Keeper at the National Museum of Ireland, Dublin, to find out more. Imagine my surprise when he informed me that, as far as he knew, no archaeological activity had been embarked upon in this particular corner of Ireland.[13] I wondered why no one had ever attempted to excavate this area, but on reflection I realized that no one before had made the connections that I had. So, to them, it was just another unimportant burial mound on a landscape littered with them. Perhaps the publication of this book may make them conduct a full archaeological and geophysical survey of the entire region.

As Scota had travelled through perilous voyages, so had I made a journey – a leap of faith from what we are told is 'fact' by many scholars to what I had unearthed by following the story of this young Egyptian princess. Surely the notion that the great Bronze Age civilizations in the eastern Mediterranean had absolutely no contact with their barbarian counterparts in western Europe can now finally be laid to rest. As I made my way to Glenscota, the time had come to consider what I had witnessed on my quest. I had discovered events that had changed my entire view of history.

If we venture back to those dark days of Akhenaten and imagine Scota as a child happily playing amongst the royal palisades of Thebes, little could she have known the strange events that would hurl her life into turmoil. In a little under five years her father Akhenaten had decimated the old religion of Egypt and had sacked the royal priesthood. He had set up his new god, the Aten, to be the single deity, sending the believers of the pantheon of older gods into hiding. He had built his new city for his new god and called it Akhetaten. Then, after these brief golden years there came tragedy. There was immense political unrest and with the rise of the ambitious Horemheb, leader of the Egyptian armed forces, ready to rally his troops against Akhenaten if need be, and finally, the great plague that brought the country to its knees and the final spur for Scota to take flight.

I also examined the different routes that Scota and her

followers would have taken to escape persecution in her homeland. I confirmed that a separate group of ancient Egyptians had possibly traversed the dangerous waters of the Aegean to leave their mark throughout Europe. In addition, they had left evidence to show their connections with the people and civilization of Mycenae. Following the ancient amber trade routes had led to the sunken ships at North Ferriby in Yorkshire. (Strangely enough, the only region of northern England where probable Egyptian faience beads have so far been unearthed also appears to have been Yorkshire.) Then there was the landing on Spanish soil and the building of their *motillas* as they struggled in vain to fight off the local tribes of barbarians.

I discovered the final tragic chain of events that made Scota flee yet another country and make her way to mainland Britain. In a hostile landscape, her happiness was only short-lived, as she was yet again made homeless and forced to take her boat and followers once more upon the open seas, travelling the few short miles to Ireland, where the final cataclysmic events of her life were to be played out.

Whether Scota had actually aimed for Britain or arrived here through sheer fluke is almost impossible to say. Perhaps this land had never been her true goal. It was only through circumstances such as the problems she and her followers encountered at Brigantia in Spain that she was forced to uproot and move even further west. Then again, it can be shown that, through trading networks, whether directly through the tin trade or indirectly through the Mycenean connection, she probably already knew of Britain's existence.

In my search for Scota, I had naturally taken many events for granted. Yet, if the truth be told, what was mind-blowing was how a simple abbot like Walter Bower, living in the Middle Ages, knew of an Egyptian princess travelling to Britain over 2000 years earlier. I was convinced that I had uncovered firm evidence for every part of the story recorded in the *Scotichronicon*. Even so, there were still many questions left unanswered. For instance, how did Walter Bower have any knowledge of the Egyptian settlement in Brigantia, when the scientific techniques required to date the *motillas* have only recently been discovered? The fact that he describes the building of Brigantia to the exact dimensions discovered by archaeologists some 500 years later is quite incredible. Moreover, when Bower was documenting the flight of Scota and the sons of Mil to Ireland, how did he know that the body unearthed by Dr O'Riordain in 1956 would have been interred with Egyptian artefacts? And when writing about the flight of Scota and Gaythelos from Egypt, how did he know about the terrible plagues inflicting the land when the Amarna Letters documenting such events were only unearthed in 1878? The only way he could possibly have known is if all these events were indeed authentic. How he came by all this information is a mystery he took to his grave. But I knew the final piece to the puzzle would be found in Ireland.

County Kerry, in the extreme south-west of Ireland, has two contrasting types of terrain: the mountainous southern part with its three hilly peninsulas of Beara, Iveragh and Dingle, and the smaller area of undulating plain in the north that stretches as far as the Shannon River estuary. It was September 1999 and I was on my way to the Dingle Peninsula. With exceptional prehistoric and early Christian remains scattered across it, it stretches westwards for 48 kilometres from the low-lying country near Tralee.[14] It is here between Tralee and Inch that the Slieve Mish range of mountains can be found, at the foot of which Scota perished at the hands of the Tuatha de Danaan.

Having left Dublin early that very morning, it had been

a long drive through some of the most dramatic scenery that I had ever witnessed. I was heading towards the town of Tralee, situated where the River Lee flows into Tralee Bay. Arriving late in the afternoon, I stopped for a moment to find my bearings. Even though it had neither any ancient ruins, nor even quaint architecture to offer, I still found it quite charming. The town has long been associated with the song 'The Rose of Tralee', the inspiration for the Rose of Tralee International Festival where, in the last week of August, Irish communities from around the world send their young women to compete in a beauty pageant. Placing the road map upon the bonnet of the car, I realized I had to travel only 5 kilometres further, south of the town, before I would arrive at my final goal – Glenscota. I was anxious to move on.

Dark clouds were already beginning to loom ominously as I drove down the steep mountain corridor. I had reached Glenscota at last. It had taken me nearly three years of painstaking research to reach this last part of the Scota story. Parking the car on the grass verge, halfway down the pass, I gazed over the ridge and could just hear the trickling of Fingal's Stream running down into the green-filled glen. Gazing into the distance, I knew that somewhere out there lay the body of Scota, far from her homeland. There would be no ornate painted tomb or ritual prayers to the Egyptian gods to welcome her passage into the underworld, just a lonely mound covered with grass in an alien land. Scota had successfully traversed the difficult political and religious waters of Egypt, only to find herself tossed on to the dangerous oceans with her followers. Her journey would finally come to an end in Ireland, a forgotten princess, lost and far from her homeland. For a while I stood there and pondered. Somewhere, in British villages, towns and cities, the descendants of Scota and her followers are living their lives, oblivious of their true origins. In time, perhaps, the old gods of Egypt will finally call them back home.

The fact that I had unearthed so many pieces of evidence, archaeological and historical, to show Egyptian settlement in the British Isles raised one question. Why had this all been ignored in academic circles? One of the main reasons, I felt, was that if such information was readily accepted then academia would rapidly have to rewrite huge chunks of history. This would throw certain traditional 'historical facts' into tremendous doubt. It is important to stress that many academics' careers are based on these 'facts' and to disprove them overnight would make these people redundant. During the research for this book, I soon discovered that some academics were quite willing to share their work off the record, but when it came to committing it to print they soon backed down and a wall of silence greeted me. None of them, it appeared, wanted to put their jobs on the line, to tell the truth. The sad reality of the matter is that we are relying on these people to tell us our history, but they seem content to operate under a veil of academic censorship.

On a Saturday afternoon in the British Museum, hordes of tourists walk nonchalantly by some of the greatest collections of artefacts from the ancient world. As cameras flash and people pose by the more famous exhibits, there stands, in the Medieval Gallery, possibly the most important piece in the entire museum. By a dimly lit case rests the ancient stone of Llywel. Unearthed in a farmer's field in Wales in 1843, it was sold to the British Museum for the meagre sum of £10.00.[15] An ornately carved piece of rock, its true importance appears to have been belittled by its placement. The most significant carving on this stone seems to have been deliberately obfuscated by the powers that be. Turned facing the wall, and impossible to view, there is a clear representation of a person dressed in Egyptian garb leaving the pyramids of Egypt on his journey to the west. Could this be the final proof of ancient Egyptian contacts with Britain? Or is this another story altogether . . . ?

❧

NOTES

Abbreviations for periodicals and series

AJA	American Journal of Archaeology
ASAE	Annales du Service des Antiquities de l'Egypte. Cairo
BSA	Annual Bulletin of the British School of Athens. London
JAOS	Journal of the American Oriental Society
JARCE	Journal of the American Research Center in Egypt. Cairo
JEA	Journal of Egyptian Archaeology. London
JRSAI	Journal of the Royal Society of Antiquaries of Ireland. Dublin
OJA	Oxford Journal of Archaeology. Oxford
PDAS	Proceedings of the Devon Archaeological Society. Devon
PPS	Proceedings of the Prehistoric Society. London
ZAS	Zeitschrift fur Agyptische Sprache und Altertumskunde. Berlin

Chapter One
THE FORBIDDEN FINDS

1. MacNeill, 'Pre-Christian Kings of Tara', *JRSAI* 57 1927, pp.153–4
2. O'Riordain, 'A Burial With Faience Beads at Tara', *PPS* 21, 1955, pp.163–73
3. Ibid

4. Ibid

5. Lucas, *Ancient Egyptian Materials and Industries*, Dover, 1962, pp. 155–156

6. Stone and Thomas, 'The Use and Distribution of Faience in the Ancient Near East and Prehistoric Europe, *PPS* 22, 1956, pp. 37-65

7. Grinsell, The Barrows of North Devon, *PDAS* 28 1970, p. 126

8. Wright, *The Ferriby Boats – Seacraft of the Bronze Age*, Routledge, 1990, pp. 1–15

9. Ibid, p. 13

10. Renfrew and Bahn, *Archaeology Theories and Methods*, Thames and Hudson, 1991, p. 16

11. Wright, op. cit., 1990, p. 16

12. Ibid, pp. 42–3

13. Ibid, pp. 44–5

14. Renfrew and Bahn, op. cit., p. 33

15. Ibid, pp. 44–5

16. Ibid, Introduction

17. Partridge, *Transport in Ancient Egypt*, The Rubicon Press, 1996, pp. 29–37

18. Ibid

19. Personal communication from Dr George Simkis, the Maritime Research Unit, UCLA

Chapter 2
THE MYSTERY OF SCOTA

1. Foster, *Picts, Scots and Gaels*, Historic Scotland/ Batsford, 1996, p. 11

2. Bower, *Scotichronicon*, translated by D.E.R Watt, Aberdeen University Press, 1993, Introduction

3. Ibid, p. 37

4. Ibid, p. 32
5. Foster op. cit., p. 14
6. Macalister, *Lebor Gabala: The Book of the Taking of Ireland*, Irish Texts Society, Dublin, vol 56, p. 1
7. Ibid, p. 52
8. Nennius, *British History and Welsh Annals*, edited by John Morris, London and Chichester, 1980, pp. 35–54
9. Ibid
10. Eusebius, *Historia Ecclesiastica*, edited by William Bright, Oxford, 1881, pp. 119–121
11. Eusebius/Jerome, *Die Chronik des Hiernyms*, Berlin 1956
12. Bower, op. cit. p. 31
13. Manetho, *Aegyptiaca*, edited by W.G. Waddell, Loeb Classic Library 1940, Harvard University Press, 1956, p. 101
14. Erichson, *Papyrus Harris*, Brussels 1993
15. Aldred, *Akhenaten – King of Egypt*, Thames and Hudson, 1988, p. 283
16. Ibid
17. Moran, *The Amarna Letters*, Johns Hopkins University Press, 1992, p. 21
18. Ibid, p. 22

Chapter 3
THE THEBAN SUPREMACY

1. Homer, *The Iliad*, book 9, translated by Alexander Pope, Oxford University Press, pp. 16–7
2. Gardiner, 'Hymns to Amun from a Leiden Papyrus', *ZAS* 42 1905, pp. 12–42
3. Parkinson, *Cracking Codes – The Rosetta Stone and Decipherment*, British Museum Press, 1999, p. 19
4. Ibid, p. 26

5. Herodotus, *The Histories*, Book 3, translated by Aubrey de Selincourt, Penguin Books, 1954, pp. 203–70

6. Watterson, *The Gods of Ancient Egypt*, Sutton Publishing, 1996, p. 9

7. Manley, *The Penguin Historical Atlas of Ancient Egypt*, Penguin Books, 1996, p. 18

8. Ibid

9. Wilkinson, *Early Dynastic Egypt*, Routledge, 1999, pp. 3–28

10. Clayton, *Chronicles of the Pharaohs*, Thames and Hudson, 1994, pp. 10–11

11. Parkinson, *Voices from Ancient Egypt*, British Museum Press, 1991, pp. 38–57

12. Tyldsley, *Hatshepsut*, Viking, 1996, p. 6

13. Parkinson, op. cit.

14. Tyldsley, op. cit., p. 41

15. Mertz, *Temples, Tombs and Hieroglyphs*, Michael O'Mara Books, 1996, pp. 178–201

16. Manley, op. cit., p. 59

17. Ibid, pp. 68–9

18. Ibid, pp. 58–63

19. Davies and Friedman, *Egypt*, British Museum Press, 1998, p. 135

20. Kaster, *The Wisdom of Ancient Egypt*, Michael O'Mara Books, 1995, pp. 91–101

21. Watterson, op. cit., pp. 11–15

22. Ibid

23. Ibid

24. Arrian, *The Campaigns of Alexander*, Book 3, edited and translated by P.A. Brunt, Loeb Classical Library, Harvard University Press, 1999, line 4

25. Kaster, op. cit., pp. 91–101

26. Aldred, *Akhenaten – King of Egypt*, Thames and Hudson, 1988, p. 70

27. Fairman, 'Worship and festivals in an Egyptian temple', *Bulletin of the John Rylands Library*, Manchester 37, 1954, pp. 165–203

28. Tulhoff, *Thutmosis III*, Munich Press, 1984, pp. 56–61

29. Helck, Otto & Westendorf, 'Amun', *Lexikon der Agyptologie*, Wiesbaden, 1975, pp. 237–48

30. *The Khonsu Cosmogony in Pyramid Studies and Other Essays presented to I.E.S. Edwards*, edited by John Baines et al, Occasional Publications 7, Egypt Exploration Society, 1988, pp. 168–75

Chapter 4
PIETY AND POWER

1. David, *Ancient Egypt*, Phaidon Press, 1975, p. 81

2. Kitchen, *Pharaoh Triumphant*, Aris and Phillips, 1982, p. 163

3. Ibid, pp. 156-9

4. Edwards, *A Thousand Miles Up the Nile*, London 1877, p. 127

5. David, *Discovering Ancient Egypt*, Michael O'Mara Books, 1993, pp. 19–21

6. Ibid, pp. 34–6

7. Shaw and Nicholson, *The British Museum Dictionary of Ancient Egypt*, British Museum Press, 1995, pp. 48–49

8. Erichson, *Papyrus Harris*, Brussels, 1933

9. Strouhal, *Life in Ancient Egypt*, Cambridge University Press, 1992, p. 22

10. Van der Horst, 'The Way of Life of the Egyptian Priests According to Chaermon' in *Studies in Egyptian Religion* by Voss, Hoens and Helde, Leiden, 1982, pp. 61–70

11. David, op. cit.

12. Strouhal, op. cit., pp. 232–233

13. Ibid
14. Van der Horst, Ibid
15. Hayes, *Cambridge Ancient History* vol 2, Cambridge University Press, 1973, p. 326
16. Shaw and Nicholson, op. cit., pp. 301–302
17. Hayes, 'Egypt Internal Affairs from Tutmosis I to the death of Amenhotep III' in I.E.S Edwards et al, *Cambridge Ancient History*, third edition, Cambridge University Press, 1973, pp. 323–9
18. Tyldsley, *Hatshepsut*, Viking, p. 95
19. Breasted, *Ancient Records of Egypt* vol II, University of Chicago, 1906, pp. 37-8
20. Ibid, pp. 37-8
21. Grimal, *A History of Ancient Egypt*, Blackwell, 1992, p. 212
22. Ibid, p. 207
23. Watterson, *Gods of Ancient Egypt*, Sutton Publishing, 1996, p. 23

Chapter Five
THE SUN KINGS

1. Herodotus, *The Histories*, book 3, translated by Aubrey de Selincourt, Penguin, 1954, pp. 203–71
2. Ibid
3. Ibid
4. El-Alfi, 'The Rivalry between Thebes and Heliopolis', *Discussions in Egyptology* 17, University College London, 1990, pp. 7–14
5. Stricker, *The Empire of Heliopolis, Proceedings of the Colloquium of the Archaeology, Geography and History of the Delta*, Oxford, 1989, pp. 293–300
6. Grimal, *A History of Ancient Egypt*, Blackwell, 1992, p. 220

7. Shaw and Nicholson, *The British Museum Dictionary of Ancient Egypt*, British Museum Press, 1995, pp. 276–277

8. Breasted, *Ancient Records of Egypt* vol II, University of Chicago, 1906, pp. 321–322

9. Gardiner, *The Tombs of Two Officials of Thutmose IV*, London, 1923, p. 13

10. Ibid

11. Clayton, *Chronicle of the Pharaohs*, Thames and Hudson, 1994, p. 27

12. Bucher, *Les Textes des Tombes de Thoutmosis III et d'Amenophis II*, Cairo, 1932, p. 24

13. Clayton, op. cit., p. 114

14. Aldred, *Akhenaten – King of Egypt*, Thames and Hudson, 1988, pp. 142–3

15. Ibid

16. Ibid

17. Assmann, 'Die Haresie des Echnaton: Aspekte der Amarna', *Saeculum*, 1972, pp. 109–26

18. Grimal, op. cit.

19. Aldred, op. cit., p. 161

20. Green, 'Queen as Goddess: 'The Religious Role of the Royal Women in the Late 18th Dynasty', In Amarna Letters vol 2, San Francisco, 1992, pp. 28–41

21. Aldred, op. cit., pp. 146–168

22. Aldred, op. cit., p. 51

23. Watterson, *The Egyptians*, Blackwell, 1998, pp. 137–8

24. Assmann, op. cit.

25. Redford, *Akhenaten, King of Egypt*, Princeton University Press, 1984, p. 47

26. Shaw and Nicholson, op. cit., p. 256

27. Redford, op. cit., p. 51

28. Ibid

29. Aldred, op. cit.

30. Johnson, 'Amenhotep III and Amarna: Some New

Considerations', *JEA* vol 82–3, Egypt Exploration Society, 1996–1997, pp. 65–83

31. Johnson, Ibid
32. Johnson, Ibid
33. Assmann, op. cit.
34. Partridge, *Faces of Pharaohs*, The Rubicon Press, 1994, pp. 118–9
35. Johnson, op. cit.

Chapter 5
HERESY

1. Hulin, 'The Amarna Period', Papers for Discussion, The Hebrew University Jerusalem 1981–2, pp. 191–209
2. Aldred, *Akhenaten – King of Egypt*, Thames and Hudson, 1998, p. 259
3. Redford, *The Heretic King*, Princeton University Press, 1984, pp. 58–9
4. Redford, 'The Sun-Disc in Akhenaten's Program: Its Worship and Antecedents', *JARCE* 15–17, 1978–80, pp. 21–75
5. Ibid, p. 62
6. Redford, 'Studies on Akhenaten at Thebes', *JARCE* 12, 1975, pp. 9–14
7. Arnold, *The Royal Women of Amarna*, The Metropolitan Museum of Art, New York, 1996, p. 24
8. Robins, *Proportion and Style in Ancient Egyptian Art*, Austin, Texas, 1994, pp. 119–48
9. Redford, 'The Sun-Disc in Akhenaten's Program', pp. 21–73
10. Ibid
11. There are a few allusions to the Aten before the reign of Akhenaten. The earliest appears to have been from the Middle Kingdom text entitled *The Tale of Sinuhe*.

12. Redford, 'The identity of the High Priest of Amun at the beginning of Akhenaten's reign', *JAOS* 83, 1963, pp. 140–1

13. Redford and Smith, *The Akhenaten Temple Project*, vol I, Warminster, 1976, pp. 1–69

14. Ibid

15. Ibid

16. Ibid

17. Ibid

18. Roberts, *Hathor Rising*, Northgate Publishers, 1995, p. 146

19. Ibid

20. Aldred, op. cit., p. 289

21. Hamza, 'The Religious Reforms of Akhenaten', *ASAE* 40, 1940, p. 540

22. Shaw and Nicholson, *The British Museum Dictionary of Ancient Egypt*, British Museum Press, 1995, p. 55

23. Redford, 'The Sun-Disc in Akhenaten's Program', pp. 21–75

24. Samson, *Nefertiti and Cleopatra*, The Rubicon Press, 1985, p. 25

25. Ibid

26. Arnold, op. cit., p. 85

27. Redford, 'The Sun-Disc in Akhenaten's Program', p. 27

28. Murnane and van Siclen, *The Boundary Stela of Akhenaten*, Kegan and Paul 1993, p. 167

29. Ibid

30. Davies, *The Rock Cut Tombs of Amarna* 6 vols, London, 1903–8

31. B. Davies, *Egyptian Historical Records of the Later 18th Dynasty*, Aris and Phillips, 1994, Facsimile, IV–VIII

32. James, *Excavating in Egypt: the Egypt Exploration Society 1822–1982*, British Museum Press, 1983, pp. 92–106

33. Ibid

34. Petrie, *Tell el-Amarna*, Aris and Phillips, 1974, pp. 41–2

35. Ibid

36. Murnane and van Siclen, op. cit., p. 167

37. Redford, 'The Sun-Disc in Akhenaten's Program', p. 27
38. Petrie, op. cit.
39. Kemp, *An Anatomy of a Civilization*, Routledge, 1991, p. 269
40. Ibid
41. Roberts, op. cit., pp. 161–2
42. Aldred, op. cit., p. 289
43. Redford, 'The Sun-Disc in Akhenaten's Program', p. 27
44. Ibid
45. Ibid
46. Ibid
47. Ibid
48. James, op. cit.
49. Aldred, op. cit.
50. Ibid
51. Redford, 'The Sun-Disc in Akhenaten's Program'
52. Arnold, op. cit., p. 52
53. Ibid, p. 55
54. Aldred, op. cit., p. 289
55. Ibid
56. B. Davies, op. cit.,
57. Arnold, op. cit., p. 12
58. Facsimile from the Berlin Museum
59. Moran, *The Amarna Letters*, Johns Hopkins University Press, 1992, p. 241
60. Kitchen, *Suppululiuma and the Amarna Pharaohs: A Study in Relative Chronology*, Liverpool University Press, 1962, pp. 11–12
61. Arnold, op. cit., p. 106
62. Redford, 'The Sun-Disc in Akhenaten's Program'

Chapter 7
Scota's Darkest Hour

1. Shaw and Nicholson, *The British Museum Dictionary of Ancient Egypt*, British Museum Press, 1995, p. 37
2. Kurht, *The Ancient Near East*, Routledge, 1995, pp. 217-8
3. Ibid, pp. 200–201
4. Schulman, *Military Rank and Title and Organization in the Egyptian New Kingdom*, Berlin, 1964, pp. 92–134
5. Trigger et al, *Ancient Egypt: A Social History*, Cambridge University Press, 1983, p. 206
6. Kurht, op. cit., pp. 217-218
7. Schulman, 'Some observations on the Military Background of the Amarna Period', *JARCE*, 3–4, 1964–5, pp. 51–55
8. Ibid
9. Ibid
10. Ibid
11. Ibid
12. El-Mahdy, *Tutankhamun: the Life and Death of a Boy King*, Headline, 1999, p. 128
13. Martin, *The Hidden Tombs of Memphis*, Thames and Hudson, 1995, pp. 35–8
14. El-Mahdy, op. cit., p. 128
15. Ibid
16. Trigger et al, op. cit., p. 202
17. Bennett, 'The Restoration Stela of Tutankhamun', *JEA 25*, 1939, pp. 8–15
18. Murnane and Van Siclen, *The Boundary Stela of Akhenaten*, Kegan and Paul, 1993, p. 169
19. Arnold, *The Royal Women of Amarna*, The Metropolitan Museum of Art, 1996, pp. 91–3
20. Aldred, *Akhenaten – King of Egypt*, Thames and Hudson, 1988, p. 293
21. Personal conversations with Egyptologist L. Gahlin at

University College, London, October 1997

22. Aldred, op. cit., p. 173

23. Ibid, pp. 280–2

24. Ibid

25. Ibid

26. Redford, 'The Sun-Disc in Akhenaten's Program', *JARCE*, pp. 21–75

27. Ibid

28. Moran, *The Amarna Letters*, Johns Hopkins University Press, 1992, Introduction

29. Ibid, pp. 90–2

30. Ibid, p. 43

31. Ibid, p. 7

32. Ibid, p. 141

33. Ibid, p. 209

34. Helck, *Die Beziehungen Agyptens zur Voderaisen*, Leiden, 1987, pp. 67–72

35. Moran, op. cit., pp. 198–214

36. Ibid, p. 107

37. Kitchen, *Suppululiuma and the Amarna Pharaohs: A Study in Relative Chronology*, Liverpool University Press, 1962, pp. 11–12

38. Moran, op. cit., p. 21

39. El-Mahdy, op. cit., p. 128

40. Moran, op. cit., p. 8

41. Ibid, p. 241

Chapter 8
ESCAPE FROM PERSECUTION

1. Ezekiel, chapter 27, verses 3–4

2. Frost, *Under the Mediterranean*, Routledge, 1963, pp. 33–9

3. Ibid

4.   Strabo, *Geography*, Loeb Classical Library XVIII, Harvard University Press, 1999, pp. 106–110

5.   Faulkner, *Egyptian Sea-going Ships*, JEA 26, 1940, pp. 3–9

6.   Nibbi, 'An Answer to Lucien Basch on Ancient Egyptian Sea-Going, Stone Anchors and Bread Offerings', *Discussions in Egyptology* 38, University College London, 1997, pp. 37–62

7.   Ibid

8.   Jones, *Boats*, British Museum Press, 1995, pp. 9–11

9.   Redford, *Egypt, Canaan and Israel in Ancient Times*, Princeton University Press, 1992, pp. 159

10. Jones, op. cit., pp. 9–11

11. Ibid

12. Ibid

13. Partridge, *Transport in Ancient Egypt*, Rubicon Press, 1995, pp. 17-20

14. Faulkner, op. cit., pp. 3–9

15. Newberry, *Notes on Sea-going Ships*, JEA 28, 1942, p. 40

16. E-mail correspondence with historian Frank Joseph Yucco, February 1999

17. Faulkner, op. cit., pp. 40–42

18. Tyldsley, *Hatshepsut*, Viking, 1996, pp. 129–154

19. Silver, *Ancient Economies*, II, New York, 1999, pp. 202–15

20. Faulkner, op. cit., p. 9

21. Silver, op. cit., pp. 205–15

22. Redford, op. cit., p. 159

23. The Thor Heyerdahl Official Website, pp. 1–3

24. Heyerdahl, *The Ra Expedition*, Allen and Unwin, 1970, p. 18

25. Alaqui and Searight, 'Rock Art in Morocco', *PPS* 63, 1997, pp. 87-101

26. Heyerdahl, op. cit., p. 18

27. Ibid

28. Ibid

29. Kemp, *An Anatomy of a Civilization*, Routledge, 1991, pp. 257-8

30. Bates, *Economic Structure of Antiquity*, Greenwood Press, 1995, pp. 20–43

31. Bower, *Scotichronicon*, translated and edited by D.E.R. Watt, Aberdeen University Press, 1993, p. 37

32. Randolph, *The Present State of the Islands in the Arches Sea of Constantinople & Gulf of Smyrna*, Athens, 1983, p. 181

33. Trianaphyllidou, *Connections Between Crete and Egypt*, Athens, 1988, pp. 95–6

34. Warren, 'Minoan Crete and Pharaonic Egypt' in *Egypt, the Aegean and the Levant*, edited by Davies and Schofield, British Museum Press, 1995, p. 10

35. Wood, *In Search of the Trojan War*, BBC Books, 1985, pp. 94–122

36. Homer, *The Iliad*, book 9 translated by Alexander Pope, Oxford University Press, 1974, pp. 240–55

37. Wood, op. cit., pp. 94–122

38. Thucydides, Loeb Classical Library, Harvard University Press, 1999, pp. 89–106

39. Ibid

40. Krzyszkowska, 'Ivory from Hippopotamus Tusk in the Aegean Bronze Age', *Antiquity* 58, 1984, pp. 123–5

41. Warren, *Minoan Stone Vases*, Cambridge University Press, 1965, pp. 125–8

42. Bietak, 'Egypt and the Minoan World' in *Egypt, the Aegean and the Levant*, edited by Davies and Schofield, British Museum Press, 1995, pp. 19–28

43. Ibid

44. Homer, op. cit., pp. 240–55

45. Pausanias, vol III, Loeb Classical Library, Harvard University Press, 1999, p. 54

46. Iakovidis, *Myceane-Epidauros*, Athens, 1989, p. 12

47. Tsountas, 'Archaeotites ek Mykenon', *Archaiologike Ephermis*, 1887, pp. 155–172

48. Immerwahr, *Aegean Paintings in the Bronze Age*,

Pennsylvania State University Press, 1990, pp. 129–73

49. Cline, 'Amenhotep III and the Aegean: a Re-assessment of Egypto-Aegean Relations in the 14th century BC', *Orientalia* 56, 1987, pp. 1–36

50. Ibid

51. Hankey, 'Stirrup Jars at El Amarna' in *Egypt, the Aegean and the Levant*, edited by Davies and Schofield, British Museum Press, 1995, pp. 116-24

52. Ibid

53. Helck, *Die Biezeihungen*, 1979, p. 97

54. Shaw and Nicholson, *The British Museum Dictionary of Ancient Egypt*, British Museum Press, 1995, pp. 69–70

55. Cline, op. cit., pp. 1–3

56. Astour, 'Aegean Place-Names in an Egyptian Inscription', *AJA* vol 70, 1966, pp. 313–7

57. Edel, *Die Ortsnamenlisten 52*, Berlin, 1966, pp. 37-40

58. Aldred, *Akhenaten – King of Egypt*, Thames and Hudson, 1988, p. 173

59. Breasted, *Ancient Records of Egypt* vol II, University of Chicago, 1906, p. 76

60. Parkinson and Schofield, 'Of Helmets and Heretics: A Possible Egyptian Representation of Mycenean Warriors On a Papyrus from El-Amarna', *BSA* vol 89, 1994, pp. 157-70

61. Moran, *The Amarna Letters*, Johns Hopkins University Press, 1992, p. 48

62. Parkinson and Schofield, op. cit., pp. 157–70

63. Ibid

64. Ibid

65. Parkinson and Schofield 'Images of Myceneans: A Recently Acquired Painted Papyrus from El Amarna' in *Egypt, the Aegean and the Levant*, edited by Davies and Schofield, British Museum Press, 1995, pp. 125–6

66. Ibid

67. Bower, op. cit., p. 37
68. Rice, *Amber – the Golden Gem of the Ages*, Litten Education Press, 1980, pp. 27–40
69. Lucas and Harris, *Ancient Egyptian Materials and Industries*, Dover, 1962, pp. 387–8
70. Rice, op. cit., pp. 108–10
71. Oppert, *The Royal Inscriptions of Mari*, London, 1876, pp. 102–10
72. Rice, op. cit., pp. 27–40
73. Ibid
74. Ibid
75. Brock, 'Amber in the Mycenean World', *BSA* 69, 1974, pp. 145–72
76. Ibid
77. Beck and Shennan, *Amber in Prehistoric Britain*, Oxbow Books, 1991, pp. 16-19

Chapter 9

BRIGANTIA

1. Fage, *The History of Africa*, Routledge, 1997, pp. 13–14
2. Shaw and Nicholson, *The British Museum Dictionary of Ancient Egypt*, British Museum Press, 1997, pp. 161–2
3. Ibid
4. Trigger et al, *Ancient Egypt: A Social History*, Cambridge University Press, 1983, p. 272
5. Personal discussion with Egyptologist Dr Bill Manley, January/February 1998
6. Manley, *The Penguin Historical Atlas of Ancient Egypt*, Penguin Books, 1996, pp. 87-8
7. Trigger et al, op. cit., pp. 272–3
8. Ibid, p. 89
9. *The Cambridge Encyclopedia of Africa*, Cambridge

University Press, 1981, pp. 79–80

10. Bower, *Scotichronicon*, translated and edited by D.E.R. Watt, Aberdeen University Press, 1993, p. 35

11. Ibid

12. Carby, *Israel, Egypt and Africa*, Hudson Group, 1990, p. 185

13. Lenz, *Timbuktu, Reise durch Morokko die Sahara und des Sudan*, Leipzig, pp. 17–54

14. Alaqui and Searight, 'Rock Art in Morocco', *PPS* 63, 1997, pp. 87–101

15. Ibid

16. Ibid

17. Ibid

18. Camp, 'Les traces d'un age de bronze en Afrique du Nord', *Revue Africaine* 104, 1960, pp. 31–55

19. Ibid

20. Alaqui and Searight, op. cit., pp. 87–101

21. Ibid

22. Graves, *Greek Myths*, Cassell, 1985, pp. 241–2

23. Herodotus, *The Histories*, book 4, translated by Aubrey de Selincourt, Penguin, 1954, p. 184

24. Taylor-Hansen, *The Ancient Atlantic*, Amherst Press, 1969, pp. 98–136

25. Ibid

26. Bower, op. cit., p. 35

27. Information kindly forwarded by the Andalusian Tourist Information Office, 1999

28. Collins, *Spain*, Oxford University Press, 1988, pp. 1–39

29. Harrison, *Spain at the Dawn of History*, Thames and Hudson, 1988, pp. 48–69

30. Boardman, *The Greeks Overseas*, Penguin, 1964, pp. 223–232

31. Harrison, op. cit., pp. 48–69

32. Strabo, *Geography* vol III, The Loeb Classical Library,

Harvard University Press, 1999, pp. 65–7

33. Harrison, op. cit.

34. Herodotus, op. cit.

35. Szynet, 'The Colonization of North Africa', *PPS*, 1978, pp. 220–4

36. Harrison, op. cit.

37. Ibid

38. Ibid

39. Lancel, *Carthage: A History*, Blackwell, 1992, pp. 231–3

40. Ibid

41. The Lady of Elche Official Website, pp. 1–3

42. Childress, *Lost Cities of Atlantis, Ancient Europe and the Mediterranean*, Adventure Unlimited, 1996, p. 267

43. Bower, op. cit., p. 39

44. Ibid

45. Castro, *Iberia in Prehistory*, Blackwell, 1995, p. 106

46. Ibid

47. Ibid

48. Jimenez, 'Excavations y trabajos arqueologicos en la pronincia de alabacete', *Informes y Memorias* 15, 1947, pp. 7–16

49. Pliny, *Natural History*, edited and translated by H. Rackham and W.H.S. Jones, Loeb Classical Library vol 37, Harvard University Press, 1999

50. *Canary Islands*, The Lonely Planet Guide, 1988, pp. 13–15

51. Ibid

52. Ibid

53. Scantos, *The Mysterious Origins of the Guanches*, 1999, pp. 1–13

54. Walker, *In Search of Cultures Past – Beyond the Beaches of Gran Canaria*, Archaeological Institute of America, 1999, pp. 1–3

55. Personal correspondence with Dr Joyce Filer, Department of Egyptian Antiquities, British Museum, June 1998

56. Herodotus, op. cit.

57. Shaw and Nicholson, op. cit.

58. Herodotus, op. cit.

59. Programme *The Cave Mummies*, Channel 4 TV, 1999

60. Ikram and Dodson, *The Mummy in Ancient Egypt*, Thames and Hudson, 1988, p. 127

61. Lehner, *The Complete Pyramids*, Thames and Hudson, 1997, p. 14

62. Edwards, *The Pyramids of Ancient Egypt*, Penguin, 1993, pp. 34–71

63. *The Cave Mummies*

Chapter 10
PROBLEMS OF PREHISTORY

1. Burgess, 'The Bronze Age' in *Renfrew's British Prehistory*, Duckworth, 1974, p. 165

2. Bradley, *The Prehistoric Settlement of Britain*, Routledge, Kegan and Paul, 1978, p. 14

3. Dyer, *Ancient Britain*, Batsford, 1990, p. 93

4. Ibid

5. Ibid

6. Marsden, *The Early Barrow Diggers*, Tempus Books, 1999, p. 7

7. Ibid, p. 10

8. Ibid

9. Personal communication with the Kent County Archives, Canterbury, July 1999

10. Ibid

11. Dyer, op. cit., p. 46

12. Ibid, p. 15

13. Atkinson, *Stonehenge*, English Heritage, 1987, pp. 21–7

14. Ibid

15. Renfrew and Bahn, *Archaeology Theories and Methods*, Thames and Hudson, 1991, pp. 286–8

16. Ibid

17. Harbison, *Pre-Christian Ireland*, Thames and Hudson, 1988, p. 27

18. Dyer, op. cit.

19. Ibid

20. Atkinson, op. cit.

21. Smith and Melluish, *Teach Yourself Ancient Greek*, Hodder and Stoughton, 1992, p. 167

22. O'Kelly, *Newgrange*, Thames and Hudson, 1982, pp. 93–102

23. Ibid

24. Armit, *Scotland's Hidden History*, Tempus, 1998, p. 4

25. O'Kelly, op. cit.

26. Burl, *Prehistoric Henges*, Shire Books, 1997, pp. 7–13

27. Armit, op. cit., p. 14

28. Bradley, op. cit.

29. Armit, op. cit., p. 14

30. Pennington, *The History of British Vegetation*, London, 1969, p. 169

31. Evans, *The Environment of Early Man in the British Isles*, Elek Books, 1975, pp. 142–6

32. Ibid

33. Butlet and van der Waals, 'Bell Beakers and Early Metal Working in the Netherlands', *Paleohistoria* 12, 1966, pp. 41–139

34. Bradley, op. cit., pp. 67

35. Fox, *Early Cultures of North West Europe*, Cambridge University Press, 1950, pp. 86-105

36. Cunliffe, *Wessex to AD 1000*, Longman, 1993, pp. 118–127

37. Pearson, *Bronze Age Britain*, English Heritage, 1993, p. 94

38. Dyer, op. cit., pp. 94–5

39. Ibid

40. Burgess, op. cit., p. 188

41. Fleming, 'Territorial Patterns in Bronze Age Wessex', *PPS* 37, 1971, pp. 154–164

42. Megaw and Simpson, *British Prehistory*, Leicester University Press, 1979, p. 178

43. Dyer, op. cit., p. 11

44. Megaw and Simpson, op. cit., p. 178

45. Ibid

46. Dyer, op. cit., pp. 94–5

47. Muckelroy, *Archaeology Underwater*, McGraw-Hill Book Company, 1980, p. 62

48. Personal communication with Gillian Hutchinson, Curator at the National Maritime Museum, Greenwich, London, June 1999

49. Fenwick and Gale, *Historic Shipwrecks*, Tempus, 1988, p. 23

50. Ibid

51. Muckelroy, op. cit.

52. Fenwick and Gale, op. cit.

53. Ibid

54. Muckelroy, 'Two Bronze Age Cargoes in British Waters', *Antiquity* LIV, 1980, pp. 100–109

Chapter 11

THE DNA ENIGMA

1. Daniel, *The Idea of Prehistory*, Penguin, 1974, pp. 100–102

2. Ibid

3. Carroll, *The Sceptic's Dictionary*, 1998, pp. 1–3

4. Ibid

5. Lombroso, *Criminal Anthropology*, New York and London, 1895, pp. 42–67

6. Carroll, op. cit.

7. Ibid

8. *Diary of Emma Andrews*, Metropolitan Museum of Art, 1999

9. Reeves, *The Complete Tutankhamun*, Thames and Hudson, 1990, pp. 20–21

10. Davies, *The Tomb of Queen Tiyi*, London, 1910, pp. 150–176

11. Smith, *The Royal Mummies*, Institut Francais D'Archeologie Orientale, Cairo, 1912

12. Samson, *Nefertiti and Cleopatra*, Rubicon Press, 1985, p. 87

13. Aldred, *Akhenaten – King of Egypt*, Thames and Hudson, 1988, p. 293

14. Brier, *Egyptian Mummies*, Michael O'Mara Books, 1996, p. 174

15. Harrison, 'The Tutankhamun Postmortem', *The Lancet*, 1973, p. 259

16. Harrison, 'An Anatomical Examination of the Pharaonic Remains Purported to be Akhenaten', *JEA* 52, 1966, pp. 95–119

17. Ibid

18. Ibid

19. Personal conversation with Dr Robson, Institute of Archaeology, University College London, 1998

20. Clarke, 'The Invasion Hypothesis in British Archaeology', *PPS* 40, 1966, pp. 21–36

21. Watson and Crick, 'A Structure for Deoxyribose Nucleic Acid', *Nature*, 1953, pp. 94–6

22. Rose, *Lifelines*, Penguin, 1997, pp. 117–8

23. Watson and Crick, op. cit.

24. Personal communication from Egyptologist Marianne Luban on DNA testing upon the Amarna royal family, Greece, September 1999

25. Renfrew and Bahn, *Archaeology: Theories and Methods*, Thames and Hudson, 1991, pp. 380–403

26. Ibid

27. Brier, op. cit., pp. 189–91

28. Personal conversation with Egyptologist Robert Partridge, Manchester 1997

29. Ibid

30. Kennewick Man Official Website, USA

31. Ibid

32. Ibid

33. David and Tapp, *The Mummy's Tale*, Michael O'Mara Books, 1992, pp. 168–9

34. Ibid

35. Ibid

36. Randall-Maciver and Wilkin, *Libyan Notes*, London, 1901

37. I. Morgan-Watkins, 'ABO Blood Group Distribution in Wales in Relation to Human Settlement', in *Genetic and Population Studies in Wales*, edited by P.S. Harper and E. Sunderland, Cardiff University Press, 1986, pp. 118–146

38. Lloyd, *A History of Wales from the Earliest Times to the Edwardian Conquest*, London, 1939

39. Owen, 'The Flemings in Pembrokeshire', *Archaeologia Cambrensis* 12, 1895, pp. 96–106

40. Morgan-Watkins, op. cit.

41. Addyman et al, *Vikings in England*, The Anglo-Danish Viking Project, 1981, pp. 15–17

42. Morgan-Watkins, op. cit.

43. Ibid

44. Brown, 'Distribution of the ABO and Rhesus blood groups in the North of Scotland', *Heredity* 20, 1965, pp. 289–303

45. Morgan-Watkins, op. cit.

46. Kherumian, *Genetique et Anthropologie des Groups Sanguins*, Paris, 1951, pp. 89–96

Chapter 12
SYMBOLS OF POWER

1. Personal communication from Steve Ottery, Curator, Isles of Scilly Museum, 1998

2. Ashbee, *Ancient Scilly*, Bayliss and Sons, 1974, pp. 216–231

3. Ibid

4. O'Neil, 'The Excavation of Knackbuoy Cairn, St Martins, Isles of Scilly', *Antiquaries Journal*, Oxford University Press, 1962, pp. 21–4

5. Ibid

6. Fox, *South-West England*, Thames and Hudson, 1964, p. 57

7. Newton and Renfrew, 'British Faience Beads Re-Considered', *Antiquity* 44, 1970, pp. 199–206

8. Personal correspondence with Gillian Varndell

9. McKerrell, 'On the Origins of British Faience Beads and Some Aspects of the Wessex-Mycenae Relationship', *PPS* vol, 38, 1972, pp. 286–301

10. Harding, *The Myceneans in Europe*, Academic Press, 1984, pp. 58–72

11. McKerrell, op. cit.

12. Shaw and Nicholson, *The British Museum Dictionary of Ancient Egypt*, British Museum Press, 1995, pp. 157–8

13. Lucas and Harris, *Ancient Egyptian Materials and Industries*, Dover, 1962, pp. 254–5

14. McKerrell, op. cit.

15. Lucas and Harris, op. cit.

16. Silvermann, *Ancient Egypt*, Duncan Baird, 1997, p. 64

17. Scheel, *Egyptian Metalworking and Tools*, Shire Books, 1989, pp. 18–20

18. Davies, *The Tomb of Rekhmire at Thebes*, Metropolitan Museum of Art Egyptian Expedition, New York, reprint 1973, pp. 53–4

19. Ibid
20. Charles, 'Where is the Tin?', *Antiquity* 49, 1975, pp. 19–24
21. Penhallurick, *Tin in Antiquity*, The Institute of Metals, 1986, pp. 15–85
22. Ibid
23. Ibid
24. Ibid
25. Ezekiel, 27, 12
26. Harrison, *Spain at the Dawn of History*, Thames and Hudson, 1992, pp. 48–92
27. Ibid
28. Ibid
29. Herodotus, *The Histories*, book 4, translated by Aubrey de Selincourt, Penguin, 1954
30. Howorth, 'The ancient mining in Galicia', *PSA VII*, 1873, pp. 128–75
31. Penhallurick, op. cit.
32. Ibid
33. Personal communication from Roger Penhallurick
34. Ibid
35. Penhallurick, in *Prehistoric Metallurgy in Cornwall Conference*, edited by Budd and Gale, Cambourne School of Mines, 1997, pp. 23–33
36. Ibid
37. Personal communication from Roger Penhallurick
38. Penhallurick, op. cit.
39. Fenwick and Gale, *Historic Shipwrecks*, Tempus, 1998, pp. 19–23
40. Carpenter, *The Pillars of Hercules*, Delacorte Press, 1966, pp. 101–129
41. Daniel, *The Idea of Prehistory*, Penguin, 1974, p. 21
42. Bochart, *Geographic Sacrara*, 1646, New York and London, pp. 89–98
43. Herodotus, *The Histories*, translated by Aubrey de

Selincourt, Penguin, 1954, p. 250

44. Pytheas, *The Voyages*, University Library Tromso, 1999, pp. 1–3

45. Tylecote, *Metallurgy in Archaeology*, London, 1962

46. Penhallurick, *Tin in Antiquity*, pp. 23–33

47. Cunliffe, 'Ictis, was it here?', *OJA* 2 (1), 1983, pp. 123–6

48. Penhallurick, *Tin in Antiquity*

49. Burgess, 'The Bronze Age', in *Renfrew's British Prehistory*, Duckworth, London, 1974, pp. 165–232

49. Laing and Laing, *The Origins of Britain*, Routledge, 1980, pp. 180–183

50. Penhallurick, *Tin in Antiquity*

52. Herodotus, op. cit. book 3, pp. 203–271

53. Shaw and Nicholson, op. cit., pp. 157–8

54. Penhallurick, *Tin in Antiquity*

55. Roeder, *Ägyptische Bronzefiguren*, Berlin, 1956, pp. 59–63

56. Powell, 'The Gold Ornament from Mold, Flintshire, North Wales', *PPS* 53, 1953, pp. 161–179

57. Laing and Laing, op. cit., p. 180

58. Powell, op. cit.

59. Ibid

60. Ibid

61. Personal communication from Andrew Halpin, Assistant Curator of the National Museum of Antiquities, Dublin 1998

62. Childe, *Dawn of Civilization*, Penguin, 1947, p. 21

63. Aldred, *Jewels of the Pharaohs*, Thames and Hudson, 1971, p. 36

64. Powell, op. cit.

65. Ibid

Chapter 13
THE LOST COLONY

1. MacNeill, *Celtic Ireland*, Dublin, 1921, pp. 225–7
2. Davies, *Mythic Ireland*, Thames and Hudson, 1996, p. 187
3. Ibid
4. Walsh, *Ireland's History in Maps*, 1996, pp. 1–4
5. Ibid
6. Beresford, *Celtic Women*, Constable, 1995, p. 23
7. *The Annals of the Four Masters*, vol I–VII, translated and edited by Dr John O'Donovan, Irish Texts Society, Dublin University, 1836
8. Ibid
9. Ibid
10. MacAlister, *Lebor Gabala: The Book of the Taking of Ireland*, vol 56, Irish Texts Society, Dublin, 1938–56, p. 1
11. Bower, *Scotichronicon*, edited by D.E.R. Watt, Aberdeen University Press, 1993, p. 112
12. Ibid
13. Personal conversation with Andrew Halpin, Assistant Curator of the National Museum of Antiquities, Dublin 1998
14. *Ireland Guide*, Moorland Publishing, 1993, pp. 215–236
15. Personal conversation with Claudia Freeman, Department of Medieval Antiquities, British Museum, 1999

BIBLIOGRAPHY

Addyman et al, *Vikings in England*, The Anglo-Danish Viking Project, 1981

Alaqui, Fatima-Zohra, and Searight, Susan, 'Rock Art in Morocco', PPS 63 pp. 87–101

Aldred, Cyril, *Akhenaten – King of Egypt*, Thames and Hudson, 1988

Aldred, Cyril, *Jewels of the Pharaohs*, Thames and Hudson, 1971

Arnold, Dorothea, *The Royal Women of Amarna*, The Metropolitan Museum of Art, New York, 1996

Armit, Ian, *Scotland's Hidden History*, Tempus Publishing, 1998

Arrian, *The Campaigns of Alexander*, edited and translated by P.A. Brunt, Book 3, Loeb Classical Library, Harvard University Press, 1999

Ashbee, Paul, *Ancient Scilly*, Bayliss and Sons Ltd, 1974

Assmann, Jan, 'Die Haresie des Echnaton: Aspekte der Amarna-Religion', *Saeculum* 23, 1972

Astour, Michael, 'Aegean Place Names in an Egyptian Inscription', *AJA* 70, 1966

Atkinson, R.J.C., *Stonehenge*, English Heritage, 1987

Baines, J. and Malek, J., *Atlas of Ancient Egypt*, Oxford, 1980

Baines, John et al, *The Khonsu Cosmogony in Pyramid Studies and other Essays, presented to I.E.S. Edwards*, Occasional Publications 7, Egypt Exploration Society, 1988

Bates, C., *Economic Structure of Antiquity*, Greenwood Press, Connecticut, 1995

Beck, Curt and Shennan, Stephen, *Amber in Prehistoric Britain*, Oxbow Books, 1991

Bennett, John, *The Restoration Stela of Tutankhamun*, JEA vol 25, 1939

Beresford, Peter Ellis, *Celtic Women*, Constable, 1995

Bietak, Manfred, 'Egypt and the Minoan World' in *Egypt, the Aegean and Levant* edited by V Davies and L Schofield, British Museum Press, 1995

Boardman, John, *The Greeks Overseas*, Penguin Books, 1964

Boece, *Historia Scotus*, 1527

Bochart, *Geographica Sacra*, 1646

Bower, Walter, *Scotichronicon*, edited and translated by D.E.R. Watt, Aberdeen University Press, 1993

Bradley, Richard, *The Prehistoric Settlements of Britain*, Routledge, Kegan and Paul, 1978

Breasted, James, *Ancient Records of Egypt*, 5 volumes, University of Chicago, 1906

Brier, Bob, *Egyptian Mummies*, Michael O'Mara Books, 1996

Brock, Helen and Harding, Anthony, 'Amber in the Mycenean World', *BSA* 69, 1974

Brown, E., 'The Distribution of the ABO and Rhesus Blood groups in the North of Scotland', *Heredity* 20, 1965

Bucher, P., *Les Textes des Tombes de Thoutmosis III et d' Amenophis II*, Cairo, 1932

Budd, Paul and Gale, David, *Prehistoric Metallurgy in Cornwall*, Cambourne School of Mines, 1997

Burgess, C., 'The Bronze Age', in *British Prehistory*, edited by Colin Renfrew, Duckworth, 1974

Burl, Aubrey, *Prehistoric Henges*, Shire Books, 1997

Butler and Van der Waals, 'Bell Beakers and Early Metalworking in the Netherlands', *Paleohistoria* 12, 1966

Camp, G., 'Les traces d'un age de bronze en Afrique du Nord', *Revue Africaine* 104, 1960

Carby, Courtland, *Israel, Egypt and Africa*, Hudson Group, 1990

Carpenter, D., *The Pillars of Hercules*, Delacorte Press, 1966

Carroll, N., *The Sceptic's Dictionary*, 1998

Castro, Maria Cruz, *Iberia in Prehistory*, Blackwell, 1995

Charles, J.A., 'Where is the Tin?', *Antiquity* vol 49, 1975

Childe, V.G., *Dawn of Civilization*, Penguin Books, 1947

Childress, David, *Lost Cities of Atlantis, Ancient Europe and the Mediterranean,* Adventure Unlimited, 1996

Clark, J.G.D., 'The Invasion Hypothesis in British Archaeology', *Antiquity* 40, 1966

Clayton, Peter, *Chronicles of the Pharaohs*, Thames and Hudson, 1994

Cline, Eric, 'Amenhotep III and the Aegean: Reassessment of Egypt-Aegean relations in the 14th century BC', *Orientalia* 56, 1987

Collins, Paul, *Spain*, Oxford University Press, 1988

Cunliffe, Barry, 'Ictis, was it here?', *OJA*, 1983

Cunliffe, Barry, *Wessex to AD 1000,* Longman, 1993

Daniel, Glyn, *The Idea of Prehistory*, Penguin Books, 1964

David, Rosalie, *Ancient Egypt*, Phaidon Press, 1975

David, Rosalie, *Discovering Ancient Egypt*, Michael O'Mara Books, 1993

David, R., and Tapp, E., *The Mummy's Tale*, Michael O'Mara Books, 1992

Davies, Benedict, G., *Egyptian Historical Records of the Later 18th Dynasty*, Aris and Phillip Ltd, 1994

Davies, Michael, *Mythic Ireland*, Thames and Hudson, 1996

Davies, N. de G., *The Rock Cut Tombs of Amarna*, 6 vols, London, 1903–8

Davies, N. de G., *The Tomb of Rekhmire at Thebes,* Metropolitan Museum of Art Egyptian Expedition, New York, reprint, 1973

Davies, Theodore, *The Tomb of Queen Tiyi*, London, 1910

Davies, Vivian and Friedman, Renee, *Egypt*, British Museum Press, 1998

Dyer, James, *Ancient Britain*, Batsford Ltd, 1990

Edel, E., *Die Ortsnamenlisten 52*, 1966

Edwards, Amelie, *A Thousand Miles up the Nile*, London, 1877

Edwards, I.E.S., *The Pyramids of Ancient Egypt*, Penguin Books, 1993

El-Alfi, Mostafa, 'The Rivalry Between Thebes and Heliopolis', *Discussions in Egyptology* 17, University College London, 1990

El-Mahdy, Christine, *Tutankhamun: the life and death of a boy-king*, Headline, 1999

Erichson, E., *Papyrus Harris*, Brussels, 1933

Esekiel, *The Old Testament*, Chapter 27, verse 3–4

Eusebius, *Historia Ecclesiastica*, edited by William Bright, Oxford, 1881

Eusebius/Jerome, *Die Chonik des Hiernyms*, Berlin, 1956

Evans, John, *The Environment of Early Man in the British Isles*, Elek Books Ltd, 1975

Fage, *The History of Africa*, Routledge, 1997

Fairman, H.W., *Worship and Festivals in an Egyptian Temple*, Bulletin of the John Rylands Library, Manchester 37, 1954

Faulkner, R.O., 'Egyptian Sea-Going Ships', *JEA* 26, 1940

Fenwick, V. and Gale, A., *Historic Shipwrecks*, Tempus Publishing, 1988

Fleming, A., 'Territorial Patterns in Bronze Age Wessex', *PPS* 37, 1971

Foster, Sally M., *Picts, Scots and Gaels*, Historic Scotland/ Batsford Ltd, 1996

Fox, Aileen, *Early Cultures of North West Europe,* Cambridge University Press, 1959

Fox, Aileen, *South-West England*, Thames and Hudson, 1964

Frost, Honor, *Under the Mediterranean*, Routledge, 1963

Gardiner, A.H., 'Hymns to Amun from a Leiden Papyrus', *ZAS* 42, 1905

Gardiner, A.H., *The Tombs of Two Officials of Thutmose IV*,

London, 1923

Graves, Robert, *Greek Myths*, Cassell Ltd, 1985

Green, L., *Amarna Letters* vol 2, San Francisco, 1992

Grimal, Nicholas, *A History of Ancient Egypt*, Blackwell, 1992

Grinsell, L.V., 'The Barrow of North Devon', *PDAS* 28, 1970

Hamza, 'The Religious Reforms of Akhenaten', *ASAE* 40, 1940

Hankey, Vronky, 'Stirrup Jars at El Amarna' in *Egypt, the Aegean and the Levant*, edited by Davies V. and Friedman R., British Museum Press, 1995

Harbison, Peter, *Pre-Christian Ireland*, Thames and Hudson, 1988

Harding, A.F., *The Myceneans in Europe*, London, Academic Press, 1984

Harrison, R.G., 'An Anatomical Examination of the Pharaonic Remains Purported to be Akhenaten', *JEA* 52, 1966

Harrison, R.G., 'The Tutankhamun Post-mortem', *The Lancet*, 1973

Harrison, Richard, *Spain – at the dawn of history*, Thames and Hudson, 1988

Hayes, W.C., 'Egypt Internal affairs from Tutmosis I to the death of Amenhotep III' in *Cambridge Ancient History* edited by I.E.S. Edwards, Cambridge University Press, 1973

Herodotus, *The Histories*, translated by Aubrey de Selincourt, Penguin Books, 1954

Heyerdahl, Thor, *The Ra Expedition*, Allen and Unwin, 1970

Homer, *The Iliad,* translated by Alexander Pope, Oxford University Press, 1974

Helck, H.R., *W Die Beziehungen Agyptens zur Voderaisen,* 1987

Helck, W., Otto, E., and Westendorf, W., 'Amun', *Lexicon der Agyptologie*, Wiesbaden, 1975

Horst Van der, P., 'The Way of Life of the Egyptian Priests According to Chaermon' in *Studies in Egyptian Religion*, Hoens, V. and Helde, Leiden, 1982

Hulin, Christopher, *The Amarna Period*, Papers for Discussion, the Hebrew University, Jerusalem, 1981–2

Iakovidis, S.E., *Mycenae-Epidauros*, Athens, 1979

Ikram, Salima and Dodson, Aidan, *The Mummy in Ancient Egypt*, Thames and Hudson, 1988

Immerwahr, S.A., *Aegean Paintings in the Bronze Age*, Pennsylvania State University Press, 1990

James, T.G.H., *Excavating in Egypt: the Egypt Exploration Society 1822–1982*, British Museum Press, 1983

Jimenez, J., 'Excavations y trabajos arquelogicos en la pronincia de alabacete', *Informes y Memorias* 15, 1947

Johnson, W., Raymond, 'Amenhotep III and Amarna: Some New Considerations', *JEA* vol 82–3, 1996–7

Jones, Dilwyn, *Boats*, British Museum Press, 1995

Kaster, Joseph, *The Wisdom of Ancient Egypt*, Michael O'Mara Books, 1995

Kemp, Barry, *An Anatomy of a Civilization*, Routledge, 1991

Kherumian, R., *Genetique et Anthropologie des groups Sanguins*, Paris, 1951

Kitchen, Kenneth, *Suppiluliuma and the Amarna Pharaohs: A Study in Relative Chronology*, Liverpool University Press, 1962

Kitchen, Kenneth, *Pharaoh Triumphant*, Aris and Phillips Ltd, 1982

Krzyszkowska, Olga, 'Ivory from Hippopotamus Tusk in the Aegean Bronze Age', *Antiquity* 58, 1984

Kurht, Amelie, *The Ancient Near East*, Routledge, 1995

Laing, Lloyd and Laing, Jennifer, *The Origins of Britain*, Routledge, 1980

Lancel, Serge, *Carthage – A History*, Blackwell, 1992

Lehner, Mark, *The Complete Pyramids*, Thames and Hudson, 1997

Lenz, O., *Timbuktu, Reise durch Moroko de Sahara und des Sudan*, Leipzig, 1884

Lloyd, J.E., *A History of Wales from the Earliest Times to the*

Edwardian Conquest, London, 1939

Lombroso, *Criminal Anthropology*, 1895

Lucas, A. and Harris, J.R., *Ancient Egyptian Materials and Industries*, Dover, 1962

MacAlister, R.A.S., *Lebor Gabala:The Book of the Taking of Ireland*, Irish Texts Society, Dublin, 1938–56

MacNeill, E., 'Pre-Christian Kings of Tara', *JRSAI* 57, 1927

MacNeill, E., *Celtic Ireland*, London, 1921

McKerrell, Hugh, 'On the Origins of British Faience Beads and Some Aspects on the Wessex-Mycenae Relationship', *PPS* 38, 1972

Manetho, edited by W.G Waddell, Loeb Classical Library, 1956

Manley, Bill, *The Penguin Historical Atlas of Ancient Egypt*, Penguin Books, 1996

Manley, John, *Atlas of Prehistoric Britain,* Phaidon Press, 1989

Marsden, Barry, M., *The Early Barrow Diggers*, Tempus Publishing, 1999

Martin, Geoffrey, *The Hidden Tombs of Memphis*, Thames and Hudson, 1995

Megaw, J.V.S. and Simpson, D.D.A., *British Prehistory*, Leicester University Press, 1979

Mertz, Barbara, *Temples, Tombs and Hieroglyphs*, Michael O'Mara Books, 1996

Morgan-Watkin, I., 'ABO Blood Distribution in Wales in relation to Human settlement' in *Genetic and Population Studies in Wales*

Moran, William, *The Amarna Letters*, Johns Hopkins University Press, 1992

Muckelroy, Keith, *Archaeology Underwater*, McGraw-Hill Book Company, 1980

Muckelroy, Keith, 'Two Bronze Age Cargoes in British Waters', *Antiquity* 54, 1980

Murnane, W. and Siclen, C.C., *The Boundary Stela of Akhenten*, Routledge and Kegan Paul, 1993

Nennius, *British History and Welsh Annals,* edited by John Morris, London and Chichester, 1980

Newberry, P.E., 'Notes on Sea-Going Ships', *JEA* 28, 1942

Newton, R.G., and Renfrew, C., 'British Faience Beads Reconsidered', *Antiquity* 44, 1970

Nibbi, Alessandra, 'An Answer to Lucien Basch on Ancient Egyptian Sea-Going, Stone Anchors and Bread Offerings', *Discussions in Egyptology* 38, University College London, 1997

O'Kelly, Michael, *Newgrange* Thames and Hudson, 1982

O'Neil, B.H., 'The Excavation of Knackbuoy Cairn, Isles of Scilly', *Antiquaries Journal*, Oxford University Press, 1962

O'Riordain, Sean, 'A Burial with Faience Beads at Tara', *PPS* 21, 1955

Oppert, *The Royal Inscriptions of Mari,* London, 186–

Owen, 'The Flemings in Pembrokeshire', *Archaeologia Cambrensis* 12, 1895

Partridge, Robert, *Transport in Ancient Egypt*, The Rubicon Press, 1996

Partridge, Robert, *Faces of Pharaohs*, The Rubicon Press, 1994

Parkinson, Richard, *Cracking Codes – The Rosetta Stone and Decipherment*, British Museum Press, 1999

Parkinson, Richard, *Voices from Ancient Egypt*, British Museum Press, 1991

Parkinson, Richard and Schofield, Louise, 'Images of Myceneans: A Recently Acquired painted papyrus from El Amarna' in *Egypt, the Aegean and the Levant* edited by Davies, V. and Friedman, R., British Museum Press, 1985

Parkinson, Richard and Schofield, Louise, 'Of Helmets and Heretics: A Possible Egyptian Representation of Mycenean Warriors on a Papyrus From El Amarna', *BSA* 89, 1994

Pausanias, Vol I–V, Loeb Classical Library, Harvard University Press, 1999

Pearson, Michael, *Bronze Age Britain*, English Heritage, 1993

Penhallurick, Roger, *Tin in Antiquity,* The Institute of Metals, London, 1986

Pennington, W.V, *The History of British Vegetation*, London, 1969

Petrie, William Flinders, *Tell el Amarna*, Aris and Phillips Ltd, 1974

Pliny, *Natural History*, edited and translated by H. Rackham and W.H.S. Jones, Loeb Classical Library, Harvard University Press, 1999

Powell, T.G.E., 'The Gold Ornament from Mold, Flintshire, North Wales', *PPS* 53, 1953

Pytheas, *The Voyages*, University Library Tromso, Sweden, 1999

Raftery, Barry, *Pagan Celtic Ireland,* Thames and Hudson, 1994

Randall-Maciver, D. and Wilkins, A., *Libyan Notes,* London, 1901

Randolph, *Creter,* 1680–87

Renfrew, Colin and Newton, R.G., 'British Faience Beads Reconsidered', *Antiquity* 44, 1970

Renfrew, Colin and Bahn, Paul, *Archaeology: Theories and Methods,* Thames and Hudson, 1991

Redford, Donald, *The Heretic King,* Princeton University Press, 1984

Redford, Donald, 'The Sun-Disc in Akhenaten's Program: Its Worship and Antecedents', *JARCE* vol 15–17, 1978–80

Redford, Donald, 'The Identity of the High Priest of Amun at the beginning of Akhenaten's reign', *JAOS* 83, 1963

Redford, Donald, 'Studies on Akhenaten at Thebes', *JARCE* 12, 1975

Redford, Donald and Smith, Ray, *The Akhenaten Temple Project vol I–III*, Warminster, 1964

Redford, Donald, *Egypt, Canaan and Israel in Ancient Times*, Princeton University Press, 1992

Reeves, Nicholas, *The Complete Tutankhamun*, Thames and Hudson, 1990

Rice, Patty, *Amber – the Golden Gem of the Ages*, Litton Education Press, 1980

Roberts, Alison, *Hathor Rising*, Northgate Publishers, 1995

Robins, Gay, *Proportion and Style in Ancient Egyptian Art*, Austin, Texas, 1994

Roeder, *Agyptische Bronzefiguren*, 1956

Rose, Stephen, *Lifelines*, Penguin Books, 1997

Samson, Julia, *Nefertiti and Cleopatra*, The Rubicon Press, 1985

Scantos, *The Mysterious Origins of the Guanchees*, 1999

Scheel, Bernd, *Egyptian Metalworking and Tools*, Shire Books, 1989

Schulman, Alan, R., *Military Rank and Title and Organization in the Egyptian New Kingdom*, Berlin, 1964

Schulman, Alan, R., 'Some Observations on the Military Background of the Amarna Period', *JARCE* vol 3–4

Shaw, Ian, and Nicholson Paul, *The British Museum Dictionary of Ancient Egypt*, British Museum Press, 1995

Silver, Morris, *Ancient Economies II*, New York, 1999

Silvermann, David, *Ancient Egypt*, Duncan Baird, 1997

Smith, G. Elliot, *The Royal Mummies,* Institut Francais D'Archeologie Orientale, Cairo, 1912

Smith, F. and Melluish, T.W., *Teach Yourself Ancient Greek*, Hodder and Stoughton, 1992

Stone, J.F.S., and Thomas, L.C., 'The Use and Distribution of Faience in the Ancient Near East and Prehistoric Europe', *PPS* 22, 1956

Strabo, *Geography*, Loeb Classical Library XVI II, Harvard University Press, 1999

Stricker, B., *The Empire of Heliopolis* – Proceedings of the Colloquium of the Archaeology, Geography and History of the Delta, Oxford, 1989

Strouhal, Eugen, *Life in Ancient Egypt*, Cambridge University Press, 1992

Szynet, *PPS*, 1978

Taylour-Hansen, *The Ancient Atlantic*, Amherst Press, 1969

Thucydides, Loeb Classical Library, Harvard University Press, 1999

Trianaphyllidou, *Baladie*, 1988

Trigger, B. et al, *Ancient Egypt: A Social History*, Cambridge University Press, 1983

Tsountas, C., *Archaeotites ek Mykenon*, Archaiologike Epherimis, 1887

Tulhoff, A., *Thutmosis III*, Munich Press, 1984

Tyldsley, Joyce, *Hatshepsut*, Viking, 1996

Tylecote, R.F., *Metallurgy in Archaeology*, London, 1962

Walsh, *Ireland's History in Maps*, 1996

Walker, A., *In Search of Cultures Past – Beyond the Beaches of Gran Canaria*, Archaeological Institute of America, 1999

Warren, Peter, *Minoan Stone Vases*, Cambridge University Press, 1965

Warren, Peter, 'Minoan Crete and Pharaonic Egypt' in *Egypt, the Aegean and the Levant*, edited by Davies V. and Freidman, R., British Museum Press, 1995

Watterson, Barbara, *The Gods of Ancient Egypt,* Sutton Publishing, 1996

Watterson, Barbara, *The Egyptians*, Blackwell, 1998

Watson and Crick, 'A Structure for Deoxyribose Nucleic Acid', *Nature*, 1953

Wilkinson, Toby, *Early Dynastic Egypt*, Routledge, 1999

Wood, Michael, *In Search of the Trojan War*, Facts on File, 1985

Wright, Edward, *The Ferriby Boats – Seacraft of the Bronze Age,* Routledge, 1990

INDEX